Voltaire and the Theatre of the Eighteenth Century

VOLTAIRE
AND THE
THEATRE OF THE
EIGHTEENTH CENTURY

MARVIN CARLSON

Contributions in Drama and Theatre Studies, Number 84

LIVES OF THE THEATRE

JOSH BEER, CHRISTOPHER INNES, and SIMON WILLIAMS, Series Advisers

Greenwood Press

Westport, Connecticut • London

Library of Congress Cataloging-in-Publication Data

Carlson, Marvin A., 1935–
    Voltaire and the theatre of the eighteenth century / Marvin
Carlson.
        p.   cm.—(Contributions in drama and theatre studies, ISSN
    0163–3821 ; no. 84. Lives of the theatre)
    Includes bibliographical references and index.
    ISBN 0–313–30302–9 (alk. paper)
    1. Voltaire, 1694–1778—Biography.   2. Dramatists, French—18th
century—Biography.   3. Theater—Europe—History—18th century.
4. Voltaire, 1694–1778—Knowledge—Theater.   I. Title.   II. Series:
Contributions in drama and theatre studies ; no. 84.   III. Series:
Contributions in drama and theatre studies. Lives of the theatre.
PQ2099.C35   1998
842′.5
[b]—DC21   98–17533

British Library Cataloguing in Publication Data is available.

Library of Congress Catalog Card Number: 98–17533
ISBN: 0–313–30302–9
ISSN: 0163–3821

First published in 1998

Greenwood Press, 88 Post Road West, Westport, CT 06881
An imprint of Greenwood Publishing Group, Inc.

Printed in the United States of America

∞™

The paper used in this book complies with the
Permanent Paper Standard issued by the National
Information Standards Organization (Z39.48–1984).

10 9 8 7 6 5 4 3 2 1

To Paul O. LeClerc

"En cultivant son jardin il faut aussi ne pas oublier son théâtre."
—Voltaire, in a letter of 1767

Contents

Illustrations

Series Foreword

Lives of the Theatre is designed to provide scholarly introductions to important periods and movements in the history of world theatre from the earliest instances of recorded performance through to the twentieth century, viewing the theatre consistently through the lives of representative theatrical practitioners. Although many of the volumes will be centered upon playwrights, other important theatre people, such as actors and directors, will also be prominent in the series. The subjects have been chosen not simply for their individual importance, but because their lives in the theatre can well serve to provide a major perspective on the theatrical trends of their eras. They are therefore either representative of their time, figures whom their contemporaries recognized as vital presences in the theatre, or they are people whose work was to have a fundamental influence on the development of theatre, not only in their lifetimes but after their deaths as well. While the discussion of verbal and written scripts will inevitably be a central concern in any volume that is about an artist who wrote for the theatre, these scripts will always be considered in their function as a basis for performance.

The rubric "Lives of the Theatre" is therefore intended to suggest both biographies of people who created theatre as an institution and as a medium of performance and of the life of the theatre itself. This dual focus will be illustrated through the titles of the individual volumes, such as *Christopher Marlowe and the Renaissance of Tragedy, George Bernard Shaw and the Socialist Theatre*, and *Richard Wagner and Festival Theatre*, to name just a few. At the same time, although the focus of each volume will be different, depending on the particular subject, appropriate emphasis will be given to the cultural and political context within which the theatre of any given time is set. Theatre itself can be seen to have a palpable effect upon the social world around it, as it both reflects the life of its time and helps to form that life by feeding it images, epitomes, and alternative versions of itself. Hence, we hope that this series will also contribute to an understanding of the broader social life of the period of which the theatre that is the subject of each volume was a part.

Lives of the Theatre grew out of an idea that Josh Beer put to Christopher Innes and Peter Arnott. Sadly, Peter Arnott did not live to see the inauguration of the series. Simon Williams kindly agreed to replace him as one of the series editors and has played a full part in its preparation. In commemoration, the editors wish to acknowledge Peter's own rich contribution to the life of the theatre.

Josh Beer
Christopher Innes
Simon Williams

Abbreviations

BV. Theodore Besterman. *Voltaire*.

GC. David Garrick. *Private Correspondence*. James Boaden, ed.

HFS. Frederick Hawkins. *The French Stage in the Eighteenth Century*.

LFT. H. Carrington Lancaster. *French Tragedy in the Time of Louis XIV and Voltaire*.

PVI. Lucien Perey and Gaston Maugras. *La Vie intime de Voltaire aux Délices et à Ferney*.

VC. Voltaire. *Correspondence*. Theodore Besterman, ed.

VLP. Voltaire. *Lettres philosophiques*.

VO. Voltaire. *Oeuvres*.

WCT. Lilian Willens. *Voltaire's Comic Theatre*.

Introduction

Born in the final years of the seventeenth century, and dying a decade before the beginning of the French Revolution, François Marie Arouet, who subsequently assumed the name Voltaire, was a central, in fact quintessential figure of the eighteenth century, so much so that this era has sometimes been called the "Age of Voltaire." At a time when French culture dominated Europe, Voltaire dominated French culture, and like Goethe, another key figure of the next generation, he was interested in and made major contributions to almost every sphere of human intellectual activity—the sciences, trade and commerce, politics, and most particularly the arts.

Despite the astonishing range of Voltaire's pursuits, indeed of his literary activities alone, the theatre maintained a central position in his interest and affection from the beginning to the end of his career. His pamphlets, novels, short stories, histories, philosophical treatises, and poems were read throughout Europe, but his first and last literary triumphs were plays: *Oedipe*, written when he was only seventeen; and *Irène*, completed when he was eighty-four. Both were produced amid the greatest public enthusiasm at the Comédie Française (the preeminent theatre in France, and indeed in Europe), and between these two, the Comédie also presented dozens of other Voltaire plays. He created a total of fifty-six, and there was rarely a period in his long life when he was not actively working on a theatrical script. During the latter part of his career, and for many years after his death, he was produced more often on the national stage (and on the stages of much of Europe) than any other serious dramatist, including Racine and Corneille, and his plays served as models for aspiring young dramatists throughout Europe.

The profession of acting was held in low esteem by both church and state in the eighteenth century; actors had neither the rights of citizens, nor access to religious ceremonies, such as marriage, baptism, or church burial. Play-writing, however, was a favored form of literary achievement, and a success-ful play could gain its author access to seats of power, especially at court, as well as literary renown—even a coveted place among the "immortals" who made up the French Academy.

Theatre occupied a central position in the social and cultural life of this period that is hard to imagine today. Theatre debates, controversies, and scandals were subjects of avid interest, and European history has probably never seen such a passion for amateur theatrical activity. Members of the royal family favored such amusements, and their example was eagerly fol-lowed by countless members of the aristocracy and many of the bourgeoisie. Voltaire was even more deeply and consistently involved in this rich amateur theatrical culture throughout his life than with the official and professional stage. As a young man he delighted in attending these private aristocratic en-tertainments, and as soon as he could afford theatres of his own at his own residences he did so, continuing to perform and direct in such venues throughout his life.

Voltaire's plays are rarely performed today, even in France, but his life-long involvement in the theatre, both amateur and professional, and his dominance in the theatrical culture of his era still make him an ideal center for a study of that culture. This would be true even if Voltaire's interests and influence were confined to France, but in fact a study of Voltaire as a man of the theatre far exceeds national boundaries. Voltaire was a truly international figure, with international fame, concerns, and influence. He was acquainted with almost every noted figure in the Europe of his time, corresponding with over 1,800 of them: kings, ministers, popes, authors, actors, musicians, shopkeepers, peasants. He lived in Switzerland, Prussia, and England in ad-dition to France, and was actively involved with the theatre in each of these countries, as well as informed about and interested in theatre in many other places, including Russia, Italy, Spain, and Denmark. He translated or adapted plays from the Spanish, Italian, Greek, and Chinese dramas, and ex-perimented with every kind of dramatic fare popular in the European theatre of his time—comedies, tragedies, sentimental plays, dramas, comic operas, operas, court spectacles, and divertissements. He lived during an era when the carefully established rules and traditions of the neoclassic French stage (involving decorum, generic boundaries, stage spectacle, and dramatic style) were beginning to be seriously challenged, and throughout his career he was torn between the possibilities and attractions of innovation and the love of tradition, a tension most famously expressed in his lifelong love/hate relationship with the work of Shakespeare.

A history of Voltaire's theatrical career and interests thus provides an entry into the whole complex world of eighteenth-century theatre—amateur and professional, traditional and innovative, French and international. Surely, the life of no other single figure during this fascinating and complex century provides a richer or more varied insight into the local, national, and international theatre of the time. In the history of theatrical culture, as in the history of culture in general, it is no misnomer to designate the eighteenth century as the "Age of Voltaire."

Chapter 1

Voltaire's Career Begins, 1694–1726

The man who would become known as Voltaire was born on Sunday, 21 November 1694 in Paris. The exact location is unknown, but it was in the parish of Saint-André-des-Arts, in the heart of the Latin Quarter. The parish church where he was christened with the name François Marie Arouet was torn down at the beginning of the nineteenth century, its site now occupied by the square that bears its name, but his birthplace probably still stands, as do most of the buildings that made up this district in his lifetime. Were Voltaire to stroll today down the parish's main thoroughfare, the rue Saint-André-des-Arts, he would find the buildings and many of their usages little changed—bakeries, cafés, small hotels. Aside from the garishness of modern commercial advertising, he would probably be most struck by (and enthusiastic about) the international flavor of these establishments—a "Muscovite" sandwich shop, Greek tavernas, Chinese restaurants, even a Tex-Mex establishment called the Tacos Loco in a restaurant formerly named L'Arléquin. And he would no doubt be amused that the district's somewhat raffish character is still clearly being maintained by Le Caméléon, a stylish discotheque, and by Chochotte, a "théâtre supererotique."

The man who would become the dominant figure in the French stage of the eighteenth century in fact could not have selected a more appropriate neighborhood in which to make his appearance, since the narrow streets around Saint-André-des-Arts had not long before his birth become established as the center of the national theatre, and Voltaire would see most of his greatest triumphs within a few streets from where he entered the world.

When François Arouet was born, professional theatre had been firmly established in Paris for some seventy years, though its early homes were all on the other side of the Seine. The first was the Hôtel de Bourgogne near the former central markets, Les Halles. Thanks to the brilliance of Racine and his leading lady, Mlle de Champmeslé, it had become unrivalled in tragedy. The plays of Corneille had established the reputation of the rival Théâtre du Marais, located in the district of that name, but after his departure this theatre turned primarily to productions stressing scenery and spectacular effects. A third theatre was located in the palace built by Cardinal Richelieu next to the Louvre that became the property of the crown after his death. This Palais-Royal theatre was the center of French comedy, shared by a company of Italian commedia actors and the French company headed by Molière.

Despite this concentration of theatrical activity on the right bank during the seventeenth century, significant hints of the future theatrical importance of the Saint-André area could be found clustered around a tiny square, the Carrefour de Buci, at one end of the district's main street, the rue Saint-André-des-Arts. A few steps north of this square, on the present rue Mazarine, the young Molière and his companions had in 1643 taken over an abandoned tennis court to establish the Illustre Théâtre, a venture which despite its proud name failed almost at once, but which initiated Molière's professional career and, it might be argued, the path that led at last to the French national theatre. A much more successful converted tennis court was located a short distance further north, in the rue Guénégaud. Here the Laffemas family staged some of the first operas in Paris; indeed, the founding date of 1669 still may be seen above the curtain in Paris' old opera house, the Palais Garnier, memorializing the founding of their establishment, as does a plaque on the building now closest to this site. A few steps on, where the street meets the Seine, a smiling statue of Voltaire now stands in a tiny park, as if welcoming visitors to his neighborhood.

The Guénégaud theatre, with the operas of Pierre Perrin, enjoyed a great but brief popularity before Jean-Baptiste Lully gained a royal monopoly on the genre in 1672 and forced this rival operation to close. Lully's growing power and support from the king had powerful effects upon the spoken theatre as well. The death of Molière in 1673 left his company dispirited and disorganized, and Lully took advantage of this opportunity to gain from the king control of the well-equipped Palais-Royal for his operas. Molière's dispossessed troupe sought refuge across the river in the recently abandoned theatre of the rue Guénégaud, where they joined forces with the declining Marais company. Molière's comedies still dominated their repertoire, but the abandoned opera machinery allowed them also to mount the popular Marais spectacle dramas.

The Bourgogne still dominated in the serious drama, but not for long. After *Phèdre*, Racine retired from the theatre to assume the post of royal historiographer, and two years later, Mlle de Champmeslé joined the theatre in the rue Guénégaud, moving into quarters in the rue Mazarine. Deprived of both its leading dramatist and interpreter, the Bourgogne faded rapidly, and in 1680, a royal decree officially merged it with the Guénégaud, creating the Comédie Française. Its opening production was Champmeslé in *Phèdre*.

The united company did not, however, enjoy its new and fairly comfortable quarters for long. A new college, founded by Cardinal Mazarin, was built just to its north on the bank of the Seine. Long viewed with deepest suspicion by the church, the theatre was considered an unsuitable neighbor and required to seek a new location. Many were suggested, only to be resisted by the local parish churches, and finally the company simply moved further down the same street, to the other side of the Carrefour de Buci but in the same parish, to create a new theatre, the first to bear the name Comédie Française. This new theatre, opened in 1689 just five years before Voltaire's birth and in the same neighborhood, was the home of the Comédie for almost all of his long life, until 1770, when it moved to new quarters in the royal palace of the Tuileries. In its honor, this little street now bears the name rue de l'ancienne Comédie (street of the former Comédie). Only a part of the stone facade of this theatre is still standing, with a plaque recalling its history and a bas-relief of the goddess Minerva. The heavy iron balcony that extended across the facade in Voltaire's time has long since disappeared. Behind the facade is a little courtyard, on the site of the former auditorium, at the back of which one could still see, early in this century, the remains of the original stage. A small bookstore had been built within it, but now, alas, has been replaced by modern apartments and a glass facade. The famous Café Procope across the street has fared much better, founded in 1684 and the favored rendezvous of artists and writers for the theatre, among whom Voltaire would become a central figure.

At the age of ten (in 1704), François Arouet was enrolled in the Jesuit College of Louis-le-Grand. Years later he wrote that the best part of the instruction there were the plays presented,[1] for Louis-le-Grand was strongly committed to the Jesuit tradition of school drama. Tragedies in Latin were presented in the entry court, with an immense tent to shelter spectators, and comedies in French on a more modest improvised stage in the library. These productions had such a reputation that Louis-le-Grand students were invited to court to perform for Louis XV.[2] The schoolboy Arouet himself composed a tragedy, *Amulius et Numitor*, of which only fragments survive, as well as a variety of odes and occasional pieces. He graduated in 1711, and soon after began work on his first major drama, *Oedipe*.

The theatrical activities and classic orientation of Louis-le-Grand unquestionably helped to inspire this project, but other influences were of equal or greater importance. Even while still at school, Voltaire began to frequent the hedonistic group of artists and poets then associated with the Temple, the old home of the French Knights Templar. A 1716 letter to one of the leaders of this group, Chaulieu, credits the Templars with criticism that "much benefitted" the new tragedy.[3] Even more important, Voltaire's godfather, the Abbé de Châteauneuf, a minor writer and diplomat, encouraged the youth's interest in literature, introducing him to some of the most elegant salons in Paris and to the world of the theatre.

Although the Comédie was condemned later in the century as being uncomfortable, crowded, and badly ventilated, when Voltaire and his godfather attended it was widely considered the most beautiful and capacious in Europe. Like most French theatres of the period, it had been converted from a former tennis court, the Étoile. The architect, François d'Orbay, divided this rectangular space into two parts: approximately one-third for the stage, the rest for the audience, which could hold as many as 2000, though half that number was considered a good attendance. Spectators entered by four doors flanked by columns. The pit, for standing patrons, was separated by a railing from a semicircular amphitheatre in the rear, with twenty rows of seats. In the pit gathered men of letters, professional men, and students. Entrance to this area was not expensive, 16–25 sous, but even so, poorer patrons attended only the free performances given to celebrate royal marriages and births or other major civic occasions. There was also a long bench in a narrow enclosure near the stage where free seating was always provided for reviewers and established dramatists. The pit was as much a social gathering place as an audience area, and was often so turbulent that a guard of soldiers always surrounded it to maintain order. Twelve large chandeliers were suspended over the pit and provided the main lighting for the theatre, as well as a steady deposit of wax on those gathered below. Patrons who preferred seats at the rear were charged 1–6 francs, according to the desirability of the location. Along the sides, which were lavishly decorated in green and gold by the designer Pizzoli, were three tiers of ornate boxes, each row containing nineteen boxes with eight chairs each. The lowest tier, with painted ceilings, rich curtains, carving, and gold leaf, accommodated members of the court, who entered free, or patrons prosperous enough to pay 35–40 francs for a box. The first box next to the stage on one side was reserved for the king, the opposite one for the queen. The next tier was occupied by the well-to-do bourgeoisie, who paid 20–30 francs. The highest boxes, at 15–20 francs, accommodated less prosperous, middle-class patrons, behind whom gathered the servants of the ladies and gentlemen below. A royal coat of arms over the proscenium attested to the patronage of the crown, since Louis in 1682 had guaranteed the company continued protection and an annual subsidy of 12,000 livres.

Certain members of the audience mixed freely with the actors, and the young Voltaire and his godfather were among this group. By modern standards, one of the strangest customs of the theatre of this period was permanent seating on the stage for aristocrats and their guests who enjoyed this sort of public display or who wanted an intimate view of the actors or, more commonly, the actresses. Although these spectators could watch from the wings, they normally preferred the exposure offered by four rows of cushioned seats on either side of the stage, separated from the acting area by a permanent iron railing. On special occasions a fifth row was added in front, and up to fifty people were allowed to stand behind. A period engraving shows members of this onstage audience peeping around the edges of the curtain to observe the less privileged spectators in the auditorium (illustration 1). Before or after the production, or in the interval between a main play and its afterpiece, this fashionable crowd would pass through a door at the side of the stage into the elegant greenroom (the *foyer des artistes*, with its polished floor, stamped velvet furniture, and portraits of house artists), to mingle with the actors and members of elegant society, exchanging gossip and witticisms.

One of the earliest anecdotes about the young Voltaire concerns a result of these backstage contacts. Around the age of ten he is said to have persuaded M. Arouet, his notoriously short-tempered father, to attend the Comédie, having previously arranged with the actor playing the title role in Brueys and Palaprat's 1691 comedy *Le Grondeur* to introduce an enraged quote from M. Arouet into his scolding part. Voltaire's father was reportedly appropriately chastened, a result one historian designates as Voltaire's "first recorded instance of an unrivalled power of ridicule" achieving its "desired result."[4] The generation of actors that worked with Molière and Racine for the most part disappeared from the stage during the years of Voltaire's childhood. The faithful La Grange, long the keeper of the theatre's records, died suddenly in 1692; Racine's last love, Mlle de Champmeslé, died in 1698, the year before the dramatist; Molière's wife, Armande Béjart, retired from the stage in 1694 and died in 1700; even the popular Baron, Molière's protege, who was generally looked to as the major link between the great period of the mid-seventeenth century and the next gen-

Illustration 1. The old Comédie Française before a performance.

eration, shocked the theatre world of Paris by retiring in 1691 at only thirty-eight years of age.

The years at the turn of the century thus saw many Comédie debuts, primarily of already established provincial actors, as the company sought to renew itself. It was this generation of actors that young François Arouet encountered on his first visits to the theatre. Pierre Beaubourg joined the company in 1693 and inherited most of Baron's roles, though not very successfully, since his approach was stiff and declamatory, and audiences missed the subtlety and nuance of his predecessor. Mlle Duclos, who made her debut this same year, became Beaubourg's usual partner in tragedy. Her measured and artificial style suited his, and introduced a period of Comédie acting that was later regarded as highly bombastic and mannered. She knew how to touch her public, however, among them the adolescent François, who selected her as one of his first romantic idols, dedicating to her his satiric poem, the *Anti-Giton* in 1714. It was a futile gesture, for the actress was then, as the young man subsequently discovered to his amused embarrassment, the mistress of the count of Uzès.

After 1699, the young Christine Desmares began sharing major tragic roles with Duclos. Desmares was the niece of the famous Mlle de Champmeslé, and had been personally trained by her. A more delicate actress than the formidable Duclos, she also achieved a significant success in comic roles; indeed, her portrait at the Comédie shows her bearing a dagger in one hand and a comic mask in the other. It was she who would create Voltaire's first tragic queen, Jocaste, though this was to be her only Voltarian role, since she retired from the stage soon after.

François Arouet unquestionably brought experiences from school, the theatre, and the world of letters to the creation of his first major drama. To these influences the world of aristocratic society must be added, early recognizing the brilliance of the young writer and providing support throughout his career. This was a period of rapid and major changes in French society, and the young François was closely connected with some of the most influential figures in it. His school days had been spent during the final years of Louis XIV, whose reign, despite a series of exhausting wars, had seen the triumph of French culture and French theatre on the European scene. In his youth, the king had dazzled his nation and, indeed, the continent with lavish entertainments, and had passionately supported the ballet and the theatre. In his final years, however, he turned to an oppressive religiosity largely under the influence of Madame de Maintenon. The theatre, like all entertainments, fell into royal disfavor, and princes of the blood, with the exception of the rather dissolute duke of Orleans, never attended.

Some grand private houses, most notably that of the duchess of Maine at Sceaux (very near to the country home of Voltaire's father), arranged regular theatrical performances, but these were now unknown at the court. In his final years, the Sun King had become widely regarded as a tyrant and a bigot, and his death in 1715 was greeted with widespread relief and even jubilation.

Louis XIV's will provided for a Council of Regency headed by the duke of Orleans to govern the country during the minority of the future Louis XV. This son, now only five, and the royal household troops were placed under the supervision of the duke de Maine, and although these arrangements predictably led to constant power struggles between supporters of the two dukes, neither faction nor its leader had any interest in maintaining the solemn tone of Louis XIV's final years. On the contrary, the Regency is remembered as one of the dissolute and scandalous periods of French history. Happily for the theatre, however, not all of the liberated energies of the period were expended in drunken revels, though these were common enough. Both the duke of Orleans and the duchess of Maine had been fascinated by the theatre, even in the inauspicious days of the old king, and the new order and their new power allowed them to expand this interest. The regent continued his strong support of the Comédie; he or members of his household attended almost every evening, encouraging new plays as well as classic revivals, and making the theatre again fashionable, to the great delight and prosperity of the actors. He also arranged for a company of Italian actors to come to Paris to replace those sent back to Italy by Louis in 1697. This company was led by Luigi Riccoboni (called Lélio) and they enjoyed great success, performing both at the refurbished Bourgogne and at the Palais-Royal on Mondays and Saturdays, when no opera was given.

The revival of theatrical activity during the Regency was accompanied by a revival of critical writings favoring this art. The common charges of immorality and corruption which had been mounted particularly by men of the church in the previous century, now almost disappeared. Doubtless when Père Courberville translated into French Jeremy Collier's famous 1698 antitheatrical tract, *A Short View of the Profaneness and Immorality of the English Stage*, his aim was to discredit the theatre, but in fact his translation had quite the opposite effect. Even by the lax moral standards of the Regency, both contemporary and classic French drama demonstrated very little of the excesses Collier condemned. Thus, the effect confirmed the French in their already generally held opinion that their cultural products were far more civilized and refined than those of the barbarians across the channel. A reissuing that same year of the Abbé d'Aubiganc's highly regarded *Pratique du théâtre*, undertaken at the request of Richelieu and first published in 1657, served as a reminder that in the golden age of French letters, the theatre had been supported and well regarded by the highest figures in the French church and state. The major new theoretical work of this generation, the Abbé Dubos' *Réflections critiques sur la poésie et sur la peinture* (1719), developed what would be the generally accepted view of theatre for at least the first half of the century: that both tragedy and comedy were beneficial in regulating the passions and improving social mores. Dubos also was an important pioneer in championing the art of acting, to which he devoted eight chapters.

The most distinguished private theatre of this period was that of the duchess of Maine, who restored the spirit of Versailles in its early days to her chateau at Sceaux with a series of elaborate festivals (the "Grand Nights"). These were arranged by Nicolas de Malezieu, who served as a kind of court poet and master of the revels, most of them including dramatic performances. Malezieu was the author of one neoclassic tragedy, *Iphigénie en Tauride*, and would both translate and declaim scenes from Sophocles, Euripides, and Terence with a skill reported worthy of the stage. Young François Arouet, intoduced to Sceaux by his godfather, was often a guest at these festivities. In a dedicatory letter to the duchess prefixed to his 1750 *Oreste*, he claimed that the idea for *Oedipe* first came to him while watching Malezieu's *Iphigénie* with the duchess in the title role. He first undertook a translation of the confession scene between Jocaste and Oedipus. Several friends and actors to whom he read this scene assured him that it was too alien to French practice, and advised him to consult Corneille's treatment of the subject, particularly in the introduction of a romantic subplot. He compromised by including a past romantic intrigue. The duchess and Malezieu agreed that the love interest was out of place, but unless the young author wished to remain satisfied with salon readings, he had to also accommodate the actors at the Comédie, to whom this addition was essential.[5]

In 1682, when Louis XIV granted a permanent annual subsidy to the Comédie, he also brought the theatre more directly under the control of the state. Traditionally, the Comédie had administered itself as a stock company, with twenty-three shares, full shares held by the leading members and parts of shares by lesser members. At the time of Louis XIV's death, the company was composed of sixteen full-share and thirteen part-share members. This system was preserved, but after 1682 the four Gentlemen of the King's Bedchamber were to determine major questions regarding the operations of the theatre. New members were proposed by the company, but only the gentlemen or the king could admit or retire them. The daily running of the theatre, however, including the selection of the repertoire, remained as it had always been, under the control of the company itself, which met each Monday to look ahead to the selections of the next two weeks and to hear possible new plays read.

The first reading of *Oedipe* before the actors was disastrous. The attack on the play was led by Pierre Beaubourg, who had inherited many of the roles of young heroes from the great Baron in the last century, and Ponteuil, who joined the company in 1701 and played mostly secondary roles. Led by these actors, the company unanimously rejected this play, which dared comparison with Corneille, contained no strong love interest or role for a young leading lady, and even included Greek choruses, created by the young poet after consulting with the famous classic scholar André Dacier.

The young author attempted to compromise, adding more sentiment in the new character of Philoctète, a former lover of Jocaste who appears in the first three acts of the play, and by reducing the choruses. The actors were now more favorable, but objections were still raised, particularly to the Jocaste/Oedipus scene of the fourth act, essentially unchanged from the Greek. Quinault-Dufresne suggested ironically that the play might be presented with its "wretched" Greek act, as a lesson to the young playwright. Finally, however, due to the influence of François Arouet's friends in society, especially the duchess of Maine, the actors agreed and the work was scheduled for performance early in 1716.

A series of political misfortunes delayed this event. The young author was suspected (probably correctly) of writing satirical verses at the expense of the duke of Orleans, the political rival of his hosts at Sceaux. He was therefore exiled from May to October of 1716 to a country house equally remote from Paris and Sceaux. Back in Paris the following year, he was accused by a police spy of penning another seditious satire. He was arrested, spent eleven months in the notorious Bastille prison, and another six months in exile from the capital. This experience undoubtedly contributed to his lifelong concern both with prisoners and with freedom of expression, but his developing literary career did not suffer. In the Bastille he continued to write and polish his *Oedipe*, which was at last presented at the Comédie on 18 November 1718, scarcely a month after his return to Paris. Soon after leaving prison, and on the brink of launching his literary career, he began to sign his letters with a new name, Voltaire, explaining in a letter of 1 March 1719, "I have been so unhappy under the name Arouet that I have taken another."[6] Henceforth it was as Voltaire that he would be known.

The long-delayed play achieved a tremendous success, the greatest in fact of Voltaire's long career. It had thirty almost consecutive performances after its opening, more than any other tragedy of the century, and Voltaire's share of the profits, over 3,000 francs, was greater than that obtained by any previous author. Houdard de La Motte, the official censor to whom all plays had to be submitted before printing or performance, hailed it as a worthy successor to Corneille and Racine, an opinion now shared by most of literary and theatrical Paris. Its success in turn inspired a parody version by Dominique at the recently reopened Comédie Italienne, the first of a type of play that would before long become a staple of that theatre.

Despite the misgivings of the Comédie actors, *Oedipe* seems to a modern reader very little different from its neoclassic models. This is hardly surprising, since the rules and practice of tragic writing had been firmly established in the previous century, and neither critics nor the public had much toleration for significant departures from them. In addition to the received body of rules, the specific plays of Corneille and Racine still dominated the repertoire, providing a living model for young dramatists. Every season saw the premiere of one, two, or three new tragedies, and for a young author like Voltaire such a production offered an opportunity for social attention and perhaps even fame. Still, few of these new works entered the ongoing repertoire, while the major tragedies of Racine and Corneille appeared season after season.

The best known of the practices characterizing this tradition are the famous three unities. The time of action cannot exceed twenty-four hours and is usually less than half of that. The place is a single location, often the palace hall so typical of Racine, or less commonly a camp, temple, or some other public place. Not only are subplots avoided, but so is most external affect. The action is established in the opening act and then allowed to develop, generally by psychological conflict, until the catastrophe. Although Aristotle and Horace continued to be cited by late seventeenth- and early eighteenth-century theorists, French neoclassic practice generally prevailed over both classic theory and practice as a model when the two did not agree. Horace's five-act structure continued to be followed, but the chorus was universally abandoned, and Voltaire's modest attempt to reinstate it was, as we have seen, strongly resisted (though in fact he gave it only fourteen lines in the play, most of them spoken by their leader and few of them substantive).

The traditional neoclassic verse form, the Alexandrine, was universally employed, except for occasional special passages, such as oracles. Oracles, prophesies, and signs were all quite frequent, as examples of the "marvelous," which neoclassic French theory encouraged as a way of heightening the power of the drama. Like the Greeks, French neoclassic dramatists favored family dramas, although even more important was a sexual love interest which, as we have seen, had become so standard a part of tragedy by the time of Voltaire that its omission was considered a major fault. The subject matter of tragedy was equally predictable. Like Corneille and Racine, new tragic authors found their subjects in the classic world, the Bible, or the Turkish empire. More recent history, even that of France, was not explored.

Voltaire's play, especially after the revisions he undertook to make it more palatable to the actors, departed very little from this highly codified tradition. Many Voltaire scholars have suggested that nevertheless the young artist left his distinctive mark even on this conventional work by infusing it with the spirit of his famous free thinking in religious and political matters. Certainly, many individual lines can be and have been cited to support such iconoclasm, such as Philoctète's "Kings, indeed, are gods / To their own subjects, but to Hercules, / Or me, they were no more than common men," or Jocaste's "These priests are not what the vile rabble think them, / Their knowledge springs from our credulity."[7]

And yet, as Voltaire scholar Theodore Besterman has pointed out, the play was passed, even praised by the official censor, performed before the king, and supported by the regent himself, who even allowed it to be dedicated to his mother. Besterman attributes the play's extraordinary success less to an open iconoclasm than to the expression of profound but still inarticulated feelings in the culture: "an increasing disgust with all forms of absolute authority, and in particular with that of the church and the throne, a disgust of which the regency was an unconscious and impermanent expression."[8] Besterman thus sees intuited in Voltaire's first great popular success themes that would only be fully politically and culturally articulated in the French Revolution, which appropriately looked to Voltaire as one of its spiritual fathers.

Voltaire's treatment follows the basic outlines of Sophocles and Corneille, but has a number of distinctive features. Both Creon and Tiersias, Oedipus' major antagonists, are gone, replaced by an unnamed high priest. The new character of Philoctète, reluctantly added by Voltaire to provide a love interest, complicates the early part of the play. He is a former lover of Jocaste, sent into exile when she married Laius, now returned to find her married to Oedipe. Voltaire does the best he can with this rather awkward new character, using his return from exile to justify the opening exposition, and making him a suspect in the death of Laius to lead Oedipus' attention in a false direction for the first three acts. The high priest's naming of Oedipe as the murderer ends this section and prepares the way for the Sophoclean fourth act, in which Oedipe discovers his guilt for the murder but not yet for incest. The arrival of a messenger from Corinth provides this final information and Oedipus rushes from the stage to kill himself. Thunder and lightning mark his death as the high priest announces the end of the plague and the pardon of Jocaste. She nevertheless stabs herself and dies, saying that the gods were guilty of her crime, not herself.

Traditionally, authors of accepted plays were permitted to cast them, although each part was doubled and the company as a whole decided who should understudy each role. Since the types of characters found in both neo-classic comedy and tragedy were generally as close to conventional practice as were the structures and themes of such plays, and since each actor tended to specialize in particular types of roles (what the English stage would later call "lines of business"), an author actually had less freedom in this matter than might appear. It is not surprising, then, that Voltaire selected for his leading role the two actors who had at first been most outspoken in rejecting his play. He first selected Ponteuil, and then, when that actor died as the play was being prepared, turned to Quinault-Dufresne, now clearly the leading tragic actor of the company.

Quinault-Dufresne, at first unsympathetic to the play, came to realize that it provided him an excellent opportunity to show his superiority to his predecessor, Beaubourg, who had played Corneille's Oedipus. Quinault-Dufresne was a tall, elegant actor, whose expressive eyes and melodic voice were much praised. His precise diction and studied movements were a relief after the bombastic delivery of Beaubourg, but for many suggested the control of a dancing master rather than the passion of a tragic actor, and the softness of his voice in quiet scenes occasionally made him almost inaudible. He went on to create many leading roles for Voltaire, who nevertheless looking back on his career judged that he possessed "only a beautiful voice and lovely features" (VC, XCVIII, 44). Quinault-Dufresne's younger brother, Maurice, who took over many of the roles formerly played by the departed Ponteuil, played Philoctète; Jocaste, as has been mentioned, was played by Christine Desmares. The magisterial Duclos might have seemed a more logical choice for the Greek tragic queen, and the choice of the gentler and more sentimental Desmares (who had triumphed in such roles as Electra and Antigone) suggests an attempt to emphasize the youthful and romantic side of this character, as Voltaire's version itself certainly does.

Oedipe was also performed at the company's old home in the Palais-Royal, since the new regent took up residence there in preference to Versailles, and made what had been the Opéra into a sort of private court theatre. Opera and ballet continued to be the main entertainments, but with the two other royal companies, the French and the Italians, appearing at least in principle one night each week. This arrangement lasted until 1723 when the new king took up residence at Versailles.[9] *Oedipe* was presented at the Palais-

Royal on 30 November before the duke and duchess, and was repeated there three more times before the following spring.

Buoyed up by this enormous success, Voltaire began work at once on a new play set in ancient Greece, *Artémire*. This time the actors were eager to produce his work, but expectations ran so high that the performance, 15 February 1720, was perhaps inevitably something of a disappointment. The play opened when the attention of Paris was focused on economic events, since the Regency was in a period of enormous monetary instability, with huge national debts left by the wars of Louis XIV and frantic financial speculation. The most notorious speculative scheme, the Mississippi Bubble, had run its dazzling course just before the opening of Voltaire's new play, leaving thousands of French households ruined. Voltaire himself had avoided the financial frenzy, but it unquestionably distracted attention from theatre events, and although in fact the production gained respectable receipts, Voltaire was dissatisfied and sought to withdraw it. At the specific request of the duchess of Orleans a second performance was given, and the actors, over Voltaire's protests, offered it six times more, but the author finally prevailed. The play was never again performed and never published. Only about 650 lines of it survive, and it has left in the national memory only a single famous couplet: "Yes, all these conquerers assembled on this shore, / Soldiers under Alexander, and kings after his death . . . " which had great currency in Napoleonic times.

For Voltaire, and for the French stage, the most memorable aspect of this production was undoubtedly the appearance of Adrienne Lecouvreur, for whom Voltaire created the leading role. After an apprenticeship in minor Parisian theatres and in the provinces, Lecouvreur made her debut at the Comédie in 1717, and was immediately recognized as a major new talent. Among her devotees from the outset was Voltaire, who wrote in 1725 that Lecouvreur had "buried Duclos" (VC, I, 335). The *Anti-Giton*, originally designed to be dedicated to Duclos, was inscribed now to the newcomer. Around 1720, Lecouvreur moved into a house near the theatre on the corner of the rue Visconti, west of Guénégaud, where Racine had died in 1699. Voltaire became a regular visitor, a close friend and, it is generally supposed, a lover of the popular young actress. The first reading of his new play occurred in her apartments there.

After the failure of *Artémire*, Voltaire turned his primarily literary attention in other directions, composing the sceptical poem *Epître à Uranie* and the epic *Henriade*, but the theatre continued to attract him. In the spring of 1723 he was at work on a new tragedy, sending a draft of it to Lecouvreur in September. He decided now to turn to a subject already known on the French stage, in tragedies by Alexandre Hardy and Tristan l'Hermite. *Mariamne* was read to and accepted by the Comédie actors before the end of the year, and presented on 6 March 1724.

During the period between Voltaire's second and third tragedies, a major change had taken place at the Comédie—the return to the stage of the beloved Michael Baron after a retirement of twenty-nine years. Now in his sixty-seventh year, he was the only surviving member of Molière's original Comédie. The precise reasons for his return remain as vague as those for his earlier departure. It has often been suggested that he sought to prove that his still considerable reputation was merited, and also that he was interested in performing with Lecouvreur, whose sensitive delivery was much more suited to his than the more bombastic style that dominated the theatre during the intervening years. His return after the Easter recess in 1720 in Corneille's *Polyeucte* was a major event, with an overflowing crowd and the regent himself in attendance. Triumphant revivals of other classic comedies and tragedies followed, along with the first Comédie production of a work by the most often revived dramatist of this period, Pierre Carlet de Chamblain de Marivaux.

Although now one of the mainstays of the classic Comédie repertoire, Marivaux was, during his lifetime, most closely associated with the Comédie Italienne. His early literary experiments were strongly influenced by Gherardi's collection of texts from this theatre, especially by those of Dufresne, and he undoubtedly followed with eagnerness the reestablishment of the Italians in Paris after 1716, especially since their repertoire now stressed French-language plays. In 1720 he provided them with two short comedies, *L'Amour et la Vérité* and *Arlequin poli par l'Amour*. The first was a failure, but the second, a fairy play of young love embellished with song and dance, proved very popular both then and since.

During this same year, Marivaux reached for a more significant literary achievement with a tragedy at the Comédie, *Annibal*. The story is a Corneillian one, concerning the conflicting responsibilities of the aging general Hannibal and Princess Laodice of Bithynia, contracted to him in a political marriage but in fact in love with the younger Roman ambassador. The story plods to a predictable stately conclusion, with honor winning out over love, and contains many attractive lines, but not even the talented Baron, supported by Mlle Desmares, could win over the Comédie audiences to this rather flat and conventional work. It was given only three times, and Marivaux decided, wisely, to devote himself henceforth exclusively to comedy. His next work, presented at the Comédie Italienne in 1722, was *La Surprise de l'Amour*, a work which established his reputation and set the pattern for the brilliant series of plays that followed. The central characters of the play are the young lovers: one created by Riccoboni, who gave him his own stage name, Lélio; and the other the countess, played by Silvia. The main action is their dawning realization of their mutual attraction, despite an initial resistance. Although traditionally the *second amoureuse* (the second female love interest; Colombine, played by Flaminia, being the first), with this part Silvia became the leading female figure in subsequent Marivaux plays, as well as in the works of other authors who followed his example, substituting psychological action and the feelings and expression of young love for the traditional physical humor of Arlequin and Colombine, now demoted to supporting roles. Silvia retains her centrality in Marivaux's next two plays, *La double inconstance* (1723) and *Le Prince Travesti* (1724), but although in each she ends up with Lélio (or the prince, a Lélio character), it is Arlequin, with his native cunning and engaging simplicity, who stands at the center of the play. Only in *La fausse suivante* (1724) do Silvia and Lélio again truly take control of the action. This play marks the end of what some Marivaux biographers have called his "Italian" period, for though he continued to write primarily for the Comédie Italienne, his subsequent plays are much less marked by the traditions of that theatre.

The 1724 production of Voltaire's *Mariamne* was presented by an outstanding group of actors, with Baron as Herod, Lecouvreur as Mariamne, and Duclos as Salome. Nevertheless, the piece did not please—the audience listened coldly to the opening acts and then began protesting. The death scene of Mariamne was ruined when a wag in the audience shouted the toast "The queen drinks" as she took up a poison cup. When the afterpiece was announced, a comedy by Hauteroche called *Le Deuil*, another shout was heard: "The wake for the new play." The disappointed Voltaire withdrew the piece after a single performance.

The failure of Voltaire's piece gave encouragement to the Abbé Nadal to present a rival *Mariamne* at the Comédie the following year. The Abbé specialized in biblical tragedies, having previously produced a moderately successful *Saül*, *Hérode*, and *Les Machabées*, but *Mariamne* was booed at its opening by the audience that called for the revival of Voltaire's work in preference. The exact grounds for this reversal of opinion are unclear. In his preface to the published version of his play, Nadal accuses Voltaire of hiring a cabal to disrupt his opening, while Voltaire responded in an open letter that the only cabal had been composed of those to whom Nadal gave free tickets, while audiences for decades had needed no cabal to protest Nadal's "burlesque verse adaptations of the Old Testament" (VC, I, 300). Whatever the truth, it was certainly not uncommon during this time for authors, actors, or their supporters to arrange for claques to attend the theatre in a group to applaud a work, or to hiss the work of rivals.

Encouraged by the indifferent reception of the work of his would-be rival, Voltaire returned to the Comédie only two months later, on 10 April 1725, with a new version of his own work, retitled *Hérode et Mariamne* to distinguish it both from his own and Nadal's previous works. In this new form, it finally achieved a substantial success, though less than that of *Oedipe*. The *Mercure*, which provided substantial reviews of productions of the period, reported that the theatre was besieged by astonishing crowds, that two-thirds of the boxes were always taken in advance whenever the play was announced, and (in an indirect recognition of the ubiquity of the cabal) that the acclamations were "too general for one to suspect that they had been purchased" (HFS, 216). One of the complaints made of the earlier version was that the two leading characters were too monolithic. In his revision, Voltaire made Herod a figure more like Shakespeare's Claudius, conscious of his crimes, but unable to reform himself. In keeping with this somewhat softer, more introspective characterization, the role was changed from Baron to Dufresne. Dufresne's previous role, Varus, the Roman governor of Syria in love with Mariamne, was now given to Dufresne's younger brother, Quinault. Voltaire also removed the offending self-poisoning of the queen onstage, remarking in a preface (surely with a touch of irony) that:

I must admit that it was against my own taste that I narrated the death of Mariamne instead of showing it, but I wished in no way to go contrary to the taste of the public. I write for them and not for myself, and so it is their feelings and not my own that I should follow. (VO, II, 164)

The success of *Hérode et Mariamne* allowed Voltaire once again to make himself visible to the highest circles of Parisian cultural and political life. Both had undergone significant changes since the death of the regent in December 1723. The duke of Bourbon had then become prime minister and he and his mistress, Madame de Prie, now dominated social, cultural, and political affairs, as the duke of Orleans had done previously. One of their major achievements was breaking off the engagement of the young Louis XV to the Spanish infanta in favor of Princess Marie Leszenska of Poland, who married the king in September of 1725. Voltaire soon became perhaps the lover and certainly one of the favored artists of Madame de Prie (others being the comic dramatist Dancourt and Riccoboni of the Comédie Italienne), and he dedicated to her a new one-act comedy, *L'Indiscret*, which premiered as an afterpiece to *Mariamne* in August.

Voltaire's unquestioned prominence as a serious dramatist has overshadowed the fact that he is also the author of seventeen comedies.[10] When his literary career began, Molière dominated the world of comedy, as Racine and Corneille did of tragedy, and the leading comic dramatists of the generation between Moliére and Voltaire, Regnard and Dancourt, essentially followed the model of the master. Although Voltaire expressed a more favorable opinion of Regnard, whose most popular works, *Le Joueur* (1697) and *Le Légataire universel* (1708) Voltaire considered on a par with the best of Molière, the leading character Damis in Voltaire's own first comedy bears a close resemblance to the chevalier de Villefontaine in Dancourt's most popular comedy, *Le Chevalier à la mode* (1688). The dashing Damis loves to brag about his amorous exploits and knowledge of high society, eventually bringing about his own downfall while offering a portrait of that society that offended some, but was greeted with amused recognition by many. The virtuous Hortense exposes his duplicity by meeting him in a mask, in a scene anticipating the famous denouement of Beaumarchais' *Mariage de Figaro*. During this same autumn, Voltaire went with Madame de Prie to the estate of the Marquis de Livrey at Bélébat, where Voltaire created a one-act ribald farce, *La Fête de Bélébat*, depicting a mock ceremony honoring the debauched curé de Courdimanche, for the entertainment of the guests. Voltaire left a description of the Aristophanic atmosphere of the performance:

> The citizens of Bélébat were seated on stools, all with laurel branches in their hands, handsome charcoal mustaches, paper bonnets in the shape of sugar loaves on their heads, with each bonnet bearing in large letters the name of one of the great poets of antiquity.

The curé himself arrived in a coach with six horses and was seated on a throne to receive pompous nonsense praise "in the style of the Academy," choric odes and a "grand play in pompous verse of which neither the actors, the author, or the curé understood anything" (VO, II, 282).

With the support of his new patroness, Madame de Prie, Voltaire saw three of his plays performed at court this fall, while the new queen accepted the dedication to her of *Oedipe* and *Mariamne*. In a letter of 17 October, Voltaire boasts that the queen wept at *Mariamne*, laughed at *L'Indiscret*, spoke familiarly to him, and granted him an annuity (VC, I, 334). At the age of thirty-one he seemed firmly established, welcomed at court and in the leading salons, and was praised and honored as the leading literary figure of his generation. Then came a sudden and totally unexpected reversal. Voltaire made the mistake of wounding a minor nobleman, the chevalier de Rohan-Chabot, by a witty riposte. According to theatrical legend, the incident took place in the theatre during a production of *Mariamne* in December of 1725, culminating in an exchange of threatening gestures between Voltaire in his box and the chevalier in his, and the on-stage fainting, real or pretended, of Lecouvreur.[11] In any case, the chevalier's response was to have Voltaire beaten a few days later in broad daylight by six of his servants while the chevalier directed their activities from his nearby carriage. Voltaire, instead of appealing to the law, employed a fencing master and announced his intention of challenging the chevalier to a duel. Unwilling to undergo the shame of such a challenge, the chevalier appealed to the duke of Bourbon to place Voltaire in the Bastille in mid-April 1726. The fact that Voltaire was widely regarded as a victim and martyr did little to assuage his feelings, and the Rohan family was determined to keep him out of the way of their threatened member. Rather than remain in the Bastille, Voltaire offered to go into voluntary exile in England, a compromise acceptable to the authorities. He was accompanied to Calais and in May 1726, landed in England, to begin a quite different phase of his complex career.

NOTES

1. Letter of 1763 to Doctor Bianchi, quoted in Henri Beaune, *Voltaire au collége* (Paris: Amyot, 1868), xciv.

2. Ibid., xcii.

3. Voltaire, *Correspondence*, ed. Theodore Besterman, 107 vols. (Geneva: Institute et Musée Voltaire, 1953–1965), I:53 (henceforward VC).

4. Frederick Hawkins, *The French Stage in the Eighteenth Century*, 2 vols. (London: Chapman and Hall, 1888), 1:136 (henceforward HFS).

5. Voltaire, *Oeuvres*, 52 vols. (Paris: Garnier, 1877), IV:81 (henceforward VO).

6. René Pomeau, *D'Arouet à Voltaire, 1694–1734* (Oxford: Oxford University Press, 1988), 117.

7. Voltaire, *Oedipus* II, iv and IV, ii in *The Works of Voltaire*, trans. William F. Fleming, 22 vols. (New York: St. Hubert Guild, 1901), 8:169 and 8:187.

8. Theodore Besterman, *Voltaire* (Chicago: University of Chicago Press, 1966), 82 (henceforward BV).

9. See Spire Pitou, "The Comédie Française and the Palais-Royal Interlude of 1716–1723," *Studies on Voltaire and the Eighteenth Century*, vol. 64 (1968): 225–64.

10. The best study of this aspect of his career is Lilian Willens, *Voltaire's Comic Theatre: Composition, Conflict and Critics*, vol. 136 in *Studies on Voltaire* (henceforward WCT).

11. Jack Richtman, *Adrienne Lecouvreur: The Actress and the Age* (Englewood Cliffs: Prentice-Hall, 1971), 88.

Chapter 2

Voltaire in England, 1726–1728

Although his English trip was in many ways as pivotal for Voltaire's intellectual development as Goethe's famous Italian journey was for his almost a century later, many aspects of it are only vaguely documented. The date of Voltaire's arrival in England is not known, nor that of his return to France, and although he certainly interacted with many of the cultural and political leaders in England at that time, many of these encounters remain similarly undocumented. The same is true of Voltaire's theatregoing. In his writings, he mentions seeing only a few specific plays in London, among them: Addison's *Cato*; Philips' version of Racine's *Andromaque*, *The Distrest Mother*; and Shakespeare's *Julius Caesar*; but he clearly saw many more. Voltaire used the theatre not only to expand his view of English culture, but to improve his knowledge of the language, at which he worked assiduously throughout his time in the country.

The most concentrated report of his observations of the English nation is his *Lettres philosophiques*, first published in English in 1733. Two of these letters, concerning comedy and tragedy, consist of observations on the English drama; the second concludes with the intriguing observation: "If you want to know English comedy, there is no other means than to go to London, to remain three years there, to learn English well, and to go to the theatre every night."[1] Clearly this conclusion is intended to reflect the experience and authority of the author, but it is equally clearly exaggerated for rhetorical effect. Voltaire arrived in England in the spring or early summer of 1726 and left sometime in the fall of 1728, so his stay was really closer to two years than three, and involved only two theatrical seasons (September to June). Even during this shorter time, it is quite clear he did not attend the theatre every night, especially at the beginning of his visit, when he was still learning English and living in virtual solitude outside London at Wandsworth, the country seat of a London merchant, Everard Falkener, whom Voltaire had met in Paris and who became a life-long friend (*Zaïre*, perhaps the best-known of Voltaire's tragedies, is dedicated to him).

Before winter, however, Voltaire moved to London, to the town house of his closest friend in England, Lord Bolingbroke. Bolingbroke is probably best known to theatre students as the wily politician who triumphs in one of Eugène Scribe's most popular dramas, *A Glass of Water*, but for students of English history he is a much more significant, although equally complex and enigmatic figure. Bolingbroke began his lifelong interest in France in 1698 and 1699 when he visited that country and acquired, it is said, an exceptional command of the language. He entered Parliament as a Tory in 1701 and soon distinguished himself by his oratorical ability. He became Secretary of State in 1710 and devoted much of his energies to seeking a peace with France ending the War of the Spanish Succession, which had begun in 1702. The intrigues surrounding this effort are treated, with much dramatic license, in Scribe's play. The glass of water itself was probably mythical, but was certainly a part of popular history of the period. Voltaire himself spoke of it, in Scribean terms, as a tiny thing that "changed the face of all Europe."[2]

Bolingbroke did obtain peace, with the Treaty of Utrecht in 1713, but only at the cost of entering into secret negotiations with France, violating public trust at home, and treaties with allies abroad. Despite wide public support for peace and the major new international power it gave to Britain, these procedures were strongly resented, and the Whig party seized upon the situation to discredit Bolingbroke and the Tories. The first production of Addison's play, *Cato*, soon after the Treaty was signed became the occasion of a major demonstration by the Whigs against the peace and against Bolingbroke. Barton Booth, the actor playing Cato, was presented with a purse of 50 guineas from Bolingbroke for "defending the cause of liberty against a dictator" (which everyone knew referred to the duke of Marlborough, Bolingbroke's arch-rival, leader of the Whigs and the British military forces in Europe). Both Whigs and Tories admired the play, competing in claiming its sentiments for their own cause.

The French negotiations were hardly Bolingbroke's only secret project. He was also deeply involved with the Jacobites, a group of British politicians who had been plotting, ever since the bloodless revolution of 1688 had removed the Catholic house of Stuart from the throne, to restore this line. Anne, who became queen in 1702, was a Stuart, though raised a Protestant, and as her reign neared its end, Bolingbroke and many leading Tories secretly urged Anne's brother, James, to give up his Catholic religion and claim the throne, while the Whigs actively supported the German George Louis of Hanover, an ally of Marlborough and enemy of the peace of Utrecht. At the death of the queen in 1714, the Whigs moved at once to seize power and proclaim George as king. Bolingbroke was dismissed from office, and inquiries started into his secret activities. He fled in disguise to France, and was soon officially banished.

Apparently planning to spend the rest of his life in exile, Bolingbroke married a French wife, purchased a country house near Orléans, and settled into a life devoted to gardening and philosophical and literary studies, quite in the manner Voltaire would later create for his Candide. Voltaire himself became acquainted with the Bolingbrokes through one of his school friends and was a guest at La Source several times in the early 1720s. Bolingbroke became not only a close friend, but a warm literary supporter of the young poet, commending his *Mariamne* in the warmest terms to Alexander Pope in a letter of 1724.[3]

In 1723 Bolingbroke was pardoned and returned to England, but his attempts to reinstate himself in politics were successfully blocked by the prominent Whig minister Robert Walpole. Bolingbroke therefore spent much of his time in an English version of his French philosophic retreat, Dawley, near Uxbridge, which became a gathering place for many of the leading literary figures of the period, most of them strongly in sympathy with the now outcast Tory party. Bolingbroke also kept a town house in Pall Mall, in the center of London's circle of power and influence, to which he always hoped to return. He was not in London when Voltaire arrived in England, but a few months later he invited Voltaire to the house in Pall Mall, where Voltaire was soon involved in a whirlwind of activities very different from his quiet life at Wandsworth: "learning English, speaking freely with both Whigs and Tories, dining with a bishop and supping with a Quaker, going to the synagogue on Saturday and to St. Paul's on Sunday, hearing a sermon in the morning and going to the theatre after dinner, passing from the court to the stock exchange."[4]

It is at this time that Voltaire's claim of nightly theatre attendance begins to be credible. Indeed there is independent confirmation of it in the history of the theatre written by Chetwood, the prompter at Drury Lane. Among the social and artistic figures Voltaire met through Bolingbroke was Colley Cibber, playwright, actor, and now codirector of the Drury Lane theatre, who arranged for Voltaire to have a complementary orchestra seat at that theatre every evening, a privilege Voltaire was pleased to accept. According to Chetwood:

His acquaintance with the Laureat [Cibber was appointed Poet Laureate in 1730] brought him frequently to the Theatre, where (he confess'd) he improved in the *English* Orthography more in a Week, than he should otherwise have done by labour'd Study in a Month. I furnish'd him every Evening with the Play of the Night, which he took with him into the *Orchestre* (his accustomed Seat): In four or five Months, he not only convers'd in elegant *English*, but wrote it with exact propriety.[5]

The modern reader should note that in the early eighteenth century the orchestra did not mean, as it does today, the high-priced audience area near the stage, but more literally the seating area for the musicians, since live music was a part of every performance. Being seated among the musicians was a mark of special privilege, like viewing the production from the wings (an area called the "slips") or even from on stage, a practice particularly associated with Gay's popular *Beggar's Opera*, but well established before that time in England, as in France. Except on benefit nights, when the actors were pleased to obtain the extra income, this custom was a constant irritation to producers of the period, especially when elaborate scenery had to be manipulated around spectators. Theatrical advertisements of the period frequently end with some variation of this, from a Drury Lane production of the 1730s: "To prevent any Interruption of the Musick, Dancing, Machinery, or other Parts of the Performance, 'tis hoped no Gentleman will take it ill, that he cannot be admitted behind the Scenes, or into the Orchestra."[6]

Possibly Voltaire attended other theatres as well, but it is almost certain that he particularly favored Drury Lane, as Chetwood's account suggests, since it was clearly the leading London theatre of the period. After the Restoration in 1660, London playhouses had been strictly limited, according to the French model, Drury Lane being one of the two official houses granted royal patents. When Voltaire came to England, the leading rival of Drury Lane was Lincoln's Inn Fields, a small Restoration theater that had closed in 1705 and stood empty until it was enlarged, reopened, and given new theatrical life after 1714 by John Rich. Drury Lane's more famous rival, Covent Garden, did not open until 1732. Although varying in size and details of decor, all of these theatres were built according to the same general pattern, slightly different from that of theatres on the continent. London generally offered a more egalitarian theatre experience, with rows of benches for seating rather than a standing pit, at least one (and in larger theatres, two) large sweeping gallery at the rear, and open boxes on the sides instead of the more private, shuttered boxes of France or Italy.

A series of unsuccessful and rapidly changing managements at Drury Lane theatre was finally replaced in 1711 by a triumvirate of actors—Colley Cibber, Robert Wilks, and first Thomas Doggett then (after 1713) Barton

Booth—which brought the theatre stability and prosperity through the 1730s. The Drury Lane patent had been revoked in 1709 under manager Christopher Rich. Rich had been removed, and since that time Drury Lane had operated under a temporary license granted by the court. With the death of Queen Anne and the shift in government power from Tories to Whigs, the license disappeared, as did the influence enjoyed by Cibber and his colleagues. They, however, adroitly enlisted the aid of Richard Steele, a friend of the theatre and well connected in Whig circles. Steele was named "supervisor" of the theatre, a purely nominal authority, but through his influence, Drury Lane regained its long-lost patent in 1715 (in effect restoring the two-patent system of the Restoration, since Christopher Rich's son, John, also possessed a patent at Lincoln's Inn Fields). The accession of George I created a much more favorable climate for theatre in London since, unlike William III and Anne, the new ruling house loved and supported the stage. After 1714, command performances and appearances by members of the royal family were frequent occurrences, especially at Drury Lane.

Cibber remained the central figure of the Drury Lane administration, a member of the company since 1690, and particularly well-known for his depiction of fops (elegant but foolish aristocrats), especially Lord Foppington, who appeared in several plays including his own popular *The Careless Husband* (1704). His adaptation of Shakespeare's *Richard III* (1699) was offered in preference to the original for more than a century after. His codirector, Robert Wilks, was a dashing romantic lead, performing elegant gentlemen in the comedies of Cibber and others, and much praised as Hamlet. Doggett, whose continual quarrels with Booth troubled the early years of the so-called triumvirate, specialized in low comic characters, though he was praised for his intelligence by no less a critic than John Dryden. Booth, who replaced him, was a rather still and formal serious actor, whose reserved style proved perfect for the rather cold neoclassic tragedies that enjoyed a popularity at this time, most notably Addison's *Cato* and Philips' *The Distrest Mother* (1712).

Voltaire's letter on English tragedy naturally begins with Shakespeare, whom he calls the "English Corneille" and the "creator of the English theatre." Shakespeare was easily the most popular dramatist at Drury Lane, represented there some forty times during Voltaire's stay, almost exclusively by the tragedies—*Hamlet, Macbeth, Julius Caesar, Richard III, King Lear, Othello*. The comedies were represented only by three productions of *The Tempest*, probably because of its potential for visual spectacle. When Voltaire went to England, neither he nor any of his countrymen had more than the vaguest knowledge of Shakespeare; the discovery that England possessed a dramatist of indisputable genius who had no feeling for the presumed universal rules of play-writing to which French classic drama was devoted presented a paradox with which Voltaire struggled throughout his life. Although in certain writings Voltaire warmly praised Shakespeare and in others attacked him almost maniacally, his overall position never departs far from that taken in an early letter. He freely admits the brilliance of Shakespeare, but argues that this very brilliance has deeply damaged the British theatre, since subsequent authors have copied not only Shakespeare's sublime passages, but also his total lack of taste and ignorance of the rules and proprieties of theatrical art, as in the strangling of Desdemona on stage and the grotesque joking of cobblers and shoemakers in *Julius Caesar* or the gravediggers in *Hamlet*. Surprisingly, Voltaire notes, this crudeness continued into the more refined age of Charles II, as in the grotesque comic scenes of Antonio and Nakki in Otway's *Venice Preserv'd* and in the prolixity of Dryden, "more fecund than judicious" (VLP, II, 79–83). Except for Addison, a special case, Voltaire mentions no other tragic authors in this essay, remarking only that he has seen a number of recent works that were "very correct, but cold" (VLP, II, 85), a criticism some historians have taken to refer to Nichols Rowe, author of *Jane Shore* and *The Fair Penitent* and among serious dramatists then second only to Shakespeare in popularity.[7] Although Shakespeare was occasionally presented at Lincoln's Inn Fields (the two theatres agreed in 1722 not to hire actors from each other, but had no agreement against the occasional duplication of classic works like *Hamlet*), Voltaire's comments on both serious and comic theatre not surprisingly more closely reflect the repertoire of Drury Lane. The only work he cites that he could not have seen performed at Drury Lane was Otway's *Venice Preserv'd*, whose single performance during his two seasons in London took place at Lincoln's Inn Fields.

Voltaire echoed the judgement of his British contemporaries by singling out for particular praise Addison's *Cato*, which a decade and a half after its initial success was still popular. Voltaire called it the first English play that was both rational and written with elegance from beginning to end (VLP, II, 85). Doubtless the enthusiasm of his patron Bolingbroke for this play helped to encourage the French writer's interest, but *Cato* possessed many features on its own to commend it to Voltaire. In an age when, as Voltaire noted, the dominant influences on new playwrights were Shakespeare and the Restoration, Addison consciously and almost uniquely departed from this tradition to seek to create a tragedy according to neoclassic and specifically French models, strictly following the unities, the limited number of characters, and the uniform high moral and rhetorical tone employed throughout. Even before the writing of *Cato*, Addison had championed these French practices in the pages of the popular *Spectator*, the periodical produced between 1711 and 1712 by Addison and Richard Steele, which was one of the great literary achievements of the period.[8] Voltaire knew this periodical in French translation, which was one of his favorite sources for learning English after his arrival in England, and which left many traces in his writing and thinking at this time.[9] Addison's decision to insert several rather banal love scenes involving Cato's children, as a concession to contemporary taste (omitted, with little loss to the action in later eighteenth-century editions) also clearly struck a responsive chord in Voltaire, who had been forced to the same expedient in his *Oedipe*. He complained that the play was seriously damaged by this addition. "The practice of introducing love inappropriately in all dramatic works came over from Paris to London in 1660 along with our ribbons and wigs," he remarks. "The women who attend plays in both places wish to hear of nothing but love. The intelligent Addison was compliant enough to soften the severity of his character according to the fashions of his times, and spoiled a masterpiece by wishing to please."[10] Voltaire, like Addison, bowed to public taste and included love scenes in most of his major works, but continued for years to complain about them. Devoted to eighteenth-century rationalism and the life of the mind, he clearly resented this interest in and emphasis upon emotional motivations.

The measured passion and declamatory moralizing of this preeminent example of English neoclassic tragedy has little appeal to modern taste, but *Cato* enjoyed a long and successful career on the British and, indeed, the international stage. It was translated into and produced in Italian, French, German, Polish, and even Latin, gaining an international popularity enjoyed by no previous British play. *Cato* remained popular throughout the century, inspiring many imitations and parodies by Gay, Fielding, and others (none of which in any way rivalled its success). George Washington arranged for the play to be presented before his troops at Valley Forge in 1777 as an inspiration in their fight against tyranny.[11] He clearly saw a parallel between his own situation and that of the Roman republican, trapped with his army by the overwhelming forces of the tyrant Julius Caesar, though one assumes that Washington hoped to avoid Cato's ultimate suicide rather than surrender. Horace Walpole memorized passages of the play to embellish his political discourse, and as late as the early nineteenth century *Cato* remained the favorite role of England's leading tragic actor, John Kemble, who called the play "the utmost sublimity of tragedy."[12]

The two leading actors in *Cato*, Anne Oldfield and Barton Booth, were ever afterward closely associated with its success. The death of the great

Restoration actor Thomas Betterton in 1710 and the retirement soon after of his usual partner, Elizabeth Barry, removed Drury Lane's two leading tragic actors, and their roles were divided among younger players of much less distinction. Then, in 1712 and 1713 appeared two new tragedies that together established Oldfield and Booth as the new company leaders, Philips' *The Distrest Mother*, and Addison's *Cato*. Chetwood reported of Booth that the role of Pyrrhus in *The Distrest Mother* "plac'd him in the seat of Tragedy, and Cato fix'd him there."[13] Precisely the same could have been said of Oldfield in the roles of Andromache and Marcia, Cato's daughter. After these successes, Booth and Oldfield, whose elegant and dignified styles fit well with each other and the general neoclassic taste of the time (Booth studied classic statuary for inspiration for his stage poses and gestures), dominated the tragic repertoire, most notably in the tragedies of Nicholas Rowe, such as *Jane Shore*, with strong central heroines and an interesting anticipation of later domestic drama hidden under historical trappings. Both Booth and Oldfield profited by this success and visibility to improve their social and professional standing. Booth became one of the managers of the theatre and Oldfield purchased a handsome house in Mayfair. Thanks to the warm interest in the theatre within the new royal house and her open liaison with Charles Churchill, a prominent young Whig aristocrat, Oldfield was welcomed in the best homes, and was on speaking terms with the royal family. There is no record of a meeting with Voltaire, but this is not unlikely, as they moved in some of the same circles, and Voltaire certainly saw and admired both her and Booth in the theatre. His visit coincided with the peak of their careers, both near their end. Booth retired at the end of 1727. Early that same year, Oldfield was occasionally forced to cancel performances because of illness, and she retired from the stage in 1729, dying soon after.

The traditional burial church for London's actors was St. Paul, Covent Garden, but Churchill, Oldfield's long-time consort, arranged for a state funeral in Westminster Abbey, more befitting the high public position she had held despite the less than conventional nature of their relationship. The inspiration may have been the funeral of Congreve in January 1729, at which Churchill had been a pallbearer. Oldfield thus became the third actor honored with burial in the great national church, her predecessors being the great Restoration actor Thomas Betterton and his wife Mary. Voltaire had returned to France when this important public ceremony took place, but he was well aware of it, and, as we shall see, used it to contrast national attitudes toward the profession of acting.

Although Booth appeared almost exclusively in tragedy, Oldfield began her career in comedy and continued to achieve equal success there. After

1700, the old, often bawdy style of comedy associated with the Restoration fell out of favor among playwrights, but certain Restoration comedy nevertheless continued to be regularly revived, and in most of these, Oldfield played the leading female role—Vanbrugh's *The Provok'd Wife* and *The Relapse*, Congreve's *The Old Bachelor*, Etherege's *The Man of Mode*. *The Provok'd Husband*, completed by Cibber from an unfinished draft by Vanbrugh, was particularly associated with Oldfield, and often chosen for her benefits. In his comments on English comedy, Voltaire follows the example of the famous attack on Restoration comedy by Jeremy Collier, remarking that the comic style is more natural than the tragic, but this naturalness "appears to us more often that of debauchery than honesty." Among the examples he gives of plays containing such offensive material is *The Provok'd Husband*, which, he notes, "is performed almost daily" in London (VLP, II, 224). Clearly this is an exaggeration, but in fact the Vanbrugh/Cibber play was given more than thirty times during Voltaire's stay, more than three times as often as the next most frequently offered work, and the total number of Vanbrugh productions surpassed that of any other author, including Shakespeare. Obviously the Drury Lane managers and public did not share Voltaire's misgivings.

Voltaire was also offended by the earthy passages in Cibber, the next most popular comic author of the period, though he judged him an excellent actor. He gave warmer praise to Congreve, whose plays, though few, "rigorously obeyed the rules of the theatre," were "full of characters nuanced with extreme finesse," while avoiding "the least crude jest." The admiring Voltaire even sought out the aging Congreve in his home in London to express his enthusiasm, much to the discomfort of Congreve, who had long retired from the public eye. His indifference to his literary reputation was profoundly shocking to the young writer, who saw it as a glory much to be desired. Congreve dismissed his writings as trifles, and begged to be regarded only as a simple gentleman. The disenchanted Voltaire haughtily informed Congreve that if he had been "so unfortunate as to be one gentleman among many" he would never have come to see him, and dismissed Congreve's attitude as shockingly misplaced humility (VLP, II, 109). The only other English dramatist Voltaire speaks of in this essay at any length is Wycherly, who had in fact disappeared from the repertory at the time of his visit, but clearly Voltaire was struck by Wycherly's interest in Molière adaptations, and these gave him an opportunity to compare the comic styles of the two countries. Not surprisingly, Wycherly is found to be too strong and crude for French taste, although Voltaire considered his plotting superior to that of Molière.

Among contemporary comic authors, Voltaire mentions only Cibber and Richard Steele, both generally favorably, but both quite briefly, reflecting the orientation of the active repertoire, which was still dominated by the dramatists of the previous century. Steele, Addison's coauthor of the influential *Tatler* and *Spectator* papers, had written in 1721 *The Conscious Lovers*, starring Anne Oldfield. This popular play was the first major example of the genre that would later be designated sentimental comedy, and it was published with an influential preface discussing the form and containing the famous phrase that the play sought a "joy too exquisite for laughter." By mid-century, sentimental comedy had become a major form, but despite its initial success, Steele's play was still quite overshadowed in the repertoire of the late 1720s by works of Vanbrugh, Farquhar, Congreve, and indeed of the Renaissance dramatists Beaumont and Fletcher. Although Voltaire himself would later create important works in the sentimental comedy tradition, he gave no attention to it at this time, rightly recognizing the English stage's continuing orientation toward more traditional comic approaches.

Voltaire's movements during the theatrical season of 1726–1727 are impossible to trace with any precision, but it is clear that he travelled about a good deal in British political, cultural, and intellectual circles. Through Bolingbroke he became acquainted with Alexander Pope, whom he visited several times at Twickenham, and Lord Peterborough, at whose home he was a houseguest for a time with Jonathan Swift, whose *Gulliver's Travels* would be the major literary event of the coming winter. Despite the bitter partisanship of English intellectual life at this period, Voltaire also actively sought out the society of Bolingbroke's dedicated enemies, the Whigs. Robert Walpole, the English ambassador whom Voltaire had appealed to in Paris, gave him access to these circles. He was a guest at Blenheim, home of Bolingbroke's old adversary the duchess of Marlborough. Through the duchess of Queensbury he was introduced to her protege, the poet John Gay, whom he later claimed as one of his closest friends in English literary circles. The wealthy Bubb Dodington invited Voltaire to his mansion in Dorsetshire and introduced him to such leading Whig literary figures as the poets Edward Young and James Thomson. Thomson was at this time devoting his efforts to the major work for which he is remembered, the poem cycle *The Seasons*, but not long after Voltaire's departure he turned to blank-verse tragedy. His first was a popular and much admired *Sophonisba*, produced at Drury Lane in 1730 and starring Anne Oldfield in her last creation before her death. Thomson's preface showed him much in harmony with neoclassic critics like Voltaire, stressing simplicity and clarity and citing Racine as his major model. Four other neoclassic tragedies followed: *Agamemnon* (1738),

Edward and Eleonora (1739), and *Tancred and Sigismunda* (1744) before Thomson's death in 1748, and the posthumous *Coriolanus* in 1749. The editor of his collected works, George Lyttleton, sent a copy to Voltaire, whose response contains a colorful and succinct statement of his views on the current French and English stages:

> I am not surpris'd yr nation has done more justice to mr Thompson's Seasons than to his dramatic performances. There is one kind of poetry of which the judicious readers and the men of taste are the proper judges. There is an other that depends upon the vulgar, great or small. Tragedy and comedy are of these last species. They must be suited to the turn of mind and to the ability of the multitude and proportion'd to their taste. Yr nation, two hundred years since, is us'd to a wild scene, to a croud of tumultuous event, to an emphaatical poetry mix'd with low and comical expressions, to murthers, to a lively representation of bloody deeds to a kind of horrour which seems often barbarous and childish, all faults which never sullyd the greak, the roman or the french stage. And give me leave to say that the taste of yr politest countrymen in point of tragedy differs not much in point of tragedy from the taste of the mob at the bear garden. T'is true we have too much of words, if you have too much of action, and perhaps the perfection of the Art should consist in a due mixture of the french taste and english energy. Mr. Adisson, who would have reach'd to that pitch of perfection had he succeeded in the amourous part of his tragedy as well as in the part of Cato, warn'd often yr nation against the corrupted tastge of the stage and since he could not reform the genius of the country, I am afraid the contagious distemper is past curing. Mr. Thompson's tragedies seems to me wisely intricated, and elegantly writ. They want perhaps some fire; and it may be that his heroes are neither moving nor busy enough. But taking him all in all, methinks he has the highest claim to the greatest esteem [spelling as in the original]. (VC, XVIII, 67)

Voltaire's social visits were by no means confined to literary figures. He also became acquainted with the most powerful man in the government, the prime minister Robert Walpole, at his home in Middlesex, though Walpole's political concerns left him little time for literary interests. The pinnacle of these visits with the highest levels of English society was achieved early in 1727, when *The Daily Journal* of 27 January reported: "Last week, M. Voltaire, the famous French poet, who was banished from France, was introduced to his majesty, who received him very graciously." So assiduously in fact did Voltaire cultivate the Court party that Pope, and later Bolingbroke and Swift as well, became convinced that he was carrying private information on their circle back to Walpole and others. From this came a distinct cooling in the relationship between Voltaire and the leaders of the Tory literary circles.

In the spring of 1727, Voltaire returned to the relative seclusion of Wandsworth, where he spent the summer and early fall in writing, primarily preparing for the English publication of his major work of this period, the epic *Henriade*. It was a turbulent summer in British political life. George I died unexpectedly in June while on a visit to the continent, and Whigs and Tories alike assumed that his departure would mean the fall of Walpole and of the virtual monopoly of Whig political power, but after several weeks of confusion Walpole survived, due in large part to the influence of the new queen, Caroline. Thus, when the new king was crowned in October, the political landscape was essentially unchanged. Coronation fever seized the capital and patrons flocked to Drury Lane to see a lavish stage coronation ceremony that was added to Shakespeare's *Henry VIII*. With this addition, the play was given thirteen consecutive performances, far more than any other Shakespeare work of the period, and for weeks after, the coronation scene was performed following almost any work the theatre presented, from *Jane Shore* to *The Way of the World*.

In November Voltaire was back in London. Bolingbroke, following the disappointment of the new Whig ascendency, had given up his town house, and in any case Voltaire seems to have seen little of the Tory literary circle at this time. He settled in more modest quarters at the Sign of the White Peruke in Maiden Lane, near the Strand and the offices of his British publishers. It is probable that he attended theatre less this season, considering the distractions of preparing the *Henriade* and some substantial essays for publication; if he did attend, it was most likely again to Drury Lane, where the complimentary admission Cibber offered would have been important in Voltaire's present very reduced circumstances. He may have attended Lincoln's Inn Fields on 15 December, however, since that is the only time during his stay in London that Otway's *Venice Preserv'd* was offered, which Voltaire criticizes in his *Lettres philosophiques*. Surely he must also have attended a production of John Gay's phenomenally successful *Beggar's Opera*, which opened at this theatre on 29 January 1728, and ran for thirty-two consecutive nights, in a period when a run of nine nights was considered excellent and one of twelve nights most unusual. Drury Lane would have been quite eclipsed had it not had the good fortune to have opened the almost equally popular *The Provok'd Husband* with Oldfield earlier this same month.

Lincoln's Inn Fields had emerged as an important theatre in 1695, when the oppressive policies of the Drury Lane manager, Christopher Rich, led to a revolt of his leading actors, who sought refuge in this small theatre dating from the early days of the Restoration. It opened auspiciously enough with Congreve's *Love for Love*, and dominated the London scene until its company moved to larger quarters in the Haymarket in 1705. Rich, who was removed from the directorship of Drury Lane in 1707, acquired the property, rebuilt the theatre and hoped to reopen it if the governmental ban against him was lifted. The new government in 1714 indeed removed the ban, but Rich died soon after and his son, John, inherited his project, received a license, and opened the theatre later that same year.

Although the company at Lincoln's Inn Fields was less distinguished than that at Drury Lane, much of their fare was similar, if not identical—Shakespearian and contemporary tragedy, comedies by Vanbrugh, Congreve, and Farquhar. The specialty of the theatre however was the pantomime, a form particularly developed by Rich. Many of these productions had harlequin as a central character, Rich being the first and most famous of a long tradition of English incarnations of this traditional commedia character. *Harlequin Sorcerer* in 1717 was the first of the Rich pantomimes and a model for most that followed. A combination of dance, music, and particularly, magic and spectacle was grafted onto familiar stories from myth and legend or even onto parodies of other stage works. One of the most popular of these offerings, the *Harlequin Dr. Faustus* in 1724, was so successful that it henceforth became a regular offering at Drury Lane as well.

The greatest success enjoyed by this theatre, or indeed by any London theatre of the century, was *The Beggar's Opera*, but there was little in the work to characterize it as a Lincoln's Inn Fields production. Indeed, part of its charm is its originality, since it essentially created a new genre, the ballad opera. The work had largely been conceived in the spring of 1727 when Gay, Pope, and Swift were together at Tickenham. Voltaire was also an occasional member of this assemblage of wits and thus aware of this project. In fact, some forty years later in Geneva Voltaire fondly recalled this period, as an English visitor reports: "He told me of his acquaintance with Pope, Swift (with whom he lived for three months at Lord Peterborough's), and Gay, who first showed him *The Beggar's Opera* before it was acted. He says he admires Swift, and loved Gay vastly."[14] Gay's literary circle enjoyed the play greatly, but few were optimistic of its success. Theatre directors were even more suspicious. Gay first approached Cibber at Drury Lane, who was uninterested. Gay then tried the more unlikely venue of the Haymarket, whose director, Aaron Hill, was an old schoolmate, but was again refused. Finally the work was accepted, without much enthusiasm, by Rich at Lincoln's Inn Fields, according to some sources because Gay's patroness, the duchess of Queensbury, guaranteed his losses.

Gay's original intention seems to have been to have the lyric sections of the work spoken, but Rich was accustomed to the musical settings of the pantomimes and urged that the lyrics be set to music, a suggestion critically supported by the duchess, who seems to have been much involved in the rehearsal process. The musical director of Lincoln's Inn Fields, Dr. Pepusch, began work writing an overture, and setting the lyrics to music, not a tremendous task, since Gay had given most of them rhythms familiar to him from traditional ballad and country dance tunes. Fifty-one of the opera's sixty-nine songs were in fact derived from popular or anonymous tunes, most of them well-known to the audience. This combination of novelty and familiarity was clearly one of the charms of the work, especially in that many of the lyrics provided parodic variations on the originals.

This web of musical references is, of course, largely lost for modern theatregoers, although Gay's exuberant work fortunately contains enough more general theatrical and dramatic values to make it still appealing. The work has also largely lost two other dimensions that gave it particular comic and parodic resonance for its contemporary audiences—its references to current politics and to the current vogue for Italian opera. As Swift observed in an article on the play in a Dublin paper:

> The author takes the occasion of comparing the common robbers of the public and their several stratagems for betraying, undermining and hanging each other, to the several arts of the politicians in time of trouble. This comedy likewise exposes, with great justice, that taste for Italian music among us, which is wholly unsuitable to a Northern climate and the genius of the people, whereby we are overrun with Italian effeminacy and Italian manners.[15]

There was a substantial English tradition of stage music before the enormous success of Italian opera at the beginning of the eighteenth century. The court masques, especially under the Stuart kings, provided a foundation and inspired operatic, masque-like productions of Shakespearian plays like *Macbeth* and *The Tempest* during the Restoration. John Blow's *Venus and Adonis* (1684) and Henry Purcell's *Dido and Aeneas* (1689) seemed to promise a particularly English style of opera, but the enormous success of Motteux's *Arsinoe, Queen of Cypress* at Drury Lane in 1705, with no speaking sections, no masques, no machines or scenic effects, and little or no probability in the plot, created a generation-long vogue for this sort of entertainment, at least among the aristocracy and monied classes. For a few years, Drury Lane and the new Queen's Theatre in the Haymarket competed in operatic production, but after 1710, Drury Lane devoted itself almost exclusively to traditional drama, while the Queen's became London's home for opera. After the coronation of George I in 1713, the Queen's Theatre was re-named the King's and George's favored composer, Handel, assumed a lead-ing position there. Although this artificial form was sung in an alien language, featured those fascinating, somewhat otherworldly figures, the castrati, and was regularly condemned by writers of the period, it remained an important, and highly visible, part of London cultural life. As Addison complained in *The Spectator* of 21 March 1711: "It does not take any great Measure of Sense to see the Ridiculousness of this monstrous Practice; but what makes it more astonishing, it is not the Taste of the Rabble, but of Per-sons of the greatest Politeness, which has establish'd it."[16] "There's nobody allowed to say, *I sing*," observed Gay in a 1723 letter to Swift, "but an eunuch or an Italian woman."[17]

The excesses of the form, and indeed its popularity with a small and self-important segment of the population made it a convenient target for Gay's satirical treatment. His political targets were equally visible, equally unrep-resentative of the general public, and equally given to excess, but obviously considerably more dangerous to ridicule. Brecht's ironic reworking of Gay's piece as *The Threepenny Opera* may help to remind modern audiences of the work's political dimension, but for a society deeply embroiled in the politi-cal struggles of the Whigs and Tories, this dimension had a much more im-mediate and specific impact. For Gay's original audiences, the often ruthless activities of Walpole and his government could readily be seen suggested by the activities of Macheath and his gang, a number of verses specifically re-lating criminal to political activities. Macheath's two "wives," Polly and Lucy, were generally thought to be a reference to Walpole's wife and mis-tress. The Prime Minister attended the opening night, and every eye turned toward his box when Lockit, played by the paunchy actor, Hall, who physi-cally resembled the corpulent Walpole, sang the words:

> When you censure the Age
> Be cautious and sage,
>   Lest the Courtiers offended should be:
> If you mention Vice or Bribe,
> Tis so part to all the Tribe;
>   Each cries: "That was levell'd at me."

Walpole had the good grace (or the political acumen) to smile approvingly at the song, and the awkward moment passed, but the enormous success of the play must have been a continuing irritation to him. When Gay offered a se-quel, *Polly*, to the Lord Chamberlain for approval, this was denied, almost certainly as a punishment for *The Beggar's Opera*, since *Polly*, set in the

West Indies to which Macheath has been transported, had nothing in it to offend the court or the Whigs. Not surprisingly, however, other authors were quick to follow up on the enormous success of *The Beggar's Opera*, and over fifty examples appeared on London stages, none of them seriously rivalling the popularity of Gay's initiating work.

Voltaire also enjoyed his major literary success in England this spring, his long-promised *Henriade* appearing in March and dedicated to Queen Caroline. The sales were excellent and Voltaire was again welcomed at court, even to intimate supper parties there. Voltaire did not again plunge into the social world, however. With his major English publishing project finished, he began to consider a return to France, where he was now arranging for the publication of the *Henriade* and other works. He again retired to Wandsworth where he spent the summer in literary projects, among which the theatre took a central position it had not held since his arrival in England, and the English influence on such activity was clear. Haunted by his exposure to the English stage in general and Shakespeare in particular, he sketched out the first act of a tragedy, *Brutus*, in English prose, and began work on *La Mort de César*, both of which he would complete soon after his return to France.

Voltaire's last letter from London is dated August 1728. In the next, February 1729, he is in Paris after an incognito stay of some time at Dieppe, gaining assurances that he would be welcome back in the capital. Voltaire had been in England for approximately two years and three months, but during this rather brief period he had become acquainted with most of the leading political and cultural figures of that country. More importantly, he gained a love and knowledge of an alternative social and literary world that would provide him with an invaluable perspective from which to view and critique his own culture and tradition in the many years to come.

NOTES

1. Voltaire, *Lettres philosophiques*, 2 vols. (Paris: Corny, 1909), II:110 (henceforward VLP).

2. Sidney Low, *Dictionary of English History* (London: Cassell, 1885), 714.

3. Elwin Whitwell, *The Works of Alexander Pope*, 10 vols. (London: Murray, 1871–1889), 7:398.

4. Quoted in Fernand Baldesperger, "La chronologie de séjour de Voltaire en Angleterre et les *Lettres philosophiques*," *Archiv für das Studium der neueren Sprachen und Literaturen* 129 (1912): 140. The other substantive study on this subject is J. C. Collins, *Voltaire in England* (New York: Harper and Brothers, 1886).

5. W. R. Chetwood, *A General History of the Stage* (London: Owen, 1749), 46n.

6. George C. D. Odell, *Shakespeare from Betterton to Irving*, 2 vols. (New York: Charles Scribner's, 1920), 1:283.

7. For example, Alexandre Beljame, *Le public et les hommes de lettres en Angleterre* (Paris: Hachette, 1897), 259.

8. See especially numbers 39, 40, 42, and 44 of *The Spectator* (14, 16, 18, and 20 April 1711), all written by Addison.

9. Baldensperger, "Chronologie du séjour," 138–39.

10. Ibid., 87.

11. Frederic M. Litto, "Addison's *Cato* in the Colonies," *William and Mary Quarterly* 23 (1966): 447.

12. James Broaden, *Memoires of the Life of John Philip Kemble* (Philadelphia: Robert H. Small, 1825), 555.

13. Chetwood, *General History*, 92.

14. Extract from the MS Journal of Major W. Broome, *Notes and Queries*, 1st series, vol. X (1854): 403.

15. Quoted in Roger Fiske, *English Theatre Music in the Eighteenth Century* (London: Oxford, 1973), 97.

16. Addison, *The Spectator*, No. 18, Wednesday, 21 March 1711.

17. Quoted in Phoebe Fenwick Gaye, *John Gay* (London: Collins, 1938), 158.

Chapter 3

Triumph in the Theatre, 1729–1743

Voltaire returned from England with two plays already partially completed, and within three years he had finished and presented them along with two others, a group that is generally regarded as the most "English" of his many dramas. *Brutus* was read to the Comédie actors and accepted in October 1729, but Voltaire withdrew it for rewriting (he wrote quickly, but was an obsessive reworker of his dramatic pieces) and it was not presented until 11 December 1730.

Voltaire had returned to find a theatre much changed during his few years of absence from France. Baron, like his master, Molière, had been striken on stage and carried home to die that same fall. Duclos retired in 1730. Both of these actors had led long and full lives; much more unexpected and tragic was the death of the popular and beloved Adrienne Lecouvreur in 1730 at the age of thirty-eight. Although Lecouvreur had long suffered from very frail health, her death was such a shock that poisoning was suspected. Voltaire, who was at her deathbed with the surgeon and her long-time lover, Maurice de Saxe, ordered an autopsy, which found no poison. This was, however, not the end of scandal surrounding this much-publicized death. Despite the fact that antitheatrical tracts were now a rarity, and the theatre was widely regarded as useful for the encouragement of public and private morality, the acting profession itself was still banned by the church in France, and actors wishing to receive any sacraments (including marriage, baptism, or final rites) had to officially renounce their profession first. Baron had done so, and was given a respectful burial at his parish church, not far from the theatre. Lecouvreur, out of conviction or weakness, did not make the required renunciation, and so was denied Christian burial, and placed hastily in the dead of night in an unmarked grave.

This example of religious intolerance infuriated Voltaire, especially when he compared the final treatment of the beloved Lecouvreur with her English contemporary, Oldfield, given the full honors of a burial in Westminster Abbey. The result was one of his most passionate and bitter attacks on official prejudice, the poem *Sur la mort de Mlle Lecouvreur*, which rhetorically inquired "Is it only in England that mortals dare to think?" The poem was naturally banned by the authorities, but widely circulated. Voltaire met with the actors of the Comédie, urging them to stop acting until their profession was given official recognition, but no such protest occurred. "They promised but did nothing," he wrote to Mlle Clairon many years later. "They preferred dishonor with a little money" (VC, XLVI, 285).

With the departure of Baron, Dufresne again became the leading male tragic actor in the company, though the older roles played by Baron were taken on by a new member, Pierre-Claude Sarrazin, and some younger ones by another newcomer, François Grandval, still in his teens. Younger still was Marie-Anne Dangeville, not quite sixteen, who began by playing children's roles, but was suddenly elevated into more mature parts by the loss of Lecouvreur. These were the actors that undertook the leading roles in *Brutus*. Sarrazin played the title role, not the friend of Caesar, but a much earlier republican hero who condemns his son, Titus (played by Grandval), to death for supporting the return of the tyrannical Tarquin. A love interest and conflict is provided by Tulle (played by Dangeville), the daughter of Tarquin beloved by Titus. The play enjoyed a moderate success, though clearly not because of its superior interpretation. During rehearsals, it is reported, Voltaire quite lost his temper with the reserved Sarrazin, who called upon the war-god Mars "like one begging the Holy Virgin to grant him a hundred-franc prize in the lottery." Clearly, Dangeville also had problems on the opening night, but Voltaire wrote her one of his most charming letters, deftly mixing flattery, encouragement, and criticism, which evidently had its effect, for he subsequently reported that she acted "like an angel" (VC, II, 145, 148).

Brutus had only a modest success in its early years, partly due to its rather undistinguished cast, but also because its republican message, perhaps the most "English" thing about it, was not very attractive to a theatre culture still largely aristocratic. As times and political attitudes changed, *Brutus* steadily grew in popularity. It was revived in 1763 to warm acclaim and became a standard revival piece during the Revolution, contributing in no small measure to establishing Voltaire as one of the patron saints of the new order. After this high-water mark, its reputation faded rapidly, and today it is primarily remembered for the lengthy prologue, "A Discourse on Tragedy," dedicated to Lord Bolingbroke and discussing in detail what Voltaire considered to be the comparative strengths and weaknesses of English and French tragedy.

The preface first discusses verse in the theatre, complaining of the restrictions it imposes: "The French writer is a slave of rhyme, forced sometimes to write four verses to express what the English can say in a single line. The English writer says whatever he wishes, the French one says whatever he is able." Yet Voltaire cannot foresee an unrhymed French drama; the weight of tradition, the training of the audience, even the structure of the language require it. Other traits of English drama, however, Voltaire would encourage in the French. One of these is the emphasis upon action, for despite the purity, elegance and finesse of French drama, "Our excessive delicacy sometimes forces us to put into recitation what we would like to display to the eye." He is quick to reject the "scenes of carnage" in Shakespeare and others, but insists that so long as the language is not neglected, spectacle can enhance it. Anticipating some of his own later "exotic" dramas, he recalls a 1702 *Montezume* by Ferrier, which opened with a "magnificent and barbarous" palace and striking costumes, but while "the spectacle charmed, there was nothing else of beauty in this tragedy." Voltaire's own attempts in this direction in *Brutus* were more modest. He introduced "not without some fear" a scene of Roman senators "in red robes, going to their meeting." He also took some liberty with unity of place (though he characterized the three unities as among the "fundamental laws of the theatre" in his preface), especially when this would achieve a strong effect, as in the fourth act when the stage opens at the rear to reveal Brutus. One other complaint made in this preface about the French theatre was the practice of placing benches for the spectators on the stage, which in practical terms encumbered the acting and scenery, and theoretically made a joke of unity of place or verisimilitude (VO, II, 311–25). Voltaire implies that the English are free of this custom, a suggestion clearly disproven by Hogarth's famous painting of *The Beggar's Opera*, which shows a similarly encumbered stage, but the custom was if anything more solidly entrenched in France, where it was closely tied to aristocratic privilege in the theatre. Voltaire continued to campaign against this abuse, and it was largely due to his ongoing campaign that the stage seating was finally abolished in 1760.

Although Voltaire's preface to *Brutus* observed that it was more difficult to write well than to seek to impress the audience with assassinations, witches, and spectres, he was fascinated by the ghost in *Hamlet* and attempted to create a similar effect in his next tragedy, *Eriphyle*, presented 7

March 1732 at the Comédie. The play was generally well received, but the climactic moment, the appearance of the ghost of Amphiaraüs at the rear of a stage lined with elegant courtiers, caused not terror but general amusement, and doubtless added to Voltaire's determination to someday rid the stage of these interlopers.

Disappointed by the reception of *Eriphyle*, which the actors decided not to revive after Easter, even though the author promised to give them all its profits, Voltaire set to work at once on a new tragedy, *Zaïre*, which was ready for performance by 13 August. English critics, including Aaron Hill, who translated the play in 1735 (for a very successful run at Drury Lane), made much of its surface resemblance to *Othello*, but the themes, language, and structure of the play in fact owe little to Shakespeare. The background is the Crusades. Zaïre, the captured daughter of a French nobleman, has been raised a Muslim in the court of the Sultan of Jerusalem. She and the Sultan Orosmane fall in love and plan to marry. Then her brother, Nérestan, arrives and her long-imprisoned father, Lusignan, is released and recognizes his two children. Misunderstanding Zaïre's interest in Nérestan, the jealous Orosmane kills her and, discovering his error, kills himself.

In a letter of 29 May 1732, Voltaire outlined his aims in writing *Zaïre*:

Everyone has reproached me for not putting love in my plays. They will have it this time, I swear, and I don't mean simple gallantry. I swear that there will be nothing so Turkish, so Christian, so full of love, so tender, so furious as what I am writing at present to please them. . . . I will paint the manners as accurately as possible, and try to put in the work the greatest pathos and interest offered by Christianity and the greatest pathos and interest offered by love. (VC, II, 322)

The first performance gained a mixed response, but as Voltaire made adjustments to the play and the actors gained in confidence, it became a major success. Gaussin played Zaïre, and Voltaire credited her with the success of the play. Dufresne played Orosmane; Grandval the brother, Nérestan; and Sarrazin the elderly and saintly Lusignan. Voltaire played this role himself when the play was revived, soon after its opening, at the private theatre of Mme de Fontaine-Martel, and in the years that followed it became his favorite part at the many private theatres he founded or supported. As an author who emerged from the Bastille to launch his literary career, and for most of his life was threatened with prison if he returned to Paris, Voltaire not surprisingly felt a special affinity with Lusignan, despotically deprived of his liberty for twenty years. The themes of capture, restraint, and imprisonment run through Voltaire's drama, and the victims of official persecution, as in the famous Calas affair late in his life, always had a claim on his sympathy.

Although *Zaïre* was not, as Voltaire claimed, the first tragedy to deal with national subjects, no predecessor had achieved much success, and it began a vogue for such themes. It has continued to be the most popular Voltaire work, revived by Sarah Bernhardt in 1874, and the only Voltaire piece performed at the Comédie in the twentieth century. In the preface, dedicated to his English friend, Falkener, Voltaire speculated that this play might be the last he would attempt: "I love literature, but the more I love it, the more irritated I become to see it ill-received. Here they perform rather too indifferently the pleasant things that a man has created with much pain" (VO, II, 540–41). In fact, however, Voltaire was on the brink of his most productive and successful decade of theatrical creation. Between *Zaïre* in 1732 and *Mérope* in 1743, he created a series of dramatic works that raised him, at least in the eyes of his century, to rival Corneille and Racine, the giants of the French tragic stage. This was a period of enormous productivity, even for the prolific Voltaire. While preparing *Zaïre*, he was also involved in putting together the first edition of his works; in researching the major historical project, *Le Siècle de Louis XIV*; and in undertaking his mock epic poem based on Joan of Arc, *La Pucelle*, which, privately circulated, was among his most scandalous and also most popular works; as well as other theatrical projects in both comedy and opera. The comedy *Les Originaux* was based on a situation similar to Molière's *Bourgeois gentilhomme*, but bore strong evidence of Voltaire's recent English theatregoing, with passages borrowed directly from Cibber, Farquhar, and Vanbrugh. This slight piece was never presented at the Comédie, but was circulated in what was becoming an important alternative theatre in France, private theatres in the homes of the aristocracy. The "Grand Nights" of the duchess of Maine at Sceaux early in the century served as a model for countless eighteenth-century aristocratic entertainments, and throughout his career Voltaire remained at least as closely associated with those as with the public theatre. Another three-act prose comedy, *L'Echange*, closely based on Vanbrugh's *The Relapse*, and completed in 1734, was a popular piece in society theatres throughout the rest of this decade. It was a particular favorite at the Château de Cirey, where Voltaire withdrew with Emilie Du Châtelet during much of the period between 1735 and 1740.

This same period saw Voltaire's first forays into yet another genre, the opera. Later in his career he would become more suspicious of opera as a rival to tragedy, but at this point it presented to him an attractive alternative and possibly a means of revitalizing tragedy, since it stressed many of those features that Voltaire felt tragedy should develop—spectacle, the picturesque, strong emotion, exoticism, and coups de théâtre. Many of Voltaire's trage- dies indeed have an operatic quality, and an astonishing number of early nineteenth-century operas were based upon them—thirteen on *Zaïre* alone.[1]

French opera of the early eighteenth century was very different from the Italian opera that was at this same time making important inroads into Eng- land, and very much closer to traditional French tragedy as a genre. Lully, the father of the form, and his librettist, Quinault, combined drama, music, ballet, and spectacle into lavish baroque entertainments, the *tragédies en musique*. These followed a rigid pattern, presenting tales of love in classic or chivalric settings in a form composed almost entirely of recitative, with only occasional formal arias in the Italian style. Central was the concept of "the marvelous," achieved by elaborate machines for divine or demonic appear- ances, magic effects, tempests, and conflagrations. Music and dance was never supposed to be simply decorative, but linked to the dramatic action. The theorist Dubos in 1719 wrote that the instrumental passages of these *tragédies lyriques* should "agitate us, calm us, move us; in short, they act upon us in the same manner as the verses of Racine and Corneille."[2]

Voltaire first tried his hand at this form in a libretto, *Tanis et Zélide*, as a kind of exercise, not meant for performance; but his second libretto, *Sam- son*, was intended for the stage, and that meant finding a composer. The gen- eration following Lully—André Campra, Marin Marais, and Michel Monté- clair—was now nearing its end, and Voltaire, with remarkable prescience, contacted a rising young composer who had not yet produced an operatic work, but who would come to dominate the operatic world of eighteenth- century France, as Voltaire did the dramatic, Jean-Philippe Rameau.[3] Ra- meau, a native of Dijon, had settled in Paris in 1722 and began his musical theatre career in the most unpromising way, creating music for sketches for fairground theatres written by a fellow native of Dijon, Alexis Piron.

Although the official Paris theatre of this time was limited to the three state houses—the Comédie Française, the Comédie Italienne (after 1716), and the Opéra—there existed throughout Voltaire's lifetime two important alternative traditions. The aristocracy, as we have already seen, developed an elaborate system of private theatres, to which Voltaire was a major contribu- tor. The rest of the population had another alternative, the theatres in the Saint-Germain and Saint-Laurent fairs at the borders of the city. The estab- lished houses of the city rightly feared the competition of the fairs, but no sooner was restrictive legislation passed than the ingenious fair performers found a way to circumvent it. Forbidden to perform comedy, they turned to opera; forbidden to speak, they sang; forbidden to sing, they mimed with printed texts dropped from the flies; forbidden to act on stage, they acted on tightropes or gave performances disguised as gymnastic exhibitions; always testing the limits of what the authorities would permit. Engaged in such constant guerrilla activity, these alternate ventures survived, and in the course of the century developed in a number of cases from crude trestle platforms to elegant permanent houses with elaborate scenic equipment. The fairs began to regularly offer imaginative combinations of dance, songs, pantomime, acrobatics, and scraps of dialogue in the 1670s, and by the early 1700s this had become standard fare, much of it provided by two prolific authors, Fuzelier and Dorneval. In 1713 they were joined by Alain René Lesage. Lesage's *Crispin rival de son Maître* (1707) and *Turcaret* (1709) were the outstanding new comedies of that decade, but the Comédie was closed to him when, after these successes, he refused to give way to the demands of the actors to make changes in his writing, and this left him with no alternative venue (the Italienne being not yet reopened) but the fairs. Under Lesage's influence, the old mixed genres of the fairs developed into the more literary and polished *opéra-comique*, which he is credited with creating.

The Piron/Rameau works provide a good example of the variety offered by the popular *opéra-comique* in the fairs of the 1720s—fairy-tale spectacles (*L'Endriague*, 1723), exotica (*Sauvages*, inspired by the display of two Louisiana indians, 1725), and harlequinades (*L'Enrôlement de Harlequin*, 1726). Still, Rameau dreamed of creating a serious opera, requesting (in vain) a libretto in 1727 from Houdar de la Motte in a letter that cites his versatility in characterizing the song and dance of the Louisiana savages in "*Les Soupirs, les tendres plaintes, les cyclopes, les tourbillons*, and *L'Entretien des muses*."[4] The wealthy patron of the arts La Riche de la Pouplinière took an interest in Rameau and, knowing that Voltaire was also interested in him, encouraged a collaboration. Montéclair's innovative *Jephté* at the Opéra in 1731 had been a great success for ten days until it was closed by the archbishop of Paris. Despite this ominous precedent, Rameau and Voltaire felt biblical subject matter could renew this genre, and proceeded with *Samson*, a subject that had been treated in 1717 and again in 1730 without protest at the Italian theatre. However, the Opéra was hesitant, Voltaire's reworkings of the libretto moved slowly, and Rameau gradually lost interest. He turned to another acquaintance from the La Pouplinière circle, the Abbé Simon-Joseph Pellegrin, librettist for some fifteen ballets and *tragédies lyriques*, among them the ill-fated *Jephté*, and with him wrote his first major success, *Hippolyte et Aricie* (1733). Rameau utilized *Samson* music in *Les Indes galantes* (1735), written with Louis Fuzelier, whom Rameau had met in the fair theatres, effectively marking the end of this project. A decade later, Voltaire and Rameau did collaborate on two court spectacles, but their combined *tragédie lyrique* remains one of the much regretted lost projects of opera history.

The dazzling success of *Zaïre* gave Voltaire the stature in Paris he had long sought. He was lavishly praised and spent six weeks at court, where the play was performed for the king and queen. Such a success naturally also aroused Voltaire's enemies and rivals. The aging and exiled poet Jean Baptiste Rousseau, long opposed to Voltaire, circulated in Paris a venomous letter attacking the play. This in turn stimulated a burlesque on contemporary writers, Rousseau in particular, from Voltaire, *Le Temple du goût*, a work somewhat similar to Pope's "Dunciad." Many besides Rousseau were wittily skewered, and the uproar was enormous. Voltaire well knew that in this climate it would be impossible to publish his *Lettres philosophiques*, full of political and religious observations that would be even more inflammatory. He therefore sought to mollify the court and Paris society with a new play which he hoped would restore the enthusiasm he had enjoyed with *Zaïre*.

The success of *Zaïre* apparently convinced Voltaire that despite his own misgivings on the matter, the public required a strong love interest in tragedy. In the words of his contemporary La Harpe: "The happy fate of this play demonstrated to the author how love ruled in the theatre and how suitable his genius was to express it; thus he decided to attempt a new work which love would dominate entirely."[5] *Adélaïde du Guesclin* was thus devoted to love, and also broke new ground by taking on a French historical subject, from fifteenth-century Brittany. In a 24 February letter, Voltaire describes the play in process as "a subject entirely French and of my own invention, where I have packed in as much as I could of love, jealousy, fury, propriety, probity, and grandeur of soul" (VC, III, 20). In his preface to *Zaïre*, Voltaire had praised the English theatre for its boldness in putting on stage kings and ancient families of the kingdom, thus giving rise "to a type of tragedy that is still unknown to us and which we need." He characterized *Zaïre* as a "feeble attempt" in this direction, and the new work clearly sought to extend this project.

The play has only four main characters: Vendôme, an ally of the English; his brother, Nemours, who supports the Dauphin; Adélaïde, beloved by Vendôme, but in love with his brother; and Coucy, a Kent-like faithful servant who saves Vendôme from murdering his brother when jealousy overcomes him. The play premiered 18 January 1734, with Dufresne as Vendôme, Gaussin as Adélaïde, and Grandval as Nemours. Despite the prominence of the love theme, however, the play was very badly received, and Voltaire withdrew it for extensive rewriting—moving the setting back to the Middle Ages; making the English into Moors; and removing some of his bolder strokes, such as having Nemours appear covered in blood, fainting on the stage, and presumably killed by offstage cannon fire. The new version, *Le Duc de Foix*, succeeded at the Comédie in 1752. Gaussin was then thirty-nine, a bit old for Adélaïde, but Vendôme was played by Voltaire's protege, Lekain, an actor clearly superior to Dufresne. Thirteen years later, Lekain enjoyed an even greater success with a version close to the original, for a public more willing to accept Voltaire's departures from classic tradition.

Eventually, then, Voltaire's historical experiment succeeded, but it did not provide him with the success he needed in 1734. Worse news soon followed. The *Lettres philosophiques* was published in April, against Voltaire's wishes and without his knowledge. The reaction he feared was not long in coming. His publisher was thrown into the Bastille, the book was burnt in Paris by the hangman, and a warrant was issued for Voltaire's arrest. Voltaire took refuge with a kindred spirit, Madame Du Châtelet, at Cirey, her remote chateau in Champagne. This remained his major home for the rest of the decade, although he did regularly return to Paris after March 1735, when his warrant for arrest was cancelled with the understanding that he would behave himself in the future.

While in England, Voltaire translated the scene containing Antony's speech over Caesar's body in Shakespeare's *Julius Caesar*, which he much admired. He had sketched out plans for a tragedy based on this play "in the English manner," but softened it according to French ideas of propriety, decorum, and tragic situation (Brutus is made the son of Caesar so that the tragedy according to classic custom can be familial, as well as political). The work was first presented in 1733 at a society theatre in a much abridged form, with only a few actors, and with the key scene of the funeral oration cut because the stage was too small for it. The first full production was in August of 1735 by pupils of the collège d'Harcourt, a quite suitable producing organization for a play that not only contained no love interest, but in fact contained not a single woman's part. Voltaire wryly commented, "I am now only a college poet. I have abandoned two theatres as too full of cabals—that of the Comédie Française and that of the world" (VC, IV, 102).

Voltaire was not likely, however, to remain long away from either of those other theatres and the recognition they offered. He was already planning his return to the Comédie with a new work, *Alzire*. Though similar in structure to *Adélaïde*, it differed greatly in treatment, and these differences clearly worked in its favor, for it opened 27 January 1736 to considerable success, both at the Comédie and subsequently at court. Again, a heroine (Alzire, played by Gaussin) is held captive by a governor (Gusman, played by Grandval), who falls in love with her though she loves a man from her own people (Zamore, played by Dufresne). There are echoes not only of *Adélaïde*, but also of *Zaïre*, since the opposing parties represent different cultures and religions. Mlle Gaussin's role is much larger here than in *Adélaïde*, increasing the work's sentimental appeal. The theme of religious tolerance proved more attractive than than of nationalism, and perhaps most important, the setting of the play in sixteenth-century Peru provided an intriguing exotic setting.

Voltaire claimed that he had opened the theatre to "a completely new world, with completely new customs" (VC, III, 327). This claim was generally accepted by Voltaire's contemporaries,[6] but it was not strictly true. The Comédie itself had offered an unsuccessful and unprinted *Montezume* by Ferrier as early as 1702, and during the 1720s a wave of exotic indian plays swept the minor theatres of Paris. The Piron/Rameau *Sauvages* of 1725 has already been mentioned (and indeed Rameau's *Les Indes galantes* at the Opéra preceded *Alzire* by a year). Louis François Delisle offered a highly popular *Arlequin sauvage* at the Comédie Italienne in 1721. All of these works contributed to the growing interest in one of the central intellectual concepts of the century, the noble savage. Jean Jacques Rousseau, who is most closely associated with this concept, remarked on the success of Delisle's play in his famous letter to d'Alembert "sur les spectacles," and Gilbert Chinard in his study on American exoticism in French literature of this period remarks that much of the success of Rousseau's ideas of the state of nature expressed in the *Discours sur l'inégalité* and the *Contract social* were in part successful because their way had been prepared by theatrical pieces like Delisle's.[7] This connection was already noted in the eighteenth century, as may be seen in D'Origny's 1788 history of the Théâtre Italien, which specifically cites the debilitating effects of society on the natural man as explained in "the beautiful discussion of this immortal Writer [Rousseau] on the origin and foundation of the inequality among men as an introduction to *Arlequin sauvage*, which also shows the contrast between our customs and those of man in a state of nature."[8]

Symbolically, the inhabitants of the new world served as a central figure for profound debates in eighteenth-century thought on the operations of history, the nature of civilization and culture, natural morality, and human progress, much of which is reflected in Voltaire's play. The opening debate in *Alzire* between Alvarez and his son, Gusman, recapitulates a debate familiar to Voltaire's audience between Gusman's heroic morality of the strongest, associated with Plutarch, Machiavelli, and among the sixteenth-century Spanish historians, with Ginés de Sepúlveda, and Alvarez's opposing Christian position that looked to St. Augustine and argued that the strongest needed to be the most just and helpful to the weak. Among the Spanish historians, Father Bartolomé de Las Casas was the leading spokesman for this position. Indeed, Voltaire's entire play may be seen as a working out of the Las Casas position, particularly the deathbed "conversion" of Gusman, so melodramatic and unlikely to a modern reader. Gusman demonstrates to his Peruvian rival and captive, Zamore, the difference between their religions by pardoning him and turning over to him both his wife, Alzire, and his rule—a textbook illustration of Las Casas' concept of the Christian combination of overwhelming strength and mercy. This is doubtless why Voltaire boasted that this "singular piece" was "a strongly Christian tragedy, which can reconcile me with some of the devout" (VC, III, 327). The passage smacks of irony, but the problem was real enough. Voltaire's outspokenness on the church and matters of faith made him many enemies and his free-thinking was not infrequently equated with an advocacy of atheism.

The "American" coloring Voltaire gave his play was much praised by contemporary critics, though it was still far from the local color so dear to the romantics. The play is full of references to Peru, Mexico, gold, temples, and tropical heat, but the speech and manners of the indians are little different from the Spanish. A new palace setting was painted for the production, but since it was stipulated that it should be useable for other plays as well, it was probably not particularly exotic, even by the taste of the period. The costumes also made only a gesture in the direction of authenticity. Voltaire stipulated traditional "Spanish" costumes for Alvarez and Gusman—short vests, black cloaks lined with red satin, red stockings, and plumes. The male indians were to wear the traditional heroic costume à la romaine, with a breastplate ornamented with a sun and a small plumed helmet, and Alzire was to have a "skirt decorated with plumes in front, a train, a coiffure, and diamonds in the buckles."[9]

Since L'Indiscret in 1725, Voltaire had offered to the Comédie only his tragedies, reserving his few attempts at comedy for the more intimate theatres of society. Partly this was because his taste in comedy ran to the farce tradition of Molière and the closely related comedy of manners of the English Restoration. By the 1730s, however, a different style of comedy had become popular in Paris, with a tonality more suited to the emotional temper of the times, and more in keeping with the current view of theatre as a school for manners. This approach was represented most prominently in the work of Philippe Néricault Destouches and Nivelle de Lachaussée. Destouches began his career with a 1710 comedy, Le Curieux impertinent, based on an episode in Don Quixote, and attained the peak of his career with Le Philosophe marié in 1727 and Le Glorieux in 1732, both comedies of character in the

Molière tradition, but distinctly softened by the same love of the sentimental that Voltaire so deplored in the audiences for his tragedies. Indeed, the preface to *Le Glorieux*, while taking the traditional position of defending comedy as a school of manners, put this in a new emotionalized setting. "I have always taken it as an undisputed maxim," said Destouches, "that however amusing a comedy might be, it is an imperfect and even dangerous work if the author does not seek in it to correct manners, to expose the ridiculous, to decry vice, and *to place virtue in so favorable a light that it draws to itself public veneration*" [italics mine].[10]

Destouches' successes prepared the way for the real master of sentimentalism in French comedy, Nivelle de Lachaussée, whose first dramatic work, *La Fausse Antipathie* in 1733, was written specifically, like Steele's *Conscious Lovers*, to demonstrate the effectiveness emotionally and morally of serious, even pathetic comedy. In its preface, Lachaussée called the theatre "a school where youth can gain lessons of wisdom and virtue while being entertained." The Jesuit priest Père Porée gave an address in 1733 at the Louis-le-Grand, the school which gave Voltaire and so many others their first taste of theatre, commending Lachaussée as a model for virtuous theatre. His success stimulated a warm debate in the literary world of Paris concerning the merits, or indeed the dramatic validity, of the new *comédie attendrissante* or *comédie larmoyante* (not on moral, but on generic grounds, as a mixture of the traditionally separate comedy and tragedy). Lachaussée, following the example of Molière, created a *Critique de la Fausse Antipathie* in 1734 defending his practice, and the considerable success of his second experiment, *Préjugé à la mode* in 1735, showed that at least the public was strongly in favor of this new approach. The mixing of genres remained a source of critical debate for the rest of the century, however, until romantic dramatists and theorists like Hugo finally forced the acceptance of this practice.

As in certain other controversial subjects (in the theatre, most notably in his attitude toward Shakespeare), Voltaire at different times in his long career took distinctly different positions on the matter of the serious comedy. He totally agreed with the idea of theatre as a school for morals, as is consistently demonstrated in his own work. His 1733 *Lettre à un Premier Commis* typically remarks: "I consider tragedy and comedy as lessons in virtue, reason, and proper behavior" (VO, XXX, 353). The mixing of genres was, however, another matter. In his 1764 *Dictionnaire philosophique*, he devotes almost half of his rather brief entry on comedy to deploring the emergence of these new sentimental works, "a bastard form which, being neither comic nor tragic, demonstrates an inability to create either tragedy or comedy." He concludes, "Authors work in the style of the *comédie larmoyante* only because it is the easiest of genres, but this very ease degrades it: in a word, the French no longer know how to laugh" (VO, XVII, 419). This same entry contains a distinctly self-serving version of "how this genre came into being." According to Voltaire, his own comedy, *Les Originaux*, was seen at one of its numerous private performances in 1732 by Mlle Quinault of the Comédie, who had just achieved a great success in *Le Glorieux*. Seeing in *Les Originaux* the possibility of "a very interesting comedy and of a totally new French genre," she asked Voltaire to make a full-length comedy of it for public performance. When he declined, she asked permission to consign the project to Lachaussée, and the result was the ground-breaking *Préjugé à la mode* (VO, XVII, 419–20).

A more likely sequence of events is that Voltaire himself was moved by the popularity of Destouches and Lachaussée, enough to shift from his allegiance to classic style in this more fashionable direction. In any case, at the suggestion of Mlle Quinault, he now created his own blend of serious and farce elements in *L'Enfant prodigue*, based on the story of the prodigal son. Mlle Quinault obligingly took the minor buffoon role of the husband-seeking baroness de Croupillac, leaving the more attractive roles of the sentimental Lisa and her sprightly maid to Gaussin and Dangeville. After *Brutus*, Dangeville devoted herself to comedy, and *L'Enfant* was the first in a series of gratifying successes she enjoyed in Voltarian comedies. Fearful of the fate of this new experiment, especially given the determination of his enemies to cause him embarrassment, Voltaire had it presented anonymously on 10 October 1736. Only in December, when his poem *Le Mondain* was suppressed by the authorities on grounds of immorality, did Voltaire publicly claim the now popular comedy, as a way of restoring his challenged reputation.

Despite his later condemnation of the genre, Voltaire's preface to *L'Enfant prodigue* provides a more comprehensive defense of it than can be found anywhere in Destouches or Lachaussée. Indeed, it anticipates many of the arguments for mixed genres later found in Diderot, Beaumarchais, even in Hugo:

> If comedy is to be the representation of manners, this piece surely fits that description. It contains a mixture of the serious and the light, of the comic and the touching. The life in men is mixed in the same way; often indeed a single event contains these contrasts. Nothing is more common than a house in which a father grumbles, a daughter, occupied with her passion, weeps, the son makes fun of both of them, and various relatives react differently to the situation. Very often there is raillery in one room and sadness in the adjacent one, and even the same person may sometimes laugh and weep about the same thing in the same quarter of an hour. (VO, III, 443)

Still Voltaire, insisting on the originality of his work, made a point of distancing himself from Lachaussée. "This is a play where one weeps a good deal and laughs no less," he admitted. "Nevertheless is it not predominantly what one calls a *comédie larmoyante* since it retains the character of true comedy."[11]

Another original element in *L'Enfant prodigue*, which Voltaire understandably did not emphasize, was the insertion of dialogues of social protest, especially between the valet and his master. In his awareness of the arbitrariness of social rank and lack of veneration for his superiors, Jasmin has been seen as a precursor of Beaumarchais' revolutionary Figaro (WCT, 76). The play brought Voltaire the success in comedy he had been seeking, with almost universal critical approval and an extended run. Unfortunately, however, before he could claim the work and print an official version, pirated editions, prepared from the manuscript used by the actors, had appeared. Voltaire had already suffered from censorship of his writing; now his popularity added new problems. For the rest of his career, official censors, printers who misprinted or openly pirated his plays, and actors who made unauthorized changes kept him in a running battle to preserve the integrity of his texts.

After presenting an average of one new Voltaire play each year between 1730 and 1736, the Comédie then offered no Voltaire premiere until 1740. Partly this was due to Voltaire's absence in Cirey and to a fascination he developed at this time for scientific reading and research, but his enthusiasm for theatre did not really diminish. He began a number of new projects that would reach fruition in the next decade, and he organized his own amateur theatre at Cirey, a passion he would continue to follow in all of his later residences. Voltaire's first dramatic project after *L'Enfant prodigue* seems to have been a new tragedy, *Mérope*, but after working on it during most of 1737, he laid it aside to take up two other tragedies, *Mahomet* and *Zulime*. He also created another opera libretto, *Pandore*, which was never performed, and two other comedies: *L'Envieux*, essentially an attack on one of the most determined of Voltaire's critics, the Abbé Desfontaines; and *La Prude*, an attempted return to a less sentimental comic style based on Wycherly's *The Plain Dealer* which, as Voltaire well knew, was itself derived from Molière's *The Misanthrope*. Both were submitted for consideration to the Comédie, but neither was accepted. *L'Envieux* was never presented, and *La Prude* received only a single performance, at Sceaux in 1747.

Most of these dramatic projects were tested at Cirey, either in readings by Voltaire himself or in actual performances, which, along with firework displays and marionettes, were a regular feature of public life at the chateau.

Mme de Graffigny, a guest at the chateau for nine weeks in 1738 and 1739, participated in these activities and commented on them in a series of long and gossipy letters that she produced almost daily, and which provide a picture of almost continual and frequently frenetic dramatic activity. On 9 February 1739, she writes:

> Today we performed *L'Enfant prodigue* and another play in three acts, which we had to rehearse. We rehearsed *Zaïre* until three in the morning; we will perform it tomorrow along with *Sérénade* [by Regnard]. We must dress our hair, get our costumes fitted, listen to an opera; what chaos! We are given charming little manuscripts to read on the fly. . . . We counted up last evening that in twenty-four hours we had rehearsed and performed twenty-three acts— comedies, tragedies, and operas. (VC, VIII, 345)

Three days later, another marathon session in celebration of Mardi Gras resulted in the rehearsal or performance of thirty-seven acts, including four complete operas and parts of two others between noon on one day and seven o'clock the following morning. After three hours of sleep, the actors were awake again to warm up with an hour of opera singing, followed by a rehearsal of *Zaïre* and a break for the women to dress their hair and costume themselves "à la Turque," following which came the actual performance of *Zaïre* with a comic afterpiece lasting until 1:30 in the morning. Graffigny's lover, Léopole Desmarets, was in the cast and left a rather grim picture of the production, which featured Voltaire and Monsieur and Madame Du Châtelet in leading roles. Voltaire reportedly did not know any two consecutive lines of his part, and became furious with his valet, who served as prompter. Mme Du Châtelet played without spirit in the same tone, scanning the verses foot by foot, while her husband broke up his speeches with no regard for the verses whatever. Others stumbled through their lines or played, like Desmarets, with scripts in hand. Oddly enough, Desmarets reports that some passages were divine, and a certain piquancy must have been provided by the fact that Voltaire and Mme Du Châtelet, whose ongoing affair was well known to all, played the tragic lovers Orosmane and Zaïre, while Du Châtelet's complaisant husband appeared as Zaïre's brother Nérestan, whose filial interest in Zaïre arouses Orosmane's mistaken jealousy (VC, VIII, 359, 363).

Voltaire's next tragedy, *Zulime*, presented at the Comédie 8 June 1740, was one of his weakest efforts, and doubtless suffered from his greater interest at this same time in completing one of his best works, *Mahomet*. Although set in Africa, the hastily written *Zulime* lacks even local color, and seems made up of parts of other works. Again the prisoner motif appears, but this time arranged to give prominence to the heroine, in keeping with Voltaire's determination to win audiences by a love interest. Zulime is a Muslim African princess whose father holds captive a secretly married Spanish prince and princess. Voltaire created many versions of this work, none of them successful, but in each one, Zulime loves the Spanish prince and at last stabs herself when she cannot win him. In the first version, the prince adds a further complication by killing Zulime's father in battle, setting up a conflict in her that clearly suggests that of Chimène in Corneille's *Le Cid*. Perhaps the most memorable thing about *Zulime* was that it was the last Voltaire play acted by Dufresne, hero in so many Voltarian tragedies, and his sister Mme Quinault, who held an equal stature in comedy and was Voltaire's closest friend and ally at the theatre. She continued to host a lively salon for many years after her retirement, at which Voltaire remained a regular guest. The title role in *Zulime* was taken by an actress recently arrived at the Comédie, Marie Dumesnil, who replaced Gaussin in tragic leads and was generally considered to be the long-awaited successor to Lecouvreur. Her arrival was apparently the impetus for Voltaire to create the final major work of this highly productive period, *Mérope*.

First, however, came *Mahomet*, Voltaire's third Mohammedan play, but his first without a Christian/Muslim conflict and the first in which religion, not love, plays the dominant role. The prophet Mahomet is presented as an unscrupulous and manipulative fanatic. Voltaire himself compared him to Tartuffe. In the central action he leads young Séide to kill Mahomet's opponent, Zopire, actually Séide's father, and poisons the young man to conceal the crime, calling both deaths acts of God. The struggle, physical and verbal, between the fanaticism of Mahomet and the humanity of Zopire and his family forms the basic conflict.

Given its subject matter, the play is not strong in local color, but it is perhaps the freest treatment Voltaire had yet given to the unities. The revelation of a new scene at the back of the stage, an effect he had used in other tragedies, was strikingly utilized here when Zopire is revealed praying at an altar and Séide enters, stabs the old man, and then is stricken with remorse (a possible echo of Hamlet?). The play begins in a Racinian neutral chamber, but soon moves on to a prison and then to other sites about the city of Mecca, stretching the unity of place no more than Corneille had done in *Le Cid*, but certainly more than a strict observance of the unities would allow.

Mahomet was accepted by the Comédie. Grandval, the specialist in older tragic roles, would of course play the prophet, but with the departure of Dufresne, there was no strong younger actor for the key role of Séide, a dilemma ultimately resolved in a surprising and quite roundabout manner. In the spring of 1739, while working on *Mahomet* at Cirey, Voltaire received a copy of a tragedy based on Mahomet's son, *Mahomet II*, the work of Jean Lanoue, author, actor, and director of provincial theatres at Rouen and Douai. Voltaire sent him an extended commentary (VC, IX, 69–74) and thought of Lanoue a year later when the king of Prussia, Frederick II, asked Voltaire to recommend a French entrepreneur to assemble a company of French actors to take up residence in Berlin. Lanoue undertook this project and spent most of a year signing up actors and incurring considerable expense, only to have the project cancelled when Frederick became involved in military campaigns. Lanoue appealed for aid to Voltaire, the intermediary, and although Frederick gave no compensation, Voltaire offered Lanoue the opportunity to premiere *Mahomet* at Lille, where he had recently become director.

This gesture turned out most happily for both. The Lille premiere in April 1741 attracted an attention unprecedented for a provincial theatre, and Voltaire was astonished at how well the work was produced and received there. Before the production, he had written to the count d'Argental that since the departure of Dufresne the theatre in Paris did not have the means to present the play, "though I would like to have at least tried out what effect it would have on stage," while at Lille "Lanoue has established a fairly passable company; he is a good actor, lacking only a good face; I confided my play to him as an honest man whose judgement I trust" (VC, XI, 80–81). A month later, he wrote in astonishment "You will think I am blaspheming when I tell you that Lanoue, with his simian features, played the role of Mahomet much better than Dufresne could have done. It is unbelievable but it is true" (VC, XI, 105).

After this success, Voltaire insisted that Lanoue take the part of Séide for the Paris premiere, which took place 9 August 1742, but even before that, word of the Lille triumph had made Lanoue the talk of Paris. He was invited to perform at court early in May and was lavishly praised by the king and queen. On 14 May he made his formal debut at the Comédie and was at once accepted as the much-needed heir to Dufresne. The first three nights of *Mahomet* in Paris, Voltaire drew some of the largest audiences of his career (interestingly, *Tartuffe* was presented the evening between the second and third performances). At the same time there was widespread protest against the play, not only from the Turkish ambassador, as might be expected, but from religious leaders and other critics who insisted that the notorious sceptic Voltaire was actually attacking Christianity under the guise of an alien fanaticism. Indeed, Voltaire was clearly attacking any religion that advanced its goals by inhumane or untruthful means, and there were plenty of lines in the play that could offer offense to religious extremists of any persuasion. Without waiting to see how this uproar would play out at court or in Parliament, Voltaire withdrew the play after these first three performances. He wittily turned the tables on his critics, however, by dedicating the play to the reigning pope, Benedict XIV, who, delighted with this negative portrayal of Islam, praised Voltaire for his "admirable tragedy," and to the confusion of Voltaire's detractors, bestowed on him an apostolic benediction and two gold medals (VO, IV, 103).

Immediately after the brief run of *Mahomet*, the Comédie offered another short-lived new tragedy, Paul Landois' *Sylvie*, scarcely noted at this time, but later remembered as an important early experiment in stage realism and middle-class drama. The type of emotional comedy represented by the work of Lachaussée and by Voltaire's *L'Enfant prodigue* was now extremely popular in France, and may have encouraged Landois' more serious experiment. The author may also have been aware of similar contemporary work in England, most notably the 1721 *Fatal Extravagance* by Aaron Hill, the leading English translator of Voltaire's plays, or the far more popular 1731 *London Merchant* by George Lillo, which later exerted an undisputed influence on Diderot in France and Lessing in Germany. The setting, a humble domestic interior, was so far from anything in the Comédie stock that new scenery had to be built, and the actors set aside 500 francs to pay for it (LFT, I, 264), but the novelty of a serious, realistic drama of everyday life did not at this time find an audience. Only with the later triumph of realism was the importance of this little work recognized.

The truncated victory of Voltaire's *Mahomet* was amply compensated for by the unqualified success of *Mérope*, premiered later this same season on 20 February 1743. The triumph was the more gratifying to Voltaire in that he had at last achieved his goal of creating a successful tragedy not involving sexual love. His emphasis instead was upon maternal devotion, but his Mérope has even less love interest than Racine's somewhat similar Andromaque, since the love of her dead husband is still a strong force in the latter, while Mérope is concerned only with placing her son on his father's usurped throne. Voltaire wrote the work with the new tragic actress Dumesnil in mind, and she unquestionably contributed to its success. The passion and naturalness of her delivery were much praised, and the audience was electrified by a key moment in the fourth act, when her son is threatened with death, as she cried out and flew across the stage to intervene, forsaking the measured pace that for a century had been traditional for tragic heroines. After the premiere, the author was called to appear on stage, the first time this honor had been accorded in the French theatre. It was the climax of Voltaire's dramatic career to-date, and of the remarkable series of works that had begun in 1732 with *Zaïre*. Voltaire would write many more plays, break important new ground, and enjoy enormous later success, but it is upon the plays of this productive decade that his reputation as a dramatist largely rests.

NOTES

1. R. S. Ridgway, "Voltaire's Operas," *Studies on Voltaire and the Eighteenth Century*, vol. 189 (1980): 122.

2. Abbé Dubos, *Réflexions critiques sur la poésie et sur la peinture* (Paris: n.p. 1719).

3. On the occasion of Rameau's first major opera, *Hippolyte et Aricie* in 1733, Campra correctly observed, "This man will eclipse us all." Dr. Hughes Maret, *Eloge historique de M. Rameau* (Dijon: n.p., 1766), note 36.

4. Quoted in Cuthbert Girdlestone, *Jean-Philippe Rameau: His Life and Work* (New York: Dover, 1957), 10.

5. Jean Françoise de La Harpe, *Commentaire sur le théâtre de Voltaire* (Paris: Maradan, 1814), 229.

6. By La Harpe, for example, who wrote, "He was the first among us to open up the New World." Quoted in Emile Deschanel, *Le Théâtre de Voltaire* (Paris: Calmann Lévy, 1888), 139.

7. Gilbert Chinard, *L'Amérique et le rêve exotique dans la littérature française au XVIIe et au XVIIIe siècle* (Paris: Droz, 1934), 231.

8. Antoine D'Origny, *Annales du Théâtre Italien*, 2 vols. (Paris: Duchesne, 1788), 1:63.

9. Quoted in H. Carrington Lancaster, *French Tragedy in the Time of Louis XIV and Voltaire*, 2 vols. (Baltimore: Johns Hopkins, 1950), 1:194 (henceforward LFT).

10. Néricault Destouches, *Oeuvres choisies* (Paris: Auguste Desrez, 1837), 663.

11. Baron de Servières, *Mémoires pour servir à l'histoire de M. de Voltaire*, 2 vols. (Amsterdam: n.p., 1785), 2:193–94.

Chapter 4

Voltaire at Court, 1743–1750

The decade of the 1740s in France was in many respects key in the reexamination of traditional ideas about social and political life that characterized the eighteenth century. A new intellectual class of writers and thinkers was appearing, mostly of middle-class background, who took Voltaire's *Lettres philosophiques* as a model for writing and action, seeking new liberty in politics, religion, and thought. They began to designate themselves *philosophes*. The legitimacy of conventional moral restrictions and codes was called into question by powerful thinkers and writers, such as: Condillac, in his *Essai sur l'origine des connaissances humaines* (1746) and *Traîté des sistèmes* (1749); La Mettrie, in his materialistic *L'Homme machine* (1747); Montesquieu, in his *Esprit des lois* (1748); Buffon, in his *Histoire naturelle*, the first volumes of which appeared in 1749; and Diderot, in his *Lettre sur les aveugles* (1749), which among other things, dared to defend atheism. The end of the decade saw the inauguration of the culminating intellectual work of the century, the great *Encyclopédie*, edited by Diderot and d'Alembert.

Voltaire stood at the center of this new ferment, the emblematic figure of the new *philosophe*, the idol of young thinkers and anathema to many conservative defenders of the old order. This preeminence was achieved, of course, largely through the power of his writings, but during this decade Voltaire also achieved a dominant position in more traditional ways: being elected to the French Academy; playing a role on the complex international scene in Europe; and moving into a prominent position at court, the intimate of the powerful royal mistress, Madame de Pompadour.

The great success of *Mérope*, despite its lack of a love interest, spurred the Comédiens to plan a production of *La Mort de César*, formerly not considered because of its all-male cast. The play, like *Mahomet*, ran into difficulties with Crébillon, the royal censor, who banned it on the night of the final rehearsal. As with *Mahomet*, his ban was overturned thanks to the influence of Voltaire's friends at court, and *La Mort de César*, originally planned for June, was presented 20 August. It had, however, only a mediocre run of seven performances.

Voltaire himself was little concerned with this venture, since he was attempting to launch a new career as a diplomat. He had, it will be remembered, prided himself on his political dexterity in England by circulating freely among the highest Whig and Tory circles. Circumstances in the 1740s provided him with the opportunity to carry out similar activities on a more European stage, an opportunity which Voltaire eagerly embraced. His entry into this international scene was provided by Frederick II, who came to the throne of Prussia in 1740, and who was involved in a long and complex relationship with Voltaire. Voltaire first heard from Frederick, who was then crown prince, in his retreat at Cirey in 1736. Frederick expressed a keen interest in Voltaire's work, and a warm correspondence and friendship developed between prince and poet. Frederick seemed genuinely fascinated by Voltaire's wit and literary skills, while Voltaire saw in the prince a potential philosopher king, far superior to the frivolous Louis XV or the dull and stolid George II, one who might serve as an example of a truly enlightened monarch, a champion of liberty and a patron of the arts.

Soon after Frederick became king, he arranged a meeting with Voltaire at Wesel and another soon after in Berlin. The aging prime minister of France, Fleury, was primarily concerned with preserving the peace in Europe and saw in Voltaire's friendship with the new prince an opportunity to explore his intentions. Voltaire thus went to Berlin partly as Fleury's agent. His visit was a success in assuring Frederick of France's peaceful intentions, but much less so in gauging Frederick's plans. Voltaire returned to France convinced that Frederick was much more concerned with cultural than military matters, and to that end encouraged Lanoue to assemble actors for Berlin, but before the year's end, Frederick surprised Voltaire and, indeed, much of Europe by embarking on a campaign that would upset the delicate balance of power established in 1713 by the Peace of Utrecht.

In 1740, the same year that Frederick became king of Prussia, the Austrian throne was inherited by Maria Theresa. Her father, Charles VI, had sought to avoid conflict over the succession by gaining support for his daughter's claim from Spain, France, Prussia, and Britain. Nevertheless, Frederick, sensing or hoping for a weakness in the new queen, invaded and rapidly occupied Silesia, the Austrian-occupied territory which lay between

them. The other European powers were less disturbed by the moral dubious-
ness of Frederick's invasion than by its challenge to the European balance of
power, and there was widespread support for a counterattack from Austria.
When this counterattack failed decisively in the spring of 1741, the prag-
matic Fleury recognized that Frederick was in Silesia to stay and concluded
an alliance with Prussia and Bavaria against Austria, whose widespread do-
mains would provide spoils for all.

This alliance and military reversal convinced Maria Theresa to conclude
an independent peace with Prussia in July 1742, leaving Frederick's French
and Bavarian allies in mid-campaign without his support. Clearly, Frederick
was not to be trusted, but neither could he be ignored, and Fleury continued
to encourage Voltaire to see what he could discover of the king's real intentions. Voltaire met him relaxing after the Treaty at Aix-la-Chapelle in September, where Frederick invited the poet to become his permanent guest in
Berlin. Voltaire never again entirely trusted Frederick (almost no one in
Europe did), but admired his determination and efficiency, as well as his apparently sincere love of literature and the arts.

Voltaire was obviously also tempted by the opportunity to play diplomat.
Fleury, who had encouraged this interest, died early in 1743, but the Duc de
Richelieu, a lifelong friend of Voltaire who had the king's ear, also saw a potential diplomatic use of Voltaire's friendship. In June, Voltaire went to Berlin, ostensibly to accept Frederick's offer of protection, but in fact on a secret
mission to warn Frederick of a possible Austrian-English alliance, to encourage strong ties between France and Prussia, and above all, to report back
any information he could on the military and financial situation of the kingdom. Voltaire remained until September, participating in a brilliant round of
balls, operas, ballets, and state occasions. He sent back voluminous and detailed reports, which were much appreciated in France, even though the wily
Frederick, doubtless aware of Voltaire's double role, evaded all the most
searching questions.

Although this project did not lead, as Voltaire clearly hoped, to further
diplomatic assignments, it did make him more visible at court, and when
Richelieu was placed in charge of organizing the festivities for the marriage
of the crown prince to Maria Theresa of Spain early in 1745, he commissioned Voltaire to create a work to celebrate the occasion. Voltaire suggested
a tragedy, but the duke insisted upon a more traditional court spectacle, what
Voltaire himself described as "one of those dramatic works in which music
makes up part of the subject, in which humor is mixed with the heroic, and in
which occurs a melange of opera, comedy, and tragedy." In such works, Voltaire complained, "It is impossible to give these three genres their due; one is

forced only to join the talents of the most distinguished artists and the only merit of the author is to promote the work of others" (VO, IV, 273–74). Nevertheless, this commission allowed Voltaire, after three failures, to produce a libretto that was certain to be performed, and to work at last with Rameau, now widely recognized as the leading composer of the period. It also provided him with a long-sought entry to the court. He moved to Versailles in January of 1745, and remained there, even being awarded the coveted prize of his own room at the palace, for most of the next two years.

Ever since Louis XIV had inaugurated his magnificent chateau and gardens at Versailles in 1664 with the famous festival *Les Plaisirs de l'Isle Enchantée*, to which Molière and Lully contributed, Versailles had remained a favored location for the sort of lavish spectacles that were the most extravagant forms of baroque court entertainment. Louis XV tended to favor more public festivals in Paris, but a lavish masked ball in 1739 marked a return to the sort of court spectacles favored in the previous century, and the marriage celebrations for the Dauphin even more closely resembled the several-day celebrations first seen at Versailles, with Voltaire and Rameau carrying on the tradition of Quinault and Lully (indeed, a revival of Quinault and Lully's *Thésée* was one of the offerings).

Voltaire and Rameau's *La Princesse de Navarre* opened the festival on 23 February 1745. A special theatre was built for the production in the riding school at Versailles, with a stage fifty-six feet deep to contain the elaborate scenery by Charles Nicolas Cochin and an auditorium and boxes which, according to Voltaire, were built with "appropriate magnificence" and yet in such a manner that "everything that was necessary for the performance could be removed in one night, leaving the room decorated for a costume ball which would be the main entertainment of the next day" (VO, IV, 273; illustration 2). Voltaire's complex plot is a typically romantic fable involving the princess Constance, who seeks refuge in disguise from her tyrannical guardian in a chateau where her lover pursues her, disguised as a servant. To a modern reader, the situation, and Constance's wavering between love and the fear of misalliance, will very likely suggest Marivaux, and especially his best-known work, *Le Jeu de l'amour et du hasard* (1730). It may well be that Voltaire took the idea from Marivaux; his works, especially his comedies, are full of similar borrowings, but it should be noted that the high regard in which Marivaux is held today developed long after his death. His contemporaries, including Voltaire, considered him a distinctly minor talent with a highly artificial style, writing light entertainments for a minor theatre, the Comédie Italienne. Still, this may have seemed to Voltaire the appropriate place to seek inspiration for *La Princesse*, which he himself characterized as

Illustration 2. Stage and auditorium constructed for *La Princesse de Navarre* at Versailles.

a "fairground entertainment." The plot in any case was only an excuse to tie together comic interludes, spectacle, ballet, verses in honor of love and Hymen, patriotic tableaux with much flag waving and rousing military anthems (despite Frederick's defection, France was still battling Austria in the low countries). The final scene featured a forest, a seascape, and a view of the Pyrenees, mountains which disappeared at the conclusion to symbolize the union of France and Spain.

The prologue to *La Princesse* was spoken by the sun, descending into a garden like those at Versailles in a flying chariot. This role was taken by a recent debutante at the Comédie, Mlle Clairon, who would become the dominant actress of her generation and the one most closely associated with Voltaire. In 1734, when Clairon was eleven, her mother moved to Paris to a house next to that of Mlle Dangeville of the Comédie, and from her window Clairon could watch the actress rehearsing her declamation and dancing. Determined to undertake that career, Clairon made her debut just two years later in Marivaux's *L'Ile des Esclaves* at the Comédie Italienne, where she remained for one year. She then left to join Lanoue, who had made his debut at the Italienne just before hers, and who was now directing a company in Rouen. Her fortunes then became entwined with those of Lanoue, who encouraged her, and she followed him to Paris and to the Comédie, becoming the understudy of her first inspiration, Mlle Dangeville. In 1743, she made her official debut, achieving her greatest success, much to the surprise of the other actors, in tragedy, which henceforth became her speciality. Her debut pieces were by Racine, Crébillon, Thomas Corneille—her triumphs with Voltaire still lay in her future.

In 1776, Voltaire wrote an autobiography which contains an amusing epigram on the success of *La Princesse de Navarre*:

My *Henry IV* and my *Zaïre*
And my American *Alzire*
Did not aquaint the monarch with my name.
I had a thousand foes and little fame
Now honors and awards upon me fall;
A fairground farce accomplished all. (BV, 640)

The king seemed to have been generally pleased with the piece, at least he requested a second performance four days later, and official honors and awards were soon heaped upon Voltaire: he was given a pension of 2,000 livres from the king, and another of 1,500 from the queen, appointed royal historiographer and the position of Gentleman in Ordinary of the Chamber. In April, he attained a long-sought election to the French Academy, the official mark of his arrival at the highest echelon of the French world of letters. Voltaire himself admitted, however, that these honors were in large part due not to the success of *La Princesse*, but to the influence of Madame de Pompadour, who in the coming years would play an important role at court and in Voltaire's career.

The costume ball for which *La Princesse*'s stage had to be taken down was one of the most lavish and famous in the reign of Louis XV. It became known as the Yew Tree Ball, since the king and six of his courtiers appeared dressed as identical yew trees, modeled on those in the Versailles park (and in the opening act of the previous night's play). The king's official mistress, Madame de Chateauroux, had recently died, and speculation about her successor was rife in the court. Thus, as the various yew trees paired off with different ladies and carried them away for flirtation in secluded corners, there was frantic speculation about which was the king. At length he was revealed, and his companion was the lively and attractive wife of a well-to-do businessman, Jeanne-Antoinette d'Etioles. Very soon, Mme d'Etioles was a daily visitor to the palace. She separated from her husband in April, and in July Louis gave her the title La Marquise de Pompadour, ending all complaints that a mere member of the bourgeoisie could hardly reside at Versailles as the official royal mistress. She now settled in for a lively and influential reign that lasted twelve years.

Soon after her marriage in 1741, Mme d'Etioles had begun inviting members of the aristocracy and leading men of letters to her Paris salon or country chateau, among them Voltaire, who became a close friend. Social life at the chateau was much to Voltaire's taste—witty conversation, readings of fashionable literature (Richardson's *Pamela* from England, translated in 1741, was a particular favorite of the company, though not of Voltaire), and of course the reading and acting of comedy and opera. Even members of the court from Versailles were from time to time attracted to these lavish theatrical productions, in which Mme d'Etioles distinguished herself both as an actress and singer. President Hénault, a favorite courtier of the queen, visited in the summer of 1742 and wrote that Mme d'Etioles

> is a perfect musician. She sang many songs with the greatest possible gaiety and taste, knows a hundred songs and performs in comedies at Etioles in a theatre as fine as the Opera and well provided with machinery and changeable scenes.[1]

The installation of Mme d'Etioles, subsequently Mme de Pompadour, as royal mistress inevitably meant a new interest at the court in literary and theatrical matters in general, and particularly in the work of Voltaire, already one of Pompadour's inner circle.

Despite the defection of Prussia, the war with Austria continued, and in May the king departed for the front in Flanders, and Mme d'Etioles for her chateau where she was joined by Voltaire and other intimates. There, Voltaire flattered her with occasional poetry, as in May after a French victory at Fortenoy: "When Louis, that charming hero / The idol of all Paris / Wins some brilliant battle / The one who should be complimented / Is the divine Etioles," or, when the king wrote conferring her new title: "Sincere and tender Pompadour / For I would give you in advance / This name that, rhyming with amour / Will soon be loveliest in France."[2]

On a more official level, Voltaire was also at work on a new court festival, another opera with Rameau, *La Temple de la Gloire*, planned to celebrate the king's victories in Flanders when he returned to Versailles in the fall after the fighting season. *La Temple de la Gloire* was presented at Versailles 27 November 1745, on the same stage which had been constructed for *La Princesse de Navarre* and with similar elaborate scenic effects—flying machines, chariots drawn by tigers, transforming scenery, temples, forests, and gardens. Voltaire attempted to add a stronger didactic element than was customary in such celebrative pieces, with an act devoted to each of three types of ruler: Bélus, who rules by terror and subjugation; Bacchus, devoted to display and self-indulgence; and Trajan, the enlightened monarch, victorious in war, generous in peace. There is a popular anecdote reporting that Voltaire received a cold rebuff from the king when asking him after the production if "Trajan were pleased" (VO, IV, 347). The story is highly doubtful, but in any case it is clear that Trajan was being put forward as a recommended royal model, though many must have felt that Bacchus was more appropriate. The work was clearly better received than *La Princesse de Navarre*, being played again at court that winter and spring and at the Opéra in Paris in December.

Richelieu felt that *La Princesse* might be more attractive if made more general in subject matter and reduced in length, but both Voltaire and Rameau avoided this assignment, claiming that they were too occupied with *La Temple de la Gloire*. Richelieu then thought of a struggling young composer, Jean-Jacques Rousseau, whom he had met at the home of that dedicated patron of the opera, M. de la Pouplinière, where the ill-fated *Samson* had been conceived. La Pouplinière had presented in concert version an operatic ballet by Rousseau which had been roundly condemned by Rameau, the reigning spirit of the house, but Richelieu found its attempt to blend French and Italian styles attractive, and sought to have it presented at Versailles.

This project did not succeed, but shortly after, when Voltaire and Rameau were unable to do the requested *Princesse* revisions, Richelieu asked the young Rousseau to undertake the project. Rousseau happily accepted this task, writing a warm letter to Voltaire asking his approval and receiving an equally warm and encouraging response. He created a new overture, converted the three-act work into a single act emphasizing military triumph more than marriage, and called it *Les Fêtes de Ramire*. The work was presented at Versailles on 22 December 1746, and was well received, but only Voltaire's name was attached to it. Rameau removed his own name and apparently prevented Rousseau's from appearing. Rousseau received neither recognition nor payment. The stress of the production put him in bed for six weeks, and by the time he had recovered, Richelieu had left for the front and his contributions were forgotten. Rousseau and Rameau were never reconciled, and their conflict would contribute importantly to the most famous musical debate of the century, the *Querelle des bouffons*, between supporters of French and Italian opera in the 1750s. The relationship between Rousseau and Voltaire was much more complicated and ambiguous, but it was never again so cordial as this first significant interchange of letters promised.

Mme de Pompadour soon realized that her continued power at court depended upon her ability to keep Louis XV entertained, and to that end, with the aid and encouragement of Richelieu, she decided to establish a permanent theatre at Versailles where she herself would perform before the king and an intimate circle. Accordingly, a gallery in the north part of the chateau adjacent to the king's private apartments was fitted up with an elegant stage and auditorium. This Théâtre de la petite galerie was later and better known as the Théâtre des petits cabinets of Versailles. The king was fascinated by the project, drawing up with Mme de Pompadour a list of regulations for the theatre covering preparation, selection of parts, and times of arrival for rehearsals (slightly less rigorous for the women). Eight men and four women of the court were selected for the first company, with more added later when the theatre began to present opera as well as comedies. There was an orchestra of twenty, most of them musicians from the king's own orchestra, and a chorus of thirteen singers. Both orchestra and chorus grew in size as the theatre became more ambitious in its productions. The tiny audience was selected by the king, and this naturally soon became a much sought-after honor.

The company began rehearsing in Paris in November, with actors from the Comédie—Lanoue, Gaussin and Dumesnil—serving as coaches. Machinists and scenic and costume designers from the Opéra were called upon to decorate this stage, aided by court artists, under the direction of Boucher, who would become the painter most associated with Pompadour's court, but who first attracted her attention by his dazzling scenic designs for the Opéra-Comique. The most famous wig-maker of the capital, Notrelle, left a catalogue of achievements, which suggests the visual range of these entertainments. He claimed to have

> exhausted the resources of his art in order to imitate the wigs of gods, of de
> mons, of heros, of shepherds, of tritons, of cyclops, of naiads, of furies, etc.
> Whatever these beings were, fictive or real, when he did not know their cus
> toms, the power of his imagination allowed him to guess what their taste
> would have been in this matter, if the fashion of wigs had existed in their time.
> And to these sublime wigs he added a collection of mustaches and bears of all
> shapes and colors, ancient as well as modern.[3]

The theatre opened 17 January 1747 with a production of Molière's *Tartuffe*, before an audience of fifteen. The interest aroused by the production
was such that one court lady obtained an army rank for a relative in exchange
for arranging with Madame de Pompadour to allow the son of the Minister of
War to appear on stage in the minor role of the policeman who arrests Tartuffe. Pompadour herself played Dorine, the sprightly maid, and the king was
delighted. Three other programs completed the first season of this theatre—Lachaussée's *Préjugé à la mode*, Dufresne's *L'Esprit de contradiction*,
and Dancourt's *Les Trois cousines* (both originally produced at the Comédie
in 1700)—and a one-act original opera, *Erigone*, with Pompadour in the title
role. The opera received a second performance, when the audience of sixteen
included for the first time the queen, who came at the king's request and can
hardly have been greatly pleased by the obvious triumph of the royal mistress,
her power clearly solidified by this new distraction. Before the second season,
the seating space was enlarged, modest dressing rooms were added behind
the stage, and a space was established for an enlarged orchestra.

Voltaire was for a time a favored author, but his welcome ended abruptly
that fall. The occasion was a card party in which Mme Du Châtelet was participating and losing heavily. Voltaire urged her to quit, indiscreetly adding
in English that others were cheating. The queen herself, however, was one of
the players, and a major scandal resulted, forcing Voltaire and Mme Du Châtelet to flee the court.

They took refuge at Sceaux, the home of the duchess of Maine, who had
encouraged Voltaire's first interest in the theatre with her entertainments
here more than thirty years before. At that time, Sceaux had been one of the
few great houses which regularly sponsored such activity, but now, partly
due to the inspiration of Pompadour's intimate entertainments at court, private theatricals were rapidly becoming the favored entertainment at almost
every great house in France, in many cases with theatres as well equipped as

the national houses in Paris. In their study of women in the eighteenth century, Edmond and Jules de Goncourt suggest the ubiquity of this activity:

> Society theatre was a fury, a madness in the second half of the eighteenth cen-
> tury. The desire to present plays seized every class, from the apartments of
> Versailles to the dramatic societies of the rue des Marais and the rue Popin-
> court. *Mimomania* reigned in high society and burst out in every corner of
> Paris. Little theatres were built in private homes, grand theatres in chateaux.
> The whole society dreamed of theatre from one end of France to the other, and
> there was not a procurer who did not want to have a stage and a company.[4]

The splendor of the great celebrations of the 1720s dimmed after the
death of their organizer, Malezieu, in 1727, but the duchess remained interested in theatre, premiering occasional new works and inviting to Sceaux
college productions of such unusual classics as Plautus' *The Captives* and
Caldéron's *Life is a Dream*. Voltaire and Mme Du Châtelet visited her in her
summer retreat at Anet in August of 1747 and organized there a production
of Voltaire's comedy *L'Echange*, long a favorite at Cirey. A much more lavish program of entertainment was organized that fall at Sceaux, with comedies, operas, and balls, during which Voltaire also created his first short
stories, or *contes philosophiques*, to entertain his hostess. Dancers were im-
ported from the Opéra for the ballet opera *Zélide* and the grand opera *Issé*, in
which Mme Du Châtelet played the leading role, as Pompadour would do
two seasons later at Versailles. Voltaire's *Comte de Boursoufle* was revived
and his *La Prude*, written a decade earlier but never performed, was premiered here with Voltaire and Mme Du Châtelet in the leading roles.

In December word came that the storm had blown over in court and that
L'Enfant prodigue was to be presented there with Pompadour in the role of
Lise, created by Mlle Gaussin. Authors were never invited to these entertainments, but the king was on this occasion so pleased that Voltaire was invited
to a second evening. The respite was a brief one. A fulsome poem praising
Pompadour aroused the antagonism of the queen and her supporters, and
once again Voltaire found himself out of favor. He retired to Cirey, then in
February to the court of Stanislas in Lorraine, officially outside of French
territory. The Peace of Vienna in 1735 had removed Stanislas from the
throne of Poland, though he retained the title of king during his lifetime, and
France, which had supported him and whose queen was his daughter, Marie,
gave him sovereignty over the province of Lorraine until his death in 1766,
when the territory reverted to France. Stanislas, himself an author and philosopher, was much more warmly disposed toward Voltaire than was his
daughter, and he was delighted to welcome the exiled poet and Mme Du

Châtelet. She performed before the court in *Issé* and *Mérope* with gratifying success. In the summer, Voltaire and Mme Du Châtelet followed Stanislas to his retreat at Commercy, with more of the inevitable operas and comedies. Among these was a new one-act farce comedy by Voltaire, *La Femme qui a raison*, full of the misunderstandings and sexually provocative situations that traditionally characterized this genre. Voltaire later expanded it to a three-act version which was only privately performed.

A major new theatrical project now occupied Voltaire's attention, his first new tragedy at the Comédie in five years. *Sémiramis* was also the first of five tragedies eventually composed by Voltaire on subjects previously treated by the reigning tragedian of the previous generation, Crébillon, and clearly intended in their totality to eclipse the older dramatist. Voltaire had many reasons for this antagonism, but his continuing unstable position at court was probably the most important. Crébillon's first tragedy, *Idoménée*, had been presented at the Comédie in 1705, and his first great success, *Atrée et Thyeste*, in 1707. Its fearsome subject established Crébillon as the master of terror, a role he willingly assumed, as may be seen in his famous comment "Corneille took heaven, Racine the earth. Only hell was left for me" (HFS, I, 41). The success of his *Electre* in 1708 made him the leader among living tragic poets; he began to be called "the French Aeschylus." *Rhadamiste et Zénobie*, his best-known work, followed in 1711. Three comparative failures—*Xerxès* in 1714, *Sémiramis* in 1717, and *Pyrrhus* in 1726—followed by the rise of a major young competitor in Voltaire, discouraged Crébillon from continuing his play-writing career. His reputation continued strong, however, and he was elected to the French Academy in 1731 and appointed royal censor in 1733.

A separate censor for theatre had been established early in the century, and the post carried considerable power, even though its decisions could be overruled by the police or various high officials at court. As we have seen, Crébillon attempted to block the performances of both *Mahomet* and *La Mort de César*, arousing a resentment in Voltaire that lasted for years. When Voltaire was commissioned in 1746, after the court performance of *La Temple de la Gloire*, to prepare a new tragedy in honor of the new crown princess, he apparently saw this as an occasion to repay Crébillon for his actions. Selecting the same subject, the Babylonian queen, Semiramis, from one of Crébillon's weaker works, Voltaire wove it together with elements of his own earlier *Eriphyle* to create a piece clearly superior to both. He anticipated a possible negative ruling from the censor by appealing to the lieutenant of police, Crébillon's superior, that the author of a previous work on the same subject might be biased. Outmaneuvered, Crébillon required only a few minor adjustments before public performance.

The unexpected death in July of the crown princess, only a year after her marriage, ruled out a premiere of *Sémiramis* at court, which Voltaire was anticipating, and moved the location to the Comédie, where his enemies and the friends of Crébillon would be freer to express their displeasure. Anticipating a battle, Voltaire purchased four hundred parterre tickets to distribute to his own forces, but clearly his opponents would also be present. Voltaire spent much of the summer preparing for the opening. He attended rehearsals when he was in Paris, and mailed instructions on acting, setting, and costumes when he was not. Once again Voltaire had challenged the accepted practices of the French tragic stage, employing his most elaborate spectacle to-date, along with special sound and lighting effects. These reached a climax with the appearance of the ghost of murdered King Ninus from his on-stage tomb in the third act when thunder rumbled, the lights dimmed, and the tomb itself shuddered as if in an earthquake. Voltaire's letters are particularly concerned with the appearance of the ghost, which he knew would cause protest. The Comédie decision to dress the ghost in black he considered ridiculous, suggesting mourning, not terror. He insisted instead upon "a totally white warrior's costume, with bronze cuirass, a golden scepter and a totally white mask like the statue in *Don Juan*" (VC, XVI, 58).

The premiere on 29 August 1748 was a major event. The part of the doomed queen was taken by Dumesnil, her evil councilor, Assur, by Lanoue, and the young lovers by Clairon and Grandval (illustration 3). As part of the celebration to honor the dauphine, Louis had promised to refurbish the Comédie for the performance at a cost of 5,000 *livres*, and his personal scenic designers were employed, Dominique and Antoine Slodtz, whose work had previously been seen only on the stages of the royal chateaux. This spectacle, the controversy, and Voltaire's reputation created a frantic opening, anticipating that of *Hernani* a century later. The *Mercure* reported that

All the boxes, even the secondary ones, were booked six weeks in advance. The day of the performance, the rue de la Comédie was filled as early as one in the afternoon by the curious, eager to see the triumph or the fall of the author. . . . Even more extraordinary, most of those forbidden entrance did not leave as long as the production lasted, but remained near the doors to hear of the success of each act from spectators who came out from time to time for a breath of air.[5]

The press of spectators insured that the stage itself would be crowded with courtiers, and as had occurred in *Eriphyle* in 1732, this prevented the ghost from gaining anything of the effect Voltaire desired. Indeed, to his horror and to the delight of his enemies, the ghost could not even push his way onstage until the sentinel guarding the tomb cried out: "Messieurs, make way

NINIAS.   SEMIRAMIS.

Publish'd by Rob.t Sayer, N.º 53 Fleet Street, London, as the Act directs, 1.t Sep.t 1777.

Illustration 3. Lekain and Mlle Dumesnil in traditional French tragic costume for Voltaire's *Sémiramis.*

for the ghost, if you please."[6] The result was that the ghost in its white regalia suggested to some less the menacing statue of the Commandatore than a surprised pastry chef.[7] The elaborate settings of the Slodtz brothers were distracting and unconvincing, opening Voltaire to the criticism that he had sacrificed logic and good taste to physical display.

Under these circumstances and with so many opponents in the auditorium, the premiere was neither a clear success nor a failure. But Voltaire did some rewriting, convinced the actors to allow fewer spectators onstage, and arranged for some reduction in the elaborate scenery. With these adjustments, and with less politicized audiences, the play enjoyed a respectable run of fifteen performances and was repeated in October before the court at Fontainebleau.

The ambiguous fate of *Sémiramis* did not satisfy Voltaire's opponents, who now engaged in a series of activities to diminish his position in French letters, with Crébillon at the center of them. After a number of years in relative obscurity, the aging poet was now promoted to a position of prominence as a representative of the higher standards of classic tragedy that the upstart Voltaire was undermining. Although less close to her than Voltaire, Crébillon also was a long-time aquaintance of Mme de Pompadour. While still in her teens she had studied singing and stage deportment with Pierre Jéliotte, the leading singer of the Paris Opéra, and elocution with his close friend, Crébillon. After her rise to power, in 1747, she arranged for Crébillon to receive a pension and a position in the Royal Library, employed him as tutor to her own daughter, Alexandrine, and arranged for a sumptuous edition of his works to be printed at state expense, an honor which Voltaire had solicited in vain.

All these marks of favor encouraged Crébillon's friends and Voltaire's enemies to promote the older poet at Voltaire's expense. For some years Crébillon had been slowly working on *Catilina*. In the summer of 1748, with *Sémiramis* in preparation at the Comédie, the director of royal entertainments provided Crébillon with an apartment in his own home where he could rapidly complete the work that would, it was hoped, eclipse that of Voltaire. On 5 September, only a week after the opening of *Sémiramis*, Crébillon's *Catilina* was given a reading at court. The king and Pompadour were delighted with it. Louis agreed to subsidize new costumes for the production, a reform that Voltaire had attempted in *Brutus* but with no financial support, and Pompadour herself persuaded Mlle Clairon to undertake the leading role of Fulvia.

As preparations went forward for the Comédie premiere of *Catilina*, a new irritation appeared for Voltaire—the announcement of a parody of his play that was to be performed at the Comédie Italienne and then at Fontainebleau. Parodies of recent tragedies and operas were hardly a novelty at the Italienne; indeed, most of Voltaire's earlier successes had generated them. In 1743, however, the Italienne and other minor theatres had been forbidden to perform such works, a ban that Crébillon had enforced as censor for the intervening five years. The fact that such a work was now approved seemed to Voltaire clear evidence that he was being singled out for ridicule on a Paris stage, and the threat of a court performance made the situation worse still. He appealed to his most influential friends. Eventually, Pompadour stopped the Fontainebleau performance, and Richelieu intervened to prevent the parody from being performed in Paris, but Voltaire's influence at court was clearly waning.

The long-running and confused War of the Austrian Succession finally came to an end in the fall of 1748. The years of fighting had accomplished little, the only clear victor being the wily Frederick, who kept Silesia, the seizure of which had started the conflict. The return of peace was greeted in France with great jubilation, and in Paris the celebrations included fireworks, illuminations, and amateur theatricals. Voltaire attended the offerings of one of these minor groups, which was performing at the Hôtel de Jabach, and was deeply impressed by the acting of the romantic lead, a young man named Lekain.

According to Lekain's own memoires, Voltaire invited him home and despite his enthusiasm for the young man's talent, expressed horror at Lekain's dream of performing at the Comédie. His reaction says much of his state of mind in the midst of the ongoing battle with his foes in the literary world and at court. Voltaire cried: "Never do that!"

> Trust me. Play comedy for your own pleasure but never make it your profession. It is the most beautiful, the rarest, the most difficult of talents, but it is now abolished by barbarians and banned by hypocrites. Perhaps someday France will value your art, but then there is no longer a Baron, a Lecouvreur, a Dangeville. Give up your project. I will lend you 10,000 francs to set you up in business.[8]

Happily for both actor and playwright, Lekain did not take this sage advice, and Voltaire, won over by his determination, extended every effort to improve his skills. He invited Lekain to move into his home on the rue Traversière, where he coached him in the delivery of tragedy. Inevitably, given Voltaire's interest in private theatricals, he began to think of showing off the abilities of his new protege, and set to work converting the second floor of his house into a small theatre for this purpose.

The premiere of Crébillon's *Catilina* on 20 December 1748 confirmed Voltaire in his suspicion that Crébillon was being promoted at his expense. Again, boxes were purchased months in advance, and the capacity opening-night audience included Pompadour, prominent members of the aristocracy, and several members of the royal family. The play enjoyed a long run, twenty performances, though most historians agree that this was more a result of court and cabal support than popular enthusiasm. Voltaire, however, enjoyed a measure of revenge when his *Sémiramis*, with a completely revised final act, was revived in the spring for six performances, giving it a total this season of twenty-one performances, one more than *Catilina*.

Before the end of the summer Voltaire would become involved again in the ongoing contest with Crébillon, but this spring another theatre project engaged him, a fresh attempt to establish himself as a comic dramatist. Bowing to the current vogue for sentimentality in general, and the British novels of Samuel Richardson in particular, he wrote *Nanine*, a comedy vaguely reminiscent of Richardson's popular *Pamela*. It is even possible that this project was not entirely unrelated to the feud with Crébillon, since Nivelle de Lachaussée, one of Crébillon's strongest supporters, had presented a stage adaptation of *Pamela* at the Comédie in 1743 which, to Voltaire's expressed delight, failed after a single performance. Voltaire's version, concerning an enlightened count who wishes to marry the peasant girl Nanine, arguing that her natural virtues and character make up for her lack of title, may also well have been intended to suggest an approval of the king's new liaison with Mme d'Etioles. A contemporary commentary on the play remarked that many dramatists at this time were inspired by the d'Etioles situation to write plays approving of love conquering class lines.[9]

Nanine was premiered at the Comédie 16 June 1749, with Mlle Gaussin in the title role. Although it was repeated eleven times, it gained little critical success, and its mixing of genres and excessive tearful sentimentality were widely condemned. One publication, *Réflexions sur le comique larmoyante*, particularly angered Voltaire and was rebutted at length in his preface to the play. Chassiron, author of the *Réflexions*, argued that sentimental and passionate love scenes were the proper domain of tragedy, not comedy. Voltaire, who had long resisted the presence of such scenes in tragedy, was thus doubly incensed. Tragedy, he argued, should deal with pity and terror, not with love, especially not with tender love, which is the business of comedy. Indeed, Voltaire suggests that the decline of comedy since Molière may be due to the invasion of its domain by tragedy. Repeating his arguments from *L'Enfant prodigue*, Voltaire insisted that human experience mixes comedy and tragedy and that comedy "can be passionate, emotional, sentimental, provided that it then arouses laughter in honest folk. If it lacks the comic and is only tearful, then it becomes a quite vicious and disagreeable genre" (VO, V, 10). Despite the indifference of its initial reception, *Nanine* became a popular piece, particularly at private theatres, later in the century as Voltaire's reputation grew. It was offered several times at court and often used by the Comédie as a backup play when another work was not ready or poorly received. After its author's death, however, it soon disappeared.

A more direct response was also among Voltaire's plans. Encouraged by his longtime supporter the duchess of Maine, and by Frederick II's complaints about historical inaccuracies in Crébillon's play (though on the whole he approved of it), Voltaire created his own version of the Catilina story, *Rome sauvée*, in eight days in August of 1749. He took special care to correct Crébillon's historical inaccuracies, having Catilina killed in battle rather than committing suicide, building up Cicero into a significant opponent, and omitting an ahistorical intriguing priest and an imaginary love plot between Catilina and Cicero's daughter, an obvious concession to the continuing desire for a romantic interest in any tragedy.

Voltaire's irritation with Crébillon was increased by the performance that month at the Comédie of a new comedy, *L'Amant précepteur*, by Jacques Duvare. The leading character, Polimatte, dabbles, as his name suggests, in everything, but specializes in theatre, where his tragedies stimulate laughter and his comedies tears. He meets a chambermaid disguised as a lady of means who proposes to study science with him in a remote chateau where they will stage theatricals and pursue their studies in art and science. The reference to Voltaire and Mme Du Châtelet was perfectly apparent, even though the actors omitted some fifty lines as particularly slanderous to the well-known couple. The fact that Crébillon had approved this comedy, including even the lines the actors themselves removed, provided Voltaire with further evidence that the censor was using his post to carry on their conflict. The attack was even more painful in that Mme Du Châtelet, Voltaire's fifteen-year companion, died in September, while Duvare's tasteless work was still on the Comédie stage.

In November, Voltaire returned to Paris and met with several actors from the Comédie, presumably to present them with his new tragedy, *Rome sauvée*. Instead, much to their astonishment, he offered them a quite different new work, *Oreste*. Apparently fearful of a direct challenge to Crébillon's most recent work, its success still fresh in the minds of the Paris public, and perhaps recalling again the difficulty of winning over that public with a play lacking a love interest, Voltaire decided on a more indirect challenge—writing a rival play, as he had done with *Sémiramis*, to one of Crébillon's earlier works, his more successful *Electre*. Both Voltaire and Crébillon follow Sophocles in the main outlines of the plot, adding a number of new characters to suit French taste. Crébillon adds a typical love and duty conflict by having his Electre fall in love with the son of Aegisthus, a complication shunned by Voltaire. Voltaire more than Crébillon generally softens the play's harsh relationships, however, introducing a certain warmth between Electre and Clytemnestra, and making Oreste's killing his mother an accident, as she seeks to protect Aegisthus.

Voltaire wrote a special curtain speech for the premiere on 12 January 1750, which began:

> Messieurs, the author of the tragedy that we have the honor to present would never have had the bold vanity to wish to compete with [Crébillon's] *Electre*, justly honored by your approval, less still against his colleague, whom he has often called his master, and who has inspired in him only a noble emulation, equally removed from disparagement or envy, an emulation compatible with friendship and of the sort that men of letters ought to feel

and continued, recalling that this "noble emulation" characterized the Greek dramatists, each of whom wrote plays on this same subject (VO, V, 88).

This transparent device had little effect. Both supporters and enemies of Voltaire came prepared for battle, and the evening was the most riotous of the many Voltaire premieres, surpassing even that of *Sémiramis*. Grandval appeared as Oreste, Clairon as Electre, and Dumesnil as Clytemnestre, but the production was swallowed up in partisan demonstrations. Following the opening, Voltaire, as was his custom, extensively revised the play, and it was given another eight performances before more receptive audiences. This was hardly the triumph Voltaire wished, though he warmly defended his work as truer to the simple and direct style of the Greek originals in an open letter on Greek tragedy to his longtime supporter, the duchess of Maine.

Voltaire naturally regarded Pompadour's support of Crébillon as a betrayal, though she appears to have had a sincere interest in encouraging the work of both poets. In any case, she made another attempt in January of 1750 to promote Voltaire's work at court in the manner most accessible to her, by a production in her petits cabinets. This venture was such a success that it had to expand into larger, though still temporary quarters in November of 1748, allowing the production of grand opera with appropriate scenery. The court painter, Cochin, has left a charming rendering of the stage and auditorium during one such performance, Campistron and Lully's *Acis et Galatée* in January of 1749 (illustration 4). Comedy, opera, and ballet were the sole fare of this theatre until January of 1750, when Pompadour selected Voltaire's

L'opéra d'Acis et Galatée sur le théâtre des Petits cabinets
D'après une gouache peinte par Cochin en 1749

Illustration 4. Lully's opera *Acis et Galatée* presented at the Petits cabinets in 1749.

Alzire for its first tragedy. It was well received and repeated two days later with Voltaire in attendance, and though he doubtless hoped for royal approbation, he had the disappointment of hearing the king loudly express astonishment that the author of *Alzire* could also have written *Oreste*.[10]

Clearly much more satisfying to Voltaire than either Comédie or court at this time was the young group of amateurs that he had assembled and personally trained in the new private theatre in his own home. To them he gave the *Rome sauvée*, which he did not dare to have presented at the Comédie, and they offered its premiere early in June before an invited audience that included several abbés, representatives from the French Academy and the world of letters (Diderot and d'Alembert), and even a few friends from court. Prominent among the latter was the Duc de Richelieu, who even arranged for costumes and properties from Crébillon's rival *Catilina* to be borrowed from the Comédie for Voltaire's use. This select performance brought the attention of the elegant world to Voltaire's private stage, and ministers, ambassadors, and the aristocracy sought entry to the subsequent performances of *Le Duc de Foix*, *Zulime*, and *Jules César*. The duchess of Maine invited the little troupe to Sceaux for a more public performance of *Rome sauvée*, which took place 22 June. There, Voltaire himself replaced the amateur actor Mandron, who had played Cicéron in his home, while Lekain appeared again as César. Lekain reported that "I do not believe it would be possible to hear anything truer, more pathetic, and more spirited than M. de Voltaire in this role. He was truly Cicero himself." The duchess was equally impressed, and while congratulating Voltaire, asked him who his young colleague, Lekain, was. "Madame," Voltaire replied, "he is the best of us all."[11] After the performance, Voltaire informed the duchess that he had decided at last to accept Frederick II's oft-repeated invitation to settle in Berlin. Despite his many successes, the triumph and recognition that he continued to seek at court and in the cultural world of Paris still eluded him, as the recent ambiguous reception of *Oreste* at the Comédie and *Alzire* at Versailles clearly proved. The Prussian court, on the contrary, seemed to offer a sanctuary with a favorably disposed monarch and none of the priests, ministers, or literary rivals that continually intrigued against him in Paris. Voltaire obtained permission from King Louis to leave the kingdom (not, apparently, very unwillingly given) and by July he was in Germany. He did not presumably expect his exile to be an extended one, but in fact he did not again see Paris until a few months before his death, twenty-eight years later.

NOTES

1. Duc de Luynes, *Mémoires sur la cour de Louis XV*, 17 vols. (Paris: Firmin Didot, 1860–1865), 6:354.

2. Both poems quoted (in French) in Jacques Levron, *Pompadour* (Paris: B. Arthaud, 1961), 43, 45.

3. Quoted in Adolphe Jullien, *La Comédie à la cour* (Paris: Firmin Didot, 1883), 152.

4. Edmond and Jules de Goncourt, *La Femme au dix-huitième siècle* (Paris: Firmin Didot, 1862), 113–14.

5. *Mercure*, September 1748, p. 224.

6. Gustave Desnoireterres, *Voltaire et la société française au XVIIIe siècle*, 8 vols. (Paris: Didier, 1871–1876), 3:204.

7. *Journal Encyclopédique*, VI (September 1756): 102.

8. Lekain, *Mémoires* (Paris: Ponthieu, 1825), 424.

9. René Louis, and Marquis d'Argenson, *Notices sur les oeuvres de théâtre*, ed. H. Lagrave, *Studies on Voltaire and the Eighteenth Century*, vol. 42 (1966): 300.

10. Jullien, *Comédie*, 221.

11. Lekain, *Mémoires*, 430–31.

Chapter 5

Voltaire and Germany, 1750–1755

In his final years as crown prince of Prussia, Frederick spent most of his time in the castle of Rheinsberg, which he had remodeled and fitted out to suit his own taste. French taste and culture was predominant among the German principalities at this time, and no one was more dedicated to it than Prince Frederick. The furnishings and gardens at Rheinsburg were in the French style, echoing the taste of Versailles. Paintings by Watteau and Lancret adorned the walls. On the ceiling of Frederick's bedroom was a painting of Minerva amid fluttering cupids holding an open book, on the pages of which were written only two names—Horace and Voltaire. Only French was spoken by Frederick and his companions, and the entertainments were in the French fashion—witty conversations on cultural and literary matters, and of course amateur theatricals, with Frederick playing the title role in Racine's *Mithridate* and Philoctetes in Voltaire's *Oedipe*. Among the other Voltaire plays known to have been presented were *L'Enfant prodigue* and *La Prude*. The castle had no theatre, so performances were given between two screens in the concert hall.[1]

Soon after moving into this retreat, in 1736, Frederick began his extensive correspondence with Voltaire, and to dream of bringing this most visible figure of contemporary French culture as the crowning evidence of Prussia's artistic significance. In 1738, under Voltaire's inspiration, Frederick began a drama in French verse, based on the *Aeneid*, but soon despaired of imitating the master, and turned instead to a refutation of Machiavelli, a rather turgid if well-meaning attack on arbitrary government and unjust wars that was widely viewed with a certain irony after Frederick's unprovoked invasion of Silesia.

It was, of course, the Silesian campaign that for most of Europe dominated its picture of the young king in the opening years of his reign, but in fact the "philosopher-king" found time for literary, scientific, and theatrical activities as well. As he noted himself in a letter to Voltaire of 14 June 1740, twelve days after his ascension, he was "busy with both hands, working at the army with the one, and at the people and the fine arts with the other." Now that he had the authority and the resources, he was determined to remake Berlin into a capital city where, as in Rheinsburg, the arts could flourish. Berlin, he predicted grandly, must become *the* theatre capital of Europe."[2] It would be a formidable task. No permanent places of performance existed in the city, and King Frederick William, Frederick's father, had sponsored only puppet shows, travelling companies of farce players featuring the popular clowns Hanswurst and Pickelhering, acrobats, and novelty acts. A particular favorite was the "strong man" von Eckenberg, who lifted cannons and whom Frederick William considered a model for his troops. Indeed, von Eckenberg was accorded the largely honorific title of Master of the King's Revels, and his license to perform in the city was regularly renewed. In the 1730s, the Pantaloon of his troupe, Peter Hilferding, set up a company of his own and also regularly appeared in traditional farces.

Frederick II was determined to change all of this. At Rheinsburg he had assembled an orchestra of fourteen musicians that would be the foundation of his court orchestra, and accompanied them on the flute in sonatas of his own composition. He now dreamed of a grand opera, surpassing that of Dresden, which had dazzled him as a boy of sixteen. Knobelsdorf, the gifted young architect who had remodeled Rheinsburg for him, was now sent to visit Dresden and other leading opera houses and, drawing upon this information, to design the best opera house in Europe for Berlin. In the meantime, Frederick's music director, Heinrich Graun, was dispatched to Italy to assemble a company of leading singers and dancers, since in opera alone Frederick looked to Dresden and Vienna for models rather than Paris, and thus to the Italian tradition. These projects moved along steadily despite the Silesian campaign, doubtless because Knobelsdorf and Graun were longtime associates of Frederick and were directly under his employ. His parallel project to establish a Berlin Comédie, organized through the intermediaries Voltaire and Lanoue, fell through, as we have seen, when Frederick was no longer able to give it his attention.

After the conquering of Silesia and the establishing of peace with Austria at Breslau in 1742, Frederick returned to Berlin and to his plans for the arts. Singers, dancers, composers, poets, and artists flocked to the capital to participate in a new golden age. The central symbol of this renaissance was

Knobelsdorf's magnificent new opera house, opened in December. Italian singers and dancers operated it under the king's personal supervision. A whole school of Italian librettists was employed, but Frederick himself chose the subject for each libretto, outlined its plot, and often extensively rewrote the finished project. Frederick's attention to military detail was famous, but his attention to artistic detail was equally thorough, as may be seen in a letter to Graun with instructions for a new opera:

> Each of the principal persons must have several important arias, all different in character. The adagio arias must be very cantabile and written so as to display the voice and delivery of the singer. In the da capo the singer can show her facility in embellishing variations. The allegro arias must contain brilliant passages. Then there must be a gallant aria, emphasized by action and a duet for the two leading singers. In these numbers 4-4 and 3-4 time are to be chiefly utilized and the pathos of French tragedy is to be observed in the delivery. The smaller measures as 2-4 and 3-8 are to be employed for the less important roles and in these the tempo di menuetto is appropriate. Care should be exercised to have contrasts by modulating from one key to another. However the minor keys are to be avoided entirely as they are too melancholy in the theatre.[3]

There were also biweekly performances of spoken French theatre at the court in 1792, with public performances on other days, although the records of the time provide little information about either the actors or the repertoire. In a November letter to Frederick, Voltaire delicately suggests that "The troupe now playing before your court is probably not like your military troupe. It is not, I believe, the best in Europe," and goes on to suggest that he might provide another promising young director, like Lanoue, to improve matters. Frederick responded: "I must admit that you have a rather accurate idea of our actors. They are really dancers, like the Cochin family, who act comedy. They perform several pieces from the Théâtre Italien and Molière passably enough, but I have forbidden them to put on the cothurnus, not finding them worthy of it" (VC, XII, 143, 150). Even so, Frederick did not accept Voltaire's offer to seek a new director, but instead employed a colorful Figaro-type wandering bohemian, the Marquis d'Argans, who in fact put together a passable, if undistinguished French company which presented the standard works of the French repertoire until the mid-1750s.

Spoken German theatre in Berlin was even more marginal. There was really no significant repertoire, and professional theatre consisted of wandering companies of mountebanks, travelling from fair to fair to present broad farce, pieces of old medieval and school drama, borrowings from the operatic and spoken theatres of Italy, Spain, France, and Italy and the colorful pageants of fairy-tale court life called *Haupt-und-Staataktionen* (chief and state plays). In the 1720s in Leipzig, the academic Johann Christoph Gottsched, working with a local company headed by Caroline Neuber, attemped to establish a German literary drama, translating French tragedies and creating an original work of his own, *Der sterbende Cato* (1731), heavily indebted to Addison's drama. Friends and disciples of Gottsched joined in his campaign, but by the early 1740s the repertoire available to a German company was still extremely small; three-quarters of it translated from the French (the most translated French dramatists, each with four plays in the repertoire, were Corneille, Marivaux, Destouches, and Voltaire, who was represented by *Brutus, Zaïre, Alzire*, and *L'Enfant prodigue*). Nevertheless, Frederick looked with favor upon a proposal in 1742 from J. F. Schönemann to establish a German company in Berlin.

Schönemann, the leading actor of this period, was a member of Neuber's company in Leipzig. When Neuber left the city, having quarreled with Gottsched in 1739 (preferring another translation of Voltaire's *Alzire* to that prepared by Gottsched's wife), Schönemann remained behind, made peace with Gottsched, and organized his own company, among the members of which were three actors who would dominate the next generation: Konrad Ackermann, Sophie Schröder, and Konrad Ekhof. The new company leased a theatre in Hamburg, but was unable to build an audience there. During the 1740s, Leipzig remained the main center for the development of a German literary theatre, thanks primarily to the continuing presence of Gottsched and the intermittent visits of Neuber. Fredrich Melchior Grimm studied with Gottsched from 1743 to 1745, unsuccessfully tried his hand at tragic composition, and after 1750 settled in Paris, where his detailed reports on the next two decades of the French stage are a major source of theatre information for that period. In 1746, Gotthold Lessing and his friend, Christian Weiss, arrived in Leipzig to study theology, and in fact spent most of their energy involved with the theatre projects of Gottsched and Neuber, translating plays by Marivaux and Regnard in exchange for free tickets to the Neuber productions. At this time, Lessing created several comedies of his own, one of which, the Molière-like *Der junge Gelehrte*, was premiered by Neuber in 1748 and presented later that same year by Schönemann in Berlin.

In Berlin, "strong man" von Eckenberg, still officially the leader of the theatre there, opposed the more academic approach championed by Schönemann, but he was overruled by Frederick, and Schönemann's company opened in Berlin in September of 1742 with Gottsched's *Cato* and a pastoral play, *Gelernte Liebe,* by Rost. The pastoral, relying heavily on song and dance, was an inexpensive substitute for opera in the popular and touring theatre until it was replaced after the middle of the century by comic opera. Schönemann also premiered, in 1743, the first German ballad opera, another precursor of comic opera, *Der Teufel ist Los*. This was a translation by C. W. von Borck of C. Coffey's *The Devil to Pay*, one of the London imitations of Gay's popular *Beggar's Opera*. Von Borck had served as the Prussian ambassador to London, and like Voltaire had frequented and much enjoyed the London theatre. He admired not only the ballad opera, but Shakespeare, and indeed was the translator of the first complete Shakespearian play into German, *Julius Caesar* in 1741. His innovations had little immediate effect, however. Shakespeare's vogue in Germany did not begin until the *Sturm und Drang* of the 1770s and the powerful Schlegel translations at the end of the century.

As Neuber had done in Leipzig, Schönemann began his Berlin productions with a ceremony officially banning Harlequin and the low comedy he represented from the stage, though like Neuber, he was soon forced by popular demand to add traditional comic afterpieces to his more ambitious offerings. A year later, Schönemann was sharing the Berlin German stage with Franz Shuch from Breslau, a specialist in traditional farce, and for the rest of the 1740s Schönemann appeared only intermittently in Berlin. Still, he offered Berlin audiences the most ambitious German repertoire of the period. To the Voltaire works played in Leipzig he added *Mahomet*, and particularly favored the new French sentimental drama—Destouches, Lachaussée, and Marivaux.

The repertoire continued to be dominated by French translations, but there were some original German works. In addition to Lessing's *Der junge Gelehrte*, Christian Gellert created a number of sentimental comedies in the French style during the 1740s and offered the first extended defense in German of this genre in his inaugural address when he joined the Leipzig University faculty in 1751. "The tears which comedy stimulates," Gellert suggested, "are like the healing rain which not only refreshes the seed but makes it fruitful."[4] J. C. Krüger, one of Schönemann's actors, translated many of Marivaux's works and created a number of original and popular comedies, the best known of them *Die Kandidaten* (1747), attacking abuses in contemporary society so sharply as to cause him some trouble with censorship.

Even fewer German tragedies were offered, but Schönemann did present in Berlin two works by the leading serious German dramatist of this generation, Johann Elias Schlegel. Schlegel was a twenty-two-year-old student in 1741 when von Borck's translation of *Julius Caesar* appeared, stimulating from him an enthusiastic essay on Shakespeare, as well as the first "patriotic" German drama, *Hermann*, dealing with early German struggles against Rome. Three years later, Schlegel went to Denmark as private secretary to the Saxon ambassador there. He arrived shortly before a key moment in Danish theatre history. Frederick V, who became king in 1746, sought, like his namesake in Prussia, to establish his capital as a center of arts and pleasure. He established six theatres, among them a French troupe, an Italian opera company, a combination German-Danish troupe, and a Danish national stage. Schlegel was inspired by this activity to write two thoughtful essays on the functions of theatre in society, and another historical tragedy which Schönemann presented, *Canut*.

Lessing settled in Berlin in the fall of 1750, making his living by journalistic essays and translations (including Caldéron's *Life is a Dream* and Crébillon's recent *Catilina*). He founded an ambitious quarterly for theatre research, "Contributions to the History and Reform of Theatre," with material on classic drama; Shakespeare; the Spanish, French, Italian, and Dutch stage, as well as the contemporary German stage, which Lessing sought to encourage as an instrument of cultural and moral improvement. In this same year, not long after Voltaire arrived in Berlin, he crossed paths with Lessing, bringing unfortunate results.

When Voltaire went to London in 1726, he found a lively, varied, and long-established theatre world, able to look back on more than a century of significant dramatic achievement. The theatre situation in 1750 Germany was more closely equivalent to England in the years just before the arrival of Marlowe and Shakespeare in the late 1500s—no established theatres, no established repertoire, only the first tentative steps toward a literary drama, and those largely based on foreign translations. Germany was not in fact a country, but a patchwork of more than three hundred kingdoms, dutchies, church-ruled states and free cities with constantly shifting alliances. Despite Frederick's enthusiasm, Berlin was still anything but a theatre center, even for his own kingdom of Prussia. Schönemann, unable to build an audience, left in 1749, and Berlin was without a German language theatre for the next four years. The French company remained, but languished as the court attention turned to the opera and court entertainments. Voltaire's attention, however, was entirely upon the court, and his letters back to France speak glowingly of the cultural life there. Under the late king, he notes, Potsdam offered military drilling fields instead of gardens, marching troops instead of music, military reviews instead of theatre, military rolls instead of libraries. Today, on the contrary, it is the home of "high spirits, pleasure and glory, magnificence and taste, etc. etc." (VC, XVIII, 107). Early in August, he commented: "I must admit that the Prussians do not create better tragedies than we do, but you would be hard pressed to create for madame the dauphine a spectacle as noble and gallant as that being prepared for Berlin," a festival "worthy in every way of those of Louis XIV" (VC, XVIII, 109).

Frederick indeed attempted to convert the royal seat at Potsdam near Berlin from a garrison town to a German Versailles, and further imitated Louis XIV in organizing in his capital the sort of elaborate allegorical and theatrical festivals that had been presented at Versailles in the late seventeenth century. Several days of celebrations were organized for the state visit of the Margrave of Bayreuth in August. Voltaire was dazzled by the "forty-six thousand glass lanterns illuminating the square," the "three thousand soldiers under arms lining all the avenues," the "four small armies of Romans, Carthaginians, Persians, and Greeks entering the lists and parading to military music," the whole concluded by a lavish dinner and a ball. Voltaire confessed he believed himself in a fairyland (VC, XVIII, 136).

A variety of theatrical entertainments were presented at this festival: comedies by Molière and Arnaud; Racine's *Iphigénie*, presented by the French actors; and an opera by Quinault; but nothing by Voltaire, probably because his arrival occurred too soon before the festival for anything to be prepared. Nevertheless, the presence of the French celebrity added extra glory to the celebrations, as Voltaire well knew, and a whole series of performances of his plays soon followed, offered not by the French company, but by the princes and princesses of the court, directed by Voltaire himself. He supervised the construction of a small theatre in the apartments of Princess Amélie, which opened with *Rome sauvée* on 22 September, with Voltaire playing the role of Cicéron and the princess playing Aurélie. This was given several performances and was followed by *La Mort de César* in October, *Sémiramis, Nanine, Mariamne*, and *Oreste* in November and December, and *Zaïre* in January. Voltaire appeared as Lusignan, and clearly enjoyed working with and directing members of the royal family. He reported to the Margrave of Bayreuth that "Prince Henry surpassed himself, the Crown Prince spoke quite distinctly, Prince Ferdinand softened his voice, Princess Amélie was quite tender and the Queen was enchanted" (VC, XIX, 10).

During these same months, Voltaire's protege, Lekain, was finding his close association with the poet a mixed blessing. He made his debut at the Comédie on 14 September 1750, playing Titus in Voltaire's *Brutus*. His acting talent was clear, but his plain features and unprepossessing garments (actors were normally expected to provide their own costumes) did not please, and moreover his close association in the public mind with Voltaire caused reactions toward him to split largely along the familiar lines of enemies and supporters of his patron.

Lekain faced opposition within the Comédie as well. Clairon reportedly did not wish to play tragedy opposite so ill-favored a hero, and Grandval, the present possessor of the leading tragic roles, reportedly saw in Lekain too powerful a potential rival. In any case, judgement on Lekain's acceptance was delayed while another promising young actor, Bellecourt, who had won fame as Nérestan in amateur performances of *Zaïre*, made his debut and was quickly accepted. The handsome Bellecourt lacked the strength for tragic roles, however, and soon settled into playing elegant gentlemen in comedy.

Lekain's second debut occurred on 30 September in a revival of Voltaire's *Mahomet*. Voltaire's friend the Comte d'Argental arranged for the play to be approved by the sympathetic young philosopher D'Alembert instead of the still reluctant Crébillon, and Lekain appeared in the youthful leading role of Seïde, while Lanoue, who had created that role nine years before, now appeared as Mahomet. A third debut, as Voltaire's Oedipe, was such an unqualified success that following the production the audience protested Lekain's continuing exclusion from membership in the company, but still the decision was delayed. The disappointed Lekain wrote to Voltaire in Berlin in October offering to come there and join the French company. Voltaire promised to apply on his behalf, but his letter was generally not hopeful, and indeed nothing came of this proposal. Between his debuts at the Comédie, Lekain continued to perform with the amateur company at the Hôtel de Jabach, but such was his growing fame that the Comédie began to lose audiences to the Jabach.

The impasse was broken when the Comédie was invited to present *Zaïre* at court and Lekain begged for the opportunity to perform Orosmane. Grandval assented, warning him (and perhaps hoping) that this presumption by an ill-favored and ill-dressed actor might well mean the end of his career. The result was an unqualified success. Mme de Pompadour praised his intelligence and emotional power, and more important, Louis XV was sufficiently moved to declare, "He made me weep, and I never weep."[5] At Louis' command, Lekain was admitted at once into the national company, though still with only half a share and few significant parts. In time, his clear superiority to Grandval would bring him most of the major tragic roles, but this required a number of years.

Although Voltaire's letters show him maintaining an interest in these Parisian theatrical intrigues, he had, as always, many ongoing projects of his own nearer at hand. His major work on French culture, the *Siècle de Louis XIV*, conceived some twenty years earlier, was at last nearing completion and, much less admirably, he was now embroiled in a long, complex, and sordid legal battle with a Berlin financier, Abraham Hirschel, involving some distinctly shady financial speculation. As the matter entered the Berlin courts, Voltaire, who was conducting his own case, realized that he would need a competent German translator. He appealed to his secretary, Richier de Louvain, a French teacher of languages in Berlin, and Richier recommended a young journalist who had studied French with him, Gotthold Lessing.

For a number of months, Lessing and Voltaire were in almost daily contact discussing this case and, it is to be hoped, occasional more exalted literary matters, since Lessing also translated some of Voltaire's minor historical writings. The case was at last settled, essentially in Voltaire's favor, by mid-February of 1751. Frederick kept a discreet distance from all of this, but privately expressed contempt for Voltaire's role in the affair. In January, at the height of the scandal, he threatened to dismiss Voltaire from Prussia entirely, and only with much difficulty were the former friends able to reestablish something resembling their previous intimacy.

His suit won and a partial reconciliation with Frederick effected, Voltaire retired from Berlin to Potsdam, where he at last completed the *Siècle de Louis XIV*. Lessing, eager to see this new work, borrowed a copy from his friend, Richier. Unfortunately, Voltaire discovered this and was enraged that the work had been passed on before it had even been seen by the royal family. His anger increased when he discovered that Lessing had unwittingly carried the book back with him to Wittenberg, where he was resuming his studies. His previous suffering from pirated editions of his work convinced Voltaire that this was Lessing's secret project. Richier was dismissed and angry letters sent to Lessing demanding the immediate return of the manuscript. Lessing immediately obliged, with a warm apology, but the damage was done. Voltaire complained to Frederick, who subsequently regarded Lessing with suspicion and prevented him from gaining any future significant success in Berlin. The loss for both Berlin and the German stage was considerable. Lessing's first major play, and the first major German drama, *Miss Sara Sampson* (a domestic drama, inspired by the work of George Lillo in England), was written by Lessing while in residence in Potsdam, but first presented in 1755 by Schönemann's leading actor, Konrad Ackermann, now in charge of his own company in Frankfurt where they were on tour. Lessing returned for a time to Leipzig, but spent most of the rest of this decade in Berlin where he wrote to a friend that he was writing plays day and night and that his smallest resolve was to write "at least three times as many dramas as Lope de Vega."[6] The Berlin stage remained inhospitable to him, however, and in 1760 he left to become a military secretary in the little garrison town of Breslau, where he wrote the first significant German comedy, *Minna von Barnhelm.*

A permanent national theatre in Germany finally was established in Hamburg in 1767, and Lessing, now well-known as a critic and playwright, was invited to serve as the theatre's resident critic and dramaturge. His collection of critical essays about this venture, the *Hamburgische Dramaturgie*, remains one of the major works of eighteenth-century dramatic theory, and laid the intellectual foundations for the modern German theatre. Lessing had a strong affinity for the English theatre and for Shakespeare, whom he claimed was closer to the spirit of Aristotle and classic practice than the rule-bound French who claimed to carry on this tradition. He seemed to take a particular pleasure in attacking Voltaire, and it is hard to resist hearing something of an echo of the unhappy memories of the Hirschel scandal and the misunderstanding over the *Louis XIV* manuscript in such passages as this, from essay number 70 of the *Dramaturgie*:

> Let a critical writer . . . first seek out someone with whom he can quarrel. Thus he will gradually get into his subject and the rest will follow as a matter of course. I frankly admit that I have selected primarily the French writers for this purpose, and among them particularly M. de Voltaire.[7]

The success of *Mahomet* encouraged the Comédie to offer at last Voltaire's *Rome sauvée*, which the author had left with them upon his departure for Berlin. It was premiered 24 February 1752 with Lanoue as Cicero, Lekain as Catilina, Grandval as César and Clairon as Aurélie. Voltaire's opponents saw no need to demonstrate against the production now that its author was far off in Prussia, and the work received a warm response, although the lack of a strong love interest remained, as always, an obstacle to the play's continued popularity. After an initial eleven performances, it was revived only rarely. At this time, though, Voltaire was quite content. The play which he had so long hesitated to bring before the public had achieved a reputable success, and equally important to him, was generally considered superior to Crébillon's version. It is not surprising that after this victory Voltaire attempted to call a halt to his extended rivalry with the older tragedian. After *Rome sauvée*, he announced, "I am going to leave Rome in peace and willingly abandon the field of battle to the troops of Crébillon."[8]

It is also not surprising that Crébillon should be unwilling to let Voltaire's success pass unchallenged, though he was never able, as Voltaire often boasted of doing, to create a play in a week or two. (In fact, Voltaire's claim needs some qualification, since he was an obsessive rewriter, continuing to make extensive changes in his plays for weeks, months, even years after the first version was completed.) Thus, though the success of *Rome sauvée* challenged the older poet to return to the field of battle with a new Roman play, *Le Triumverat*, it required him another two years to complete.

Lekain was, in the eyes of most commentators, overshadowed by Lanoue and Grandval in *Rome sauvée*, but on 17 August 1752 he was finally given the opportunity to create a new Voltaire role, the leading part in *Le Duc de Foix*, and he achieved a gratifying success in this totally reworked version of *Adélaïde du Guesclin*, which had been so badly received in 1734. His reputation was now steadily growing.

Events at the Opéra this summer quite overshadowed Lekain's success, however. In August and September, an Italian troupe headed by Eustachio Bambini made a guest appearance and enjoyed enormous success with renditions of Italian comic operas, particularly Pergolesi's *Serva padrona*. Until this point, Italian operatic practice had made few inroads into France, but several pamphlets championing the simple and direct Italian opera at the expense of the cumbersome and artificial French opera had appeared earlier this year, and now a major controversy erupted over the relative merits of the two national musical traditions. Jean-Jacques Rousseau, who became a central figure in this dispute, thus describes the situation in his *Confessions*:

> All Paris was divided into two parties as heated as if it were a question of politics or religion. The more powerful and numerous one, made up of the rich, the important, and the women, supported French music. The other, livelier, more spirited was made up of the real connoisseurs, the men of talent and genius. Its little faction gathered at the Opéra under the Queen's box. The others filled the rest of the house, but their principal location was under the King's box. That is how the parties came to be known as the "King's Corner" and the "Queen's Corner."[9]

Thus began the famous *Querelle des bouffons*, taking its name from the Italian form, the *opera buffa*. Rousseau clearly favored the Italians, but at first he seems to have attempted a conciliatory role. In the spring of 1752, he conceived the idea of introducing his countrymen to this genre by writing an *opéra bouffe* in the Italian style, but using the familiar French shepherds and shepherdesses, and preaching a conservative social message quite unlike the mixture of classes sanctioned by *La serve padrona*. The result was *Le Devin du village* which, despite the unfamiliarity of its approach, was not only accepted by the Opéra, but presented on 17 October in a command performance at Fontainebleau. This was a great success, as was the Opéra premiere on 1 March 1753. Soon after, however, Rousseau called down a storm of protest by publishing the most extreme and inflammatory brochure of the

Querelle des bouffons, his *Lettre sur la musique française*, which called French singing "continual barking" and French music devoid of harmony and expression, concluding "the French have no music and cannot have any."[10] The other philosophers who had attacked French opera had at least made an exception for Rameau, but Rousseau, long antagonistic toward the leading French composer, soon began singling him out for personal attack. The controversy now focused on Rousseau himself. The musicians at the Opéra burned him in effigy, a campaign was mounted to drive him from France, and although he was banned from the Opéra by the municipal authorities, he continued to attend with a bodyguard. The conflict between Rousseau and Rameau continued until the death of the latter in 1764. Accommodation was impossible because two opposed theories of music, indeed of political, social, and experienced reality were involved. Rameau represented the old school of Cartesian rationalism, seeing music as a mathematical and abstract system in which logical harmonies were more important than melodic lines. Rousseau felt this attitude particularly French, hence their inability to create true music, which he saw as the authentic voice or expression of human feeling or experience. He saw harmony as an invention of the mind, melody as the voice of nature. Music historians place the advent of romanticism in the early nineteenth century, but in music, as in much romantic thought, Rousseau clearly prepared the way, stressing the lyrical expression of feeling over formal principles of composition.

Le Devin du village thus marks a new direction, but it was a direction Rousseau did not himself pursue. He had achieved success in opera and on a much less modest scale, in the theatre, since his comedy *Narcisse* was presented at the Comédie on 18 December 1752 and was warmly applauded, even though the author himself pronounced it a failure. There was a paradox in these undertakings that clearly caused Rousseau some discomfort. If music was impossible in France, why attempt to write French operas, even reformed ones? If, as he argued in his philosophic writings, modern society had become more interested in entertainment than in the pursuit of virtue, why encourage this tendency with theatrical amusements? In the preface to *Narcisse,* he attempted to resolve these contradictions, to defend his musical and theatrical activity by shifting the blame to his public. In a society already corrupted, the distractions of music and theatre may prevent worse alternatives: "When it is no longer a question of leading people to do good, one may at least distract them from doing evil, one must occupy them with foolish pleasures to keep them from evil actions, one must amuse them rather than preach."[11] The argument is not very convincing, and Rousseau himself did not long pursue it. He had come to Paris dreaming of success in the theatre and in music, but no sooner had he began to achieve this than he turned away, to devote himself henceforth to the critical examination of himself and his society. He would not write a new *Brutus* or *Cato* for this generation, but would seek to become its Brutus or Cato.

The entrepreneur who most profited from the *Querelle des bouffons* was the canny Jean Monnet. Monnet had already shown himself as a skilled theatre administrator, becoming director of the Opéra-Comique, one of the leading theatres at the Saint-Laurent and Saint-Germain fairs, in 1743. There he assembled a remarkable company, including: the orchestra leader Rameau, who, as we have seen, had built his reputation in the fair theatres and who was soon in collaboration with Voltaire on *La Princesse de Navarre*; the costumer and scene designer Boucher, who created court spectacles for Mme de Pompadour and who would become one of the century's best-known artists; the comic actor Préville, who would end at the Comédie, considered the century's greatest comedian and the originator of Beaumarchais' Figaro; the ballet master Dupré, who brought with him his pupil, Noverre, who would revolutionize French dance; and most important for the genre of comic opera itself, the author and stage manager Charles Simon Favart, who would both establish and create a European vogue for this new genre including, among the sources for his popular offerings, several works by Voltaire.

The combined talents of this company brought all Paris to Monnet's theatre, with the result that both the Comédie Française and the Comédie Italienne protested against the competition. Only a year after his direction began, Monnet's theatre was closed by the authorities. For a time he became director of the provincial theatre in Lyons, and in 1749, with the encouragement of Garrick and Rich, assembled a company of French actors to perform at the Little Theatre in the Haymarket in London. Patriotic Englishmen protested these performances (as patriotic Frenchmen would protest the better-known English performers in Paris in 1827), and the venture failed. In 1750, Monnet was back in Paris, where friends at court succeeded in reestablishing him as director of the Opéra-Comique. He had just opened a new and luxurious theatre at the Saint-Germain fair in 1752 when the *Querelle des bouffons* erupted. Monnet and his colleague, Favart, saw a unique opportunity in this controversy, and Favart began to develop French plays based on Italian themes, working with French composers influenced by Italian music. The resulting blend proved enormously popular, and in the 1750s Favart emerged as an author of enormous popularity and the developer of a new mode of French comic opera.

Had Voltaire been in Paris in the summer of the *Querelle*, he would have undoubtedly enrolled himself on the side of the reformers, which included many of his intellectual companions, but in far-off Prussia he paid little attention to this debate over musical style, one of the few subjects concerning which he seems to have had little curiosity. Moreover, his attention was at this moment focused on another dispute, much more near at hand and closer to his own interests. It involved two of the leading figures in the Prussian intellectual world: the mathematician Samuel König, a member of the Berlin Academy; and Pierre Louis de Maupertuis, who had been appointed head of the Academy upon Voltaire's recommendation, but whose overbearing and tyrannical manner increasingly aroused Voltaire's anger. As a result of a scientific quarrel, Maupertuis had König expelled from the Academy. Even though Frederick supported Maupertuis, Voltaire entered the fray, and after several pamphlets, produced a work that, like Rousseau's *Lettre*, brought him to the center of the debate. This was one of his wittiest and sharpest satires, the *Diatribe du docteur Akakia*, a savage attack on Maupertuis that delighted Europe and enraged Frederick. The book was burned in Berlin, and the warm relationship between Voltaire and the king was clearly finished. Voltaire received permission to leave Berlin in March and made a leisurely retreat from Germany, reaching Mayence, a city outside Frederick's realm, on 7 July 1753. In time their friendly correspondence resumed, but he would never see the Prussian king again.

In the complex web of German principalities with their frequently shifting political loyalties, there were still many courts that would be happy to attract a figure of Voltaire's prominence to testify to their cultural and artistic distinction, whatever tensions existed between him and the powerful courts of France and Prussia. Charles Theodore, elector of the Palatinate, whose capital was Mannheim, invited him to recover from his recent unhappy experiences in his summer castle at Schwetzingen, another of those countless small imitations of the castle and gardens of Versailles that dotted eighteenth-century Germany.[12]

There, Voltaire passed most of August engaged in the whirl of court life and entertainment that he loved: "French comedy, Italian comedy, Italian grand opera, *opera buffa*, ballets, conversations, elegance, grandeur, simplicity" (VC, XXIII, 120). And since, as he remarked, "there is no better way to receive an author than to perform his works," a series of his plays were also offered—*Alzire, Nanine, Zaïre*, and *L'Indiscret*, with, of course, the author himself deeply involved in the rehearsals and staging (VC, XXIII, 133–34). This reimmersion in theatrical activity spurred him again to think of dramatic composition. To his friend, d'Argental, he wrote: "The elector palatine has paid me the compliment of having me stage four of my plays. This has reawakened an old passion, and although I am at death's door I have drawn up a plan for a new play quite full of love. I am quite ashamed of it, it is the dream of an old fool" (VC, XXIII, 145–46). The play, which was to become *L'Orphélin de la Chine*, would indeed open a new period of dramatic productivity and experimentation, but the work went slowly, and his letters of the fall and winter of 1753 often ironically or pathetically comment on the unlikelihood of a man of his years and physical condition attempting a tragedy of love.

Hoping that he would soon obtain permission from Louis to return to Paris, Voltaire sought refuge in early October, as he had six years before, in King Stanislas' province of Lorraine, on the edge of France. At his urging, Mme Denis appealed to Mme de Pompadour to intercede on his behalf with the king, but Louis had no desire for Voltaire to return, and he had to seek refuge elsewhere. He toyed with the idea of going back to England, or even travelling to America, but by the spring of 1754 he had decided upon Switzerland, a Protestant republic with a certain reputation for tolerance, also conveniently close to France.

On 11 November he departed for Geneva. He stopped over for five days in Lyons with his old friend the Duc de Richelieu, and received a taste of his old glory. The Lyons theatre performed his plays in his honor, and when he appeared there in his box he was greeted with enthusiastic applause. Word also came of his continuing success in Paris, where revivals of his works were now being given almost unqualified praise. Mme de Pompadour was unable to obtain permission for Voltaire to return, but she did arrange for a court performance of *Mariamne* in August which was highly successful, as were revivals at the Comédie of *Le Duc de Foix* in November and *Nanine* in December. Equally gratifying, word came of the very indifferent success of what was to be Crébillon's last play and his final attempt to recapture the Roman battlefield from Voltaire. *Le Triumverat* opened at the Comédie 23 December with Clairon, Lekain, Grandval and Lanoue in the leading roles. Although the work contains some of the scenes of horror that first established Crébillon's reputation, as well as visual spectacle that recalled Voltaire's innovations in this area, the reception, even from Crébillon's previous supporters, was cool. With Voltaire gone, and *Rome sauvée* two years in the past, the play could not even stimulate the interest of partisan enthusiasm. Voltaire confined himself to a few contemptuous comments in his letters, and seemed content to keep to his vow of putting this particular quarrel behind him. Unhappily, though, a final confrontation with his old enemy still lay ahead.

During the month of January 1755, Voltaire sought a property of his own in Switzerland and permission, as a nominal Roman Catholic, to settle in this

Protestant stronghold. At last, early in February, he obtained the permission and a lifetime lease on a property near Geneva, which he christened "Les Délices." He was now sixty-one years of age and ready to embark upon the last great phase of his creative career.

NOTES

1. Jean-Jacques Olivier, *Les Comédiens Français dans les cours d'Allemagne au XIIIe siècle*, 2 vols. (Paris: Société Française d'Imprimerie, 1902), 2:25.

2. Gerhard Wahnrau, *Berlin: Stadt der Theater* (Berlin: Henschelverlag, 1957), 55.

3. Quoted in Nathan Ausubel, *Superman: The Life of Frederick the Great* (New York: Ibes Washburn, 1931), 495.

4. Christian Fürchtegott Gellert, "Pro Comoedia Commovente Commentatio," *Gesammelte Schriften*, 6 vols. (Berlin: Walter de Gruyter, 1994), 5:171.

5. F. J. Talma, "Quelques Réflexions sur Lekain," in *Mémoires de Lekain* (Paris: Ponthieu, 1825), v.

6. Thomas William Rolleston, *Life of Gotthold Ephraim Lessing* (London: W. Scott, 1889), 85.

7. Gotthold Lessing, *Lessings Werke*, eds. J. Peterson and W. von Olshausen, 25 vols. (Berlin: Bong, 1925–35), 5:297.

8. Quoted in Paul O. LeClerc, *Voltaire and Crébillon père: History of an enmity*, *Studies on Voltaire*, 115 (1973):116.

9. Jean Jacques Rousseau, *Confessions* (Paris: Georges Crès, 1904), 261–62.

10. Quoted in Lester G. Crocker, *Jean Jacques Rousseau*, 2 vols. (New York: Macmillan, 1968), 243.

11. Jean Jacques Rousseau, "Préface" to *Narcisse*, *Oeuvres complètes*, 23 vols. (Paris: P. Dupont, 1823-26), 10:279.

12. See Hans Rall, *Kurfürst Karl Theodor* (Mannheim: Wissenschafsverlag, 1994), 65–66.

Chapter 6

Voltaire and the *Philosophes*, 1755–1760

Voltaire renamed his new home "Les Délices," because, he said, "there is nothing more delightful than to be free and independent." He had learned how important a certain flexibility in movement was to freedom, and Les Délices was well situated in that respect—within the republic of Geneva, but almost on the border of the Sardinian province of Savoy and half an hour's ride from France along the Lyon road. So long accustomed to the pleasures of the city and court, Voltaire now threw himself enthusiastically into the life of the lord of a country manor. He tore down walls to improve the view, planned new rooms, expanded the gardens. He wrote in March that his conversation was no longer of literature, politics, and culture, but of "masons, carpenters, and gardeners" (VC, XXVI, 159). But, while Voltaire was no longer circulating in the world, the world would, during the following years, begin coming to him. A visit to one of the philosopher's homes in Switzerland became a necessary part of a European tour for any traveller with a truly deep regard for contemporary culture.

The first guest at Les Délices, in April of 1755, was Lekain, now firmly established as a leading actor in Paris and freed from the Comédie because of the annual Easter closing. In his letter of invitation, Voltaire warned: "You will find me become a mason, carpenter, gardener; only you will be able to restore me to my proper calling" (VC, XXVI, 174). Indeed, Lekain's arrival did inspire a desire to stage some theatre and *Zaïre* was rehearsed and performed in one of the large rooms of the house. According to Voltaire, almost the entire council of Geneva was in the large audience and, "I have never seen so many tears; never were Calvinists so tender" (VC, XXVI, 192). Mme Denis and Lekain played the leading roles, with Voltaire in his favorite part of Lusignan. The group also did a reading of his most recent work, *L'Orphélin de la Chine*, and Lekain returned to Paris hoping soon to stage it at the Comédie. In his enthusiasm over this visit, Voltaire decided to follow the custom of so many of his aristocratic hosts and install a permanent theatre in his home. He began fitting up a gallery of Les Délices with a stage, having scenery painted, and theatrical costumes gathered. He announced an opening with *Alzire*, to be followed by *L'Orphélin de la Chine*, presented by a company of amateurs drawn from the youth of Geneva. The threat of regular theatre and worse yet, the participation of their children, stirred the town council to action, and on 31 July, citing city ordinances of 1732 and 1739 (hitherto not rigorously enforced, which banned all theatrical representations, public and private, from the city), they required Voltaire to give up his project.[1] Voltaire gave in with surprising humility, but this was doubtless in large part because he anticipated another alternative. He had also purchased a smaller winter home, Monrion, in Lausanne, a much more liberal community with an substantial international population and a passion for the theatre. Within a few months of his arrival there, Voltaire had assembled a dedicated group of amateurs and was giving regular productions, which were a source of delight to a faithful and substantial local audience. Among them was the young Edward Gibbon, who spent the years 1753 to 1758 in Lausanne and became so enraptured by the productions of *Zaïre*, *Alzire*, *Zulime*, *L'Enfant prodigue*, and Racine's *Iphigénie* that he became devoted to the French theatre, even at the cost of that "idolotry for Shakespeare . . . inculcated from our infancy as the first duty of an Englishman."[2]

Apparently wishing to avoid the partisan demonstrations aroused at the Comédie by his earlier rivalry with Crébillon, Voltaire resisted the staging of *L'Orphélin de la Chine* there until Crébillon's *Triumverat* was no longer in the repertoire. By mid-1755, the way seemed clear and the new work was submitted to the police for approval. A possible obstacle remained when Crébillon, as usual, was asked by the police to serve as censor, but this time his corrections were relatively minor, consisting of a few lines excised because they hinted at the natural religion of deism.

L'Orphélin de la Chine opened at the Comédie on 20 August 1755. It was one of the greatest successes of Voltaire's career, with patrons besieging the theatre for tickets hours before the doors opened and violent quarrels over their distribution. The opening night had an income of 4,717 livres, at a period when 1,000 was considered a good house, with an attendance of 1,308 when 600 was considered a success. Voltaire created his two leading roles specifically for Clairon and Lekain, and continued to send them detailed notes on interpretation after the play opened. Clairon was highly praised from the outset, but Lekain suffered, as he often did, from a weak vocal delivery. On 6 September, the highly successful production was suspended, reportedly because Lekain had been wounded by his sword. In fact, however, Lekain seems to have felt the need for some personal coaching from his mentor, since he spent the rest of September at Les Délices. The result was a much improved performance, both in Paris and in October before the court at Fontainebleau. Indeed, the role became one of Lekain's most popular, regularly performed the rest of his life.

In his preface to *L'Orphélin de la Chine*, Voltaire credits his inspiration to the fourteenth-century Chinese play, *The Orphan of the House of Chao*, one of the many plays created during the Yuan period, the first great flowering of Chinese drama. The play had been translated into French and published in 1735, but Voltaire is careful to distance himself from his oriental source. This, he admits, is highly sophisticated compared to the crude farces being produced at France in the fourteenth century, but not compared to the achievements of the classic French stage. "The action of the Chinese play," he complains, "lasts seventy-five years, as in the monstrous farces of Shakespeare and Lope de Vega that have been called tragedies; it is a series of incredible events" (VO, V, 297). Clearly for Voltaire, the main attraction of this story was the opportunity to examine, in yet another exotic setting, one of his favorite themes—conflicts in love and morality involving characters from different cultures. In the end, not surprisingly, *L'Orphélin de la Chine* is much closer to *Alzire* and *Zaïre* than it is to *The Orphan of the House of Chao*, but the major difference is a significant one. In these earlier plays, to which *Mahomet* could be added, the ideals of western Christianity, at least in its best manifestations, were shown to be superior to the emotionality and fanaticism of other cultures. Certainly this position helped Voltaire, widely suspected of being a freethinking rationalist, in his frequent debates with the censor, but he probably also hoped that dramas like *Alzire* would encourage the humane rather than the fanatical side of Christianity itself. *L'Orphélin*, involving the confrontation of two non-Christian cultures, but still dealing with moral issues, demonstrated the existence of a natural morality in the world beyond Christian influence. In this sense, the play was much closer to Voltaire's own philosophy of the natural connection between reason and morality, and in fact much more subversive of a conservative ecclesiastical position than the few supposed references to deism dutifully excised by Crébillon.

While the original play had been set seven centuries earlier and dealt with family feuds and vengeance, Voltaire placed it at the time of Genghis Khan, the actual time of the Chinese play's creation, and made the tyrant and the orphan not members of rival families, but of rival races, the Mongols and the

Chinese. Genghis Khan, having conquered China, seeks to exterminate the last traces of the Chinese royal family. Zamti, to whom the child has been left, wants to substitute his own son to save the prince. His distraught wife, Idamé, urges him to kill her as well. The conqueror, who has already been smitten by the beautiful Idamé, overhears this offer and is so impressed by her heroism that he spares the child. *L'Orphélin* allowed Voltaire once again to demonstrate the existence of a natural morality outside of Christianity.

Among theatre historians, *L'Orphélin de la Chine* is remembered primarily for its innovations in scenery and costume. French opera had become increasingly devoted to visual spectacle in the eighteenth century. Servandoni, who became the leading scenic artist of the Opéra in 1728, established ten years later a Salle des Machines in the Tuileries palace devoted entirely to visual spectacle, but this by no means lessened the taste for such display in the Opéra itself. In the 1740s, the constant search for new sources of spectacle led authors and choreographers, as well as Servandoni and his sometime collaborator (and after 1746 his successor) the painter Boucher, to seek out oriental subjects. The most famous of these spectacles was Rameau's *Les Indes Gallantes*, but one of the first ballets by Noverre brought "chinoiserie" to the Opéra stage in *Les Fêtes des Chinoises* (1744). The settings for spoken tragedy, however, had for the past century remained essentially simple and somber, often simply reusing the same elements again and again. Voltaire was a pioneer in seeking greater visual variety in spoken tragedy, and like the creators of the baroque operas, he often turned to exotic and oriental subjects to achieve this. Wishing *L'Orphélin* to set a new standard for authenticity of scenic atmosphere, he contributed all his own profits for new scenery and costumes. Under the direction of Fouré, a student of Servandoni, twelve men worked day and night from 28 July until 17 August to construct and paint a sumptuous Chinese setting.

The costuming for the production was as ground-breaking as the setting, although here the major credit seems to go not to Voltaire, but to his leading actors Clairon and Lekain (illustration 5). For the costumes as for the settings, Voltaire picked a respected painter, Joseph Vernet, but Voltaire's instructions were hardly revolutionary, asking for costumes that would be both "Chinese enough and French enough not to arouse the spectators to laughter."[3] Modern theatre histories frequently cite this production as the beginning of a break from the traditional "tragic" dress of classic France, according to which all men in leading roles wore stiff skirts (*tonnelets*), helmets and high plumes, while the women wore large hoop skirts (*paniers*), elbow-length gloves, and diamond-studded wigs regardless of nationality, period, or social position. This claim, however, requires some modification.

Illustration 5. Lekain in his costume for *L'Orphélin de la Chine*.

The contemporary review of the production in the *Mercure* indeed reported that here Clairon had dared "to be the first to suppress the *panier*" and that Mlle Hus (in one of the smaller roles) "had the courage to imitate her"; and Grimm, in his *Correspondence littéraire*, praised Clairon both for the suppression of *paniers* and for her natural delivery.[4] Both written and iconographic evidence, however, indicate that Clairon was preceded in this reform by Mme Favart, the popular leading lady of the Opéra-Comique, who discarded traditional costume in September of 1753 for the role of Bastienne in the pastoral *Les Amours de Bastien et Bastienne*, a parody of Rousseau's *Le Devin du village*. Her husband reported that she broke the tradition of actresses playing even peasant heroines "with large *paniers*, heads heavy with diamonds, and elbow-length gloves" to appear "in a woolen dress like that of actual villagers, unadorned hair, a simple golden cross, bare arms, and wooden shoes" (illustration 6).[5] This was a bold and significant step, but since it was carried out at the theatre associated with parody and light entertainment, it left the major citadels of tradition, the Opéra and the Comédie Française, still unaffected. Thus Clairon's appearance in untraditional dress in 1755, while not literally the first on the French stage, was still of paramount importance, since it was the first on the "official" national stage. (One may recall the symbolic importance, three quarters of a century later, of Hugo's *Hernani* at the Comédie, with features that had long been accepted at the minor boulevard theatres, but which were considered far more shocking and innovative at the conservative national house.) Not wishing their amateur stage to lag behind the Comédie in this innovation, Mme Denis wrote to Lekain in November asking him to send appropriate costumes to Monrion for her and Voltaire to perform *L'Orphélin* (PVI, 132).

Costume reform was clearly "in the air" in the mid-1750s in Paris. On 7 October, the Abbé Philippe de la Garde presented before the Court at Fontainebleau (and subsequently at the Opéra) an *Alceste*, in which the leading singer, Chassé, and the other performers not only discarded the traditional *tonnelets*, plumed helmets, and symmetrically arranged costumes of baroque opera heroes for dress more suggestive of antiquity, but also utilized a large number of extras to present what was considered an unprecedentedly authentic siege scene and funeral procession.[6] Thus Lekain, like Clairon, had a recent precedent for his break with costume tradition in *L'Orphélin de la Chine*, but that does not detract from the significance of this change at the Comédie itself. The radicalness of the change was somewhat muted by the exoticism of Voltaire's subject, but as the decade went on, Clairon and Lekain took the bolder step of introducing similar changes into the more familiar repertoire. Early in 1756, Lekain shocked the Comédie audiences by

Illustration 6. Mme Favart in *Bastien et Bastienne*.

emerging from Ninus' tomb in a revival of Voltaire's *Sémiramis* "with sleeves rolled back, arms bloody, hair disordered, and eyes starting," an effect even Voltaire considered rather "too English," and a far cry from the ordered dress and demeanor of a traditional baroque hero (VC, XXX, 86). Clairon also continued to appear in more standard roles without the traditional panoply of *paniers*, fringed gloves, plumes and voluminous wigs, most notably as the oriental Princess Roxane in Racine's *Bajazet* and in Crébillon's *Electre*, where she was much praised for her unostentatious costume—of a simple slave's habit, her hair loose, and long chains upon her arms.[7]

These innovations were encouraged by Philippe de la Garde, author of the innovative *Alceste* of 1754, who became responsible for the spectacle section of the major periodical *Mercure* in 1758, where he carried on a steady campaign for costume reform, especially at the Opéra, until his death in 1767. The series of innovations in scenic effects and particularly in costume during the 1750s, with the Comédie *L'Orphélin de la Chine* at their center, is highly impressive, with each step requiring the overcoming of a tenacious and long-standing cultural tradition. Nevertheless, the ideal of authentic historic or realistic costume did not become firmly established on the French stage until well into the nineteenth century, with the triumph of romanticism (which, however, credited Lekain and Clairon as early pioneers in this reform). The immediate followers of Lekain and Clairon did not pursue this course, and a 1778 print purporting to show Clairon in *L'Orphélin de la Chine* wearing huge paniers and a traditional wig is unquestionably modeled on Mme Vestris, her successor (illustration 7). Vestris, like most of the leading Comédie actors of her generation, stoutly resisted the efforts of the young François-Joseph Talma to reintroduce Lekain and Clairon's authentic approach on the eve of the Revolution.

Although he was interested in specific visual moments in his productions, Voltaire was on the whole more concerned with vocal than physical delivery, and his coaching of both Lekain and Clairon for *L'Orphélin* reflects this. Although the language of *L'Orphélin* still seems stiff and artificial enough to modern ears, by the standards of the time it was considered ground-breaking in its clarity and simplicity. Voltaire worked very hard for this effect, and he emphasized with both Clairon and Lekain the importance of stressing the meaning of the lines rather than seeking a traditional rhetorical effect. Clairon, who in any case surpassed Lekain in vocal skill, was clearly much more successful at this and was warmly praised for the naturalness of her speech by champions of realism like Diderot.

Illustration 7. Tragic actress, probably Mme Vestris, as Idamé in *L'Orphélin de la Chine*.

Lekain's vocal problems doubtless caused him to concentrate on them, and there is little evidence that he sought in his acting, as he did in his costume, to depart from tradition. On the other hand the aging, sixty-six-year-old Sarrazin, who much to Voltaire's displeasure was assigned the major secondary role of Zamti, was said to have attempted to give a "Chinese" flavor to his interpretation, though just how he did this is not clear. Clairon also clearly attempted to depart from convention. Witnesses remark on her "strange gestures," such as resting a hand, or even two on her hips or placing a closed fist on her temple for minutes at a time (a gesture that would eventually become a cliché in the melodrama theatre).[8]

One of the spectators at *L'Orphélin* was a young Paris lawyer with a passion for the theatre, Claude-Pierre Patu, who reported on it in a letter to his idol, the great English actor, David Garrick. Patu found *L'Orphélin* "warm, interesting, and generally written in the standard Voltaire style," but he was shocked by Voltaire's flippant dismissal of Shakespeare in the preface, which he was certain would "revolt" Garrick, and which Patu feared would cause great damage, due to Voltaire's influence.[9] All of the leading figures of the generation of actors that Voltaire had seen in England had died or retired by the early 1730s, and a significant new generation, led by David Garrick, emerged in the next decade. Since his stunning debut as Richard III in 1741, Garrick had become lionized in England, launching a striking new acting style that seemed to contemporaries vastly more natural and emotional than the more formal and declamatory approach of the previous generation. Garrick became director of Drury Lane in 1747, and in June and July of 1751 visited Paris, where he met many of the leading figures of the theatrical and literary world. He also gave occasional after-dinner performances of the dagger scene from *Macbeth*, which dazzled his hosts. Charles Collé wrote that his face expressed "all the passions one after the other" without any grimacing, offering a kind of "tragic pantomime" that was far beyond the ability of any French actors, including the revered Lekain and Clairon.[10]

Patu did not meet Garrick in 1751, but three years later he made a pilgrimage to London to see his idol's performances of Shakespeare, and afterward wrote to Garrick regularly to report on the French cultural scene. Fearing the effect on French readers of Voltaire's harsh comment on Shakespeare, Patu paid a visit to Ferney in November of 1755, hoping, with the naivete of the youthful enthusiast, that he could bring Voltaire to a better understanding of Shakespeare's genius. He took with him his friend, Palissot, an aspiring young poet whose first comedy, *Les Trois Tuteurs*, was written this year, following Patu's recommendation by using English models. Although Palissot would gradually become associated with Voltaire's literary enemies, at this time, like most poets of his generation, he avidly wished Voltaire's approval, and the famous author received what he called "the two little poets from Paris" with amused conviviality (VC, XXVIII, 115). Both of the "little poets" were charmed by their reception, and Patu reported to Garrick that although Voltaire continued to confer on Shakespeare such mixed epithets as "amiable barbarian" and "delightful madman," the philosopher seemed sincerely moved by Patu's reading of passages from *Romeo and Juliet*. Patu hopefully concludes, "I have little doubt that I should bring him round to my way of thinking on the subject, if I had time to make a longer stay at Geneva" (GC, II, 409). Alas, poor Patu had little time left for any of his many projects to promote English culture in France. Always in poor health, he died in Italy the following summer, his last letter to Garrick concluding with the Ghost's plea to Hamlet: "Adieu, remember me." Voltaire, who even in his period of warmest admiration for the freedom and imagination of Shakespeare always considered him rather a barbarian, was still touched by Patu's youthful enthusiasm, after whose death he wrote, "I sadly miss little Patu; he loved the arts and had a guileless soul" (VC, XXXII, 136).

To the modern reader, this little tribute calls up deeper resonances. In the same month that Patu visited Voltaire, the great earthquake struck Lisbon, shaking not only that city, but the European psyche. One of the first literary reactions to this catastrophe was Voltaire's 1756 *Poem on the Disaster of Lisbon*, raising the philosophic questions that Voltaire would develop three years later in his most beloved work, *Candide*. The great earthquake figures prominently in the novel, but perhaps little Patu, with his engaging enthusiasm and his melancholy end, also made a not insignificant contribution, reflected in Voltaire's characterization of him as a "guileless soul" (*âme candide*).

In January of 1756, Voltaire was back at his winter home in Lausanne, but in the somber aftermath of the great earthquake there was little revelry, and the usual theatrical activity was sharply curtailed. As always, however, Voltaire had many projects to occupy him, including entries for the great philosophic enterprise of the era, the encyclopedia project of Diderot and D'Alembert.

Voltaire was not one of the organizers of the famous *Encyclopédie*, but he was closely associated with the venture and its editors intellectually and politically. He was sufficiently close to both Diderot and D'Alembert to invite them to the private showing at his home of *Rome sauvée* in June of 1750 before his departure for Germany, and the "Preliminary Discourse" written by D'Alembert announcing the venture the following year contained high praise for Voltaire's inspiration. A few months later, D'Alembert was selected as censor to approve Voltaire's *Mahomet* for public performance. Voltaire, in turn, referred in his 1751 *Siècle de Louis XIV* to the projected *Encyclopédie* as an "immense and immortal" work (VO, XIV, 153). From 1752 onward, Voltaire and D'Alembert corresponded regularly, and by 1754 Voltaire had become a regular contributor, eventually creating some forty-three articles, the majority of them on matters of style and literature, such as "Taste," "Genius," and "Imagination."[11] The work was by this time widely recognized as the central intellectual project of the *philosophes*, and as such it was a focus of attacks not only from major figures in the church, but from more conservative figures in the world of letters who resisted its challenges to authority and tradition. One of the leaders of this latter group was the influential journalist Fréron. Fréron was a major supporter of the young Palissot, who visited Voltaire with Patu in the fall of 1755, and with Fréron's encouragement, Palissot became one of the most visible of the literary figures in the anti-*philosophe* camp.

The first hint of this appeared soon after Palissot's visit to Ferney. He was requested by King Stanislas to provide a comedy for the festivities marking the opening of a new city hall and the inauguration of a statue of Louis XV at Nancy. Palissot created a one-act diversion, *Le Cercle ou les origineaux*, inspired by Molière's early court entertainment for Louis XIV, *Les Fâcheux*. Molière's piece is little more than a series of portraits of foolish characters from his period, and Palissot followed this pattern, but included among his ten characters three that were in the eyes of many unmistakable satires on: Voltaire (M. Volcan, an affected poet), Mme Du Châtelet (Araminte, a learned lady enamored of Volcan), and Rousseau (Blaise-Gille-Antoine, a moody, sensitive, reclusive philosopher). The play aroused a storm of protest (in part orchestrated, it appears, by D'Alembert), but somewhat surprisingly it focused upon the presumed attack on Rousseau. The king was under some pressure to ban the play or discipline the author, but Rousseau magnanimously quieted things down by writing a letter excusing the comedy as merely a youthful *jeu d'ésprit*. As for Voltaire and the apparent references to the departed Châtelet, Palissot rather ingenuously denied that any such references were intended, and Voltaire somewhat uncharacteristically let the matter pass without comment. Palissot, informed by Fréron of D'Alembert's campaign against him, increasingly distanced himself from the writers for the *Encyclopédie*, though he tried to continue on warm terms with Voltaire.

This was a delicate matter, since Voltaire was now growing more and more closely associated with the *Encyclopédie* project. D'Alembert paid a visit to Ferney in August of 1756, when the volume in preparation was the seventh, devoted to the conclusion of the F entries and all of the Gs. Voltaire seized the opportunity presented by his writing an article on coldness of literary style (*froideur*) to strike back at his old adversary, Crébillon, citing lines from his tragedies as examples. The most famous article in this volume of the *Encyclopédie*, however, and one of the most fateful in the history of that monumental work, was the direct result of D'Alembert's visit. Usually the *Encyclopédie* devoted little space to sovereign states—England received three-quarters of a column, Spain one column, Denmark seventeen lines. France itself was covered in a mere 900 words. The entry on Geneva over-shadowed all of these, containing four double-columned pages. D'Alembert seems to have intended to be complimentary to the Genevese, or at least to praise their virtues that he felt the French should emulate, but he succeeded only in infuriating both the Catholics of Paris, who resented his praise of Calvinism, and the Protestants of Geneva, who felt he had portrayed them as having totally rejected revealed religion.

The encyclopedia project had gained many opponents in conservative circles in France. An attempted assassination of the king in January of 1757 was said by many to have resulted from the freethinking and challenge to tra-ditional authority represented by the *philosophes*, and a royal proclamation issued in April warned all French publishers against printing anything that might encourage seditious thinking. The seventh volume of the *Ency-clopédie* appeared this fall, and its Geneva article provided a focus for such protest. More careful censorship was called for, and D'Alembert was so widely attacked that, against Voltaire's advice, he resigned from the *Ency-clopédie*, leaving the enterprise to Diderot.

Far from being overwhelmed by this responsibility, Diderot at this critical moment in his own career and in the life of the *Encyclopédie* made the sud-den and rather surprising decision to launch himself as a playwright, pre-senting to the Comédie and publishing a major new drama, *Le fils naturel*. Diderot was hardly a newcomer to the theatre. He was, like Voltaire, edu-cated in a Jesuit college with a strong interest in the theatre. There he studied Racine, Corneille, and the classic tradition so thoroughly that, as he later re-ports, he developed his interest in pantomime by watching works he knew with his ears covered. As a young man he frequented the theatre and even considered becoming an actor, an interest reflected in a lengthy section on the current stage in his early novel *Les bijoux indiscrètes*. Even so, his turn to play-writing in 1757 was unexpected and caused much comment.

It was widely assumed that this new venture reflected Diderot's interest in making himself a candidate for election to the French Academy, which had recently accepted D'Alembert, and this is not unlikely, since play-writing was still, as it had been for Voltaire, a major path to such literary renown. Diderot was not content, however, to simply follow traditional dramatic style; he wanted to make his mark as a significant innovator in the theatre, and he presented *Le fils naturel* as a new approach to theatre, explained in a series of accompanying prefaces. Diderot planned the play for production at the Comédie, indeed assigned the roles to particular Comédie actors in the published version, which appeared in February of 1757, but to his great disappointment, it was not accepted, and at this time was staged only in a private production at Saint-Germain-en-Laye outside of Paris, in fact the presumed actual setting of the play.

The play nevertheless caused a great stir in Parisian intellectual circles. Supported by the encyclopedists as a work of genius and equally strongly attacked by their opponents, it soon gained a European reputation, appearing not only in twenty-five French editions by 1800, but in translations in Germany, Russia, Italy, Holland, Spain, and Denmark. In fact, the innovations Diderot argued for in the prefaces and demonstrated in the play were not as revolutionary as they appeared to many. In his prefaces, Diderot refers approvingly to two English precursors, Lillo's *The London Merchant* and Moore's *The Gamester*, the latter of which Diderot translated into French in 1760. Both had been popular in England, Lillo especially so, but neither had inspired much imitation there. There were also less well-known precursors in France, such as Landois' 1742 *Sylvie*, also mentioned by Diderot in his prefaces, and Mme de Graffigny's 1750 *Cénie*.

Many of the theoretical arguments advanced by Diderot had also been anticipated, especially by his close friend, Grimm, in the *Correspondence littéraire*. Nevertheless, it was Diderot's plays and prefaces that provided the central stimulus for a new sort of serious theatre in France and eventually throughout Europe. This theatre, which Diderot first named *genre sérieux*, and later *drame*, dealt with middle-class characters from contemporary life in domestic settings, depicted with realistic scenery and costumes, action and dialogue, with the aim common in *philosophe* writing of moral instruction. Although Grimm's prediction that Diderot had opened the way to the theatre of the future seemed exaggerated given the modest stage history, then and later, of his plays, their example and theory in fact fulfilled this bold prophesy, leading to the main line of modern realistic drama, of Hebbel, Ibsen, and countless others.[12]

Fréron and Palissot, inveterate opponents of the encyclopedists, predictably led the attacks on Diderot's new play. Central to these attacks was a charge of plagiarism, since Fréron discovered that Diderot's work was heavily indebted to a comedy, *Il vero amico* by the Venetian playwright Carlo Goldoni. Goldoni had only recently emerged into the public consciousness in Paris, or for that matter in Italy. His bold, and successful, promise to provide no less than sixteen new comedies in a single season (1750–51) to the San Angelo Theatre in Venice made him the talk of the Italian theatre world. One of the lesser plays produced during that remarkable year was *Il vero amico*, inspired in part by Molière's *The Miser*. Goldoni's major concern was to provide to the Italian public a literary alternative to the traditional and still highly popular *commedia dell'arte*, drawing upon Molière and other modern writers to create a more realistic Italian comedy of everyday life. The rather grotesque miser remains a major figure in Goldoni's play, but attention shifts to the young lovers, and especially to the tension generated when the young heroine and the best friend of the young hero find themselves attracted to each other.

Not surprisingly, this more sentimental part of the plot was what attracted the attention of Diderot, or to be more precise, of Grimm, who suggested to Diderot that he use it as the basis for an example of the new sort of serious play of everyday life that interested them both. Diderot accordingly left out the miser figure entirely and concentrated upon the sentimental triangle, creating a play very close to Goldoni in its first half, but then moving in a distinctly different direction, away from comic complications and toward moral discussion. Fréron nevertheless noted the similarity, and planned to publish a spurious letter from Goldoni protesting the theft. He was dissuaded by the royal director of publications, Malesherbes, who reasonably felt that one plagiarism hardly justified another. Fréron then simply published almost identical passages from the two plays, leaving his readers to draw their own conclusions. Palissot went much further, publishing in late 1757 a widely read pamphlet, *Petits Lettres sur les grands philosophes*, the main feature of which was an extended attack on Diderot and his play.

Even more serious than these personal attacks, the next year saw the appearance of one of the best-known critical statements on the theatre from this century—Rousseau's *Lettre à d'Alembert sur les spectacles*, inspired by the notorious Geneva article from the *Encyclopédie*. Rousseau believed that the Geneva article was really essentially the work of Voltaire, and although he was probably mistaken about this, the influence of Voltaire upon it was considerable, especially in the full column which D'Alembert devoted to arguing against the ban on theatre in this city. Although Rousseau's article covers many of his concerns, and has been considered a kind of prologue to the works of his mature period, the majority of it is devoted to rebutting this defense of theatre. Rousseau was, of course, no stranger to the theatre world in Paris either as a contributor or an audience member, but that world also represented to Rousseau the sensual, what he called the feminine side of his nature, whereas he saw Geneva as a community still virtuous and virile, which could only be corrupted and weakened by the display, luxury, and sensual appeal the theatre offered. Rousseau at first planned to attach a commentary on Plato's objections to the theatre to his letter, but even without this, many of his complaints are clearly derived from the Greek theorist—the suspicion of actors as imitators, the pandering of the dramatist to the vanity and prejudices of his audience, the sterility of the emotions raised, the drawing of attention from the real world of social obligations to that of fiction. In conclusion, Rousseau proposes another sort of entertainment more suitable to a virile republic—great public celebrations of civic and domestic virtues. Although the Genevans did not take this particular advice, its influence on subsequent theatre history, especially in France, was considerable. The project of mass republican celebrations proved especially appealing to the leaders of the French Revolution and the great Revolutionary Festivals grew directly from Rousseau's advice in his letter to D'Alembert.

The kind of arguments advanced by Rousseau against the theatre had been voiced in one form or another by a long tradition of antitheatrical writers in France and elsewhere, but Rousseau's prominence and rhetorical skill gave this attack particular importance, as did the fact that it came from a writer popularly assumed to be numbered among the *philosophes*. An attack from among this company on the theatre, a cultural activity normally championed by them, and, by implication on the *Encyclopédie*, their central intellectual project, caused an enormous stir. For Voltaire, it only provided additional proof of the advantages of being outside the artistic and philosophical antagonisms of Paris. "I have several comedies and tragedies in my portfolio," he wrote in 1757, "but I will not show them to the Parisian audiences. It is my fresh wine and I will drink it with my friends" (PVI, 187). The amateur theatres at Les Délices and Monrion remained very busy.

Diderot, beleaguered both as editor of the *Encyclopédie* and as dramatic author, now chose to devote his major attention to the latter project, publishing in November of 1758 a new play based on his own family experiences, *Le Père de famille*, with a lengthy preface dedicated to Grimm. The preface did not engage the general moral questions raised by Rousseau except by its reiteration of the social benefits of theatre. The major part of the lengthy discussion instead considered in detail the implications of Diderot's new realistic approach for plot, dialogue, incident, genre, character, decor, costume, pantomime, and gesture. These concerns were clearly articulated in the play itself, which made extensive use of tableaux, disjointed and emotional language, and detailed scenic descriptions and stage business. Although it was not produced at the Comédie until 1761, it was, like *Le fils naturel*, very widely read and translated, making a considerable international impact.

Probably the most influential supporter of Diderot's theories outside France was Lessing in Germany, who shared Diderot's interest in Lillo and Moore, translated a selection of Diderot's writings into German, and called Diderot "the most philosophic mind which has concerned itself with drama since Aristotle."[13]

Diderot's passion for realistic illusion onstage naturally led him, like Voltaire, to deplore the long-standing practice of allowing one-third of the stage to be taken up by permanent seating for aristocratic spectators, mostly seated on benches behind a railing on either side, but often spilling out into the playing area itself. In a letter to Mme Riccoboni, leading actress of the Comédie Italienne, Diderot complained that this "ridiculous," practice led to "false scenery" and "bad theatre." "We cannot even decorate the rear of the stage," he remarked, "because there are so many people back there. They must all be removed, so that the entire stage can be decorated."[14]

The major resistance to this change came not from those who normally sat onstage, but in fact from the actors, who would rather put up with the inconvenience of these interlopers than lose the considerable profit from their seats. Lekain carried on a lonely battle against his colleagues, but it was not until a wealthy aristocrat and amateur of the theatre, the comte de Lauraguais, promised a sum to indemnify the actors that the permanent seating was finally removed from the stage. This took place during the annual Easter closing of 1759, and the theatre staged the same work, Châteaubrun's spectacle-play *Les Troyennes*, just before and after the closing to point out the difference. The newly open stage was covered by swarms of Greek soldiers with the vast expanse of the burning city of Troy behind, a spectacle that gained universal admiration for its beauty and truthfulness.[15] The example of the Comédie encouraged other theatres, in France and abroad, to adopt this reform. In England, Garrick, who like Voltaire had long complained of the pernicious effect of this practice on scenic and acting illusion, increased the offstage seating at Drury Lane to make up for lost income and abolished stage spectators soon after the Comédie, in 1762.

The fact that the new Diderot play had the same title as another of Goldoni's famous "sixteen comedies" of 1750, *Il padre di famiglia*, naturally raised again the question of plagiarism, although these two plays were even further apart than *Vero amico* and *Fils naturel*. Two contributors to the *Encyclopédie*, Deleyre and Forbonnais, undertook to demonstrate this by publishing at this time faithful French translations of the two plays in question so that readers might actually compare them with Diderot. When the translations were published, however, it was with an accompanying preface by a certain "Etienne Bleichnnarr." The German means "pale fool,"—a pun on the name Palissot, and indeed the essay was an extended satire on the anti-*philosophes* in general, and on Palissot and his own essays and prefaces in particular. Only many years later was the true author of this scandalous essay revealed to be Diderot's friend Grimm (the German pun should have been a clue), but at the moment many suspected Diderot himself and the "Affair of the Dedications" added to the controversy swirling about him.

In the spring of 1760, Paris resounded with rumors of a daring new play to be presented at the Comédie directly attacking the *philosophes*. The author was unknown, but Fréron read the play to the actors in March and his support led most to suspect, correctly, that Palissot was its creator. Over the objections of Mlle Clairon and a few others, *Les Philosophes* was accepted and the censor, Voltaire's old enemy Crébillon, passed it without requiring changes of any sort.

 The play's opening on 2 May was one of the most eagerly awaited of the century and the crowd was enormous. The play was very well received and Palissot hailed by many as a new Molière. Certainly the play evoked his work, especially *les femmes savantes*. Rosalie, the heroine, loves Damis, but her mother, the affected Cydalise, who has surrounded herself by ridiculous *philosophes*, prefers one of their number, Valère, closely modeled on Helvétius, who was at this moment if not the best-known, in the eyes of many the most notorious of the *philosophes*. His materialist masterwork, *De l'esprit*, conflating the motivations of humans and animals and arguing that morality was a cultural constuction, had appeared in 1758, scandalizing the court, the church, and conservative thinkers in general, and had been burned by the public executioner. At times the *philosophes* in Palissot's play are merely ridiculous, as in the most famous scene in the final act when Crispin, modeled on Rousseau, enters on all fours chewing a lettuce. At others, they gather and plot like a cabal of Tartuffes. Diderot appeared as Dortidius, but as usual, Palissot spared Voltaire, even singling him out for praise in the preface to the published play, which attempted to separate him from the rest of the *philosophe* party.

Naturally, so partisan a work stimulated a storm of pamphlets and other plays both supporting and attacking Palissot's position, and even though Palissot had attempted to keep him out of the debate, the *philosophes* inevitably wanted to engage Voltaire, as their most effective polemicist. As early as 6 May, d'Alembert appealed to him to respond, and in fact Voltaire, who had remained fairly disengaged from the ongoing intellectual debates in Paris, decided to enter the fray; perhaps because he indeed felt that Palissot had gone too far and needed reining in, perhaps because he felt that the Comédie should not have accepted the work, or perhaps because his long-term antagonism toward Crébillon was reawakened—toward a censor who had been so severe with possible offensive passages in his own work, now winking at so obvious and personal an attack on individuals closely associated with Voltaire.

In any case, he followed d'Alembert's suggestion to withdraw in protest his *Médine*, a new version of *Zulime*, which was at that moment in rehearsal at the Comédie, and began to consider offering the theatre instead a work that would directly respond to the growing anti-*philosophe* manifestations. One possibility lay immediately at hand, an odd experimental play, *Socrate*, that Voltaire had published under a pseudonym the previous year. Thematically the piece was ideal, and d'Argental wrote to Voltaire in May urging him to submit it to the Comédie. In the wake of the controversy over *Les Philosophes*, both Palissot and Fréron had shifted from styling the dramatist a new Molière to calling him a modern Aristophanes, partly in response to those who consider his satires on individuals beneath the dignity of the national stage. A play defending Socrates, a respected philosopher unjustly mocked by the Greek dramatist, seemed an almost perfect response, and Voltaire began at once reworking the play to make the parallels even more specific.

Its appropriate theme, however, did not compensate for *Socrate*'s serious problems. The sufferings of the enlightened philosopher at the hands of Voltaire's usual enemies, the priests and magistrats, were depicted seriously and emotionally, but the work as a whole was comedic, mixing scenes of gross buffoonery with serious intellectual discussions. Voltaire had attempted in the preface to justify the work's unusual mixture of tonality and of elevated and common people by claiming that it was in fact a translation from the English, who were known to be given to such eccentricities. According to this preface, Addison had first conceived the idea of such a play but had turned instead to Cato on the advice of Steele and passed on his outline to James Thomson, just then beginning his series of neoclassic tragedies. As his final work, Voltaire claimed, Thomson, who in fact had created only quite regular tragedies on the French neoclassic model, created this *Socrates* following the advice of friends who urged him to follow a more Shakespearian model. If Voltaire expected this bizarre and totally untrue genealogy of the play to disarm criticism of the printed version, he was disappointed. Fréron called it a monstrous and grotesque mixture of genres and even the potentially more sympathetic Grimm characterized it as "barbarous, false, and gothic."[16] It is interesting, and quite possibly significant, that Voltaire a decade later would employ these same adjectives in his own notorious attacks on Shakespeare, but whatever his feelings about English dramatic style in 1760, it was clear that *Socrate*, without extensive reworking, was itself too open to attack on other grounds to be an effective response to Palissot. Voltaire began converting it to verse and elevating its tone, but by mid-June realized that this would take many more months, and wrote to d'Argental that he had decided to submit to the Comédie another, simpler work that he had been writing on the side, the comedy *L'Ecossaise*. The reworked *Socrate*, with even clearer references to the *philosophe* controversy, was published in 1761 but never staged. The subject continued to appeal to the *philosophes*, however. In 1762, Sauvigny created a *Mort de Socrate* which was filled with clear allusions to the Palissot affair, but it was only approved for performance the following year after most of this material was removed (the character of Aristophanes was excised completely). Even Diderot in his *Essai sur la poésie dramatique* considered developing the subject as a philosophical drama, but he never pursued this project.

Although Voltaire's comedy *L'Ecossaise* was also presented as a translation of a recent English play, by a "M. Hume," *L'Ecossaise* (first appearing under the title *Le Caffé*) was widely assumed to be his work, and a secondary character, the corrupt journalist Frélon (French for "wasp"), was immediately recognized as a satire on Palissot's mentor, Fréron. Perhaps in order to demonstrate their even-handedness after accepting so openly partisan a work as *Les Philosophes*, the Comédie actors accepted it at once and Crébillon, apparently in the same spirit, approved it, requiring only that the name of the journalist be changed. It was therefore changed to the English word "wasp," but the association remained clear. The play, presented on 26 July, had little more artistic merit than Palissot's, but it appealed to the same passions of the moment and enjoyed a comparable success. Fréron may himself have decided to turn the tables on the *philosophes* by playing Socrates on this occasion. There is a famous anecdote of Socrates reportedly standing in the audience during the performance of Aristophanes' *Clouds* so that the original could be compared with his satiric treatment onstage. In any case, Fréron sat prominently in the orchestra on the opening night and provided in his *Année littéraire* the best surviving report of the performance.[17]

Aside from the satiric scenes, *L'Ecossaise* sought to appeal to the popular love of sentimentality, with tender love scenes, emotional family encounters, and virtue triumphant. The printed version included a dedicatory letter and a preface. The letter, to the Comte de Lauraguais, praised him for his eternal service to the arts in general, and tragedy in particular, by purging the stage of spectators and thus preparing the way for future geniuses to unite "suitable scenic spectacle" with "fearful and convincing action" and "beautiful and natural poetry" (VO, V, 426). The preface cited Goldoni and

Diderot as models, praising them for their attention to the truthful depiction of men and society. Certainly the comedy's domestic situations, generally sentimental tone, and moral conclusion could all be found in Diderot's theory and practice, but also in Voltaire's own earlier experiments in sentimental comedy, such as *Nanine* and *L'Enfant prodigue*. *L'Ecossaise*, however, is Voltaire's first play which contains the kind of detailed instructions for acting, tableaux, stage settings, and even costumes that were particularly associated with Diderot's dramas.

As for Goldoni, Lessing later suggested that Frélon was based on the scandal-mongering busybody Don Marzio in Goldoni's 1750 *La Bottega del caffè*, and other critics noted echoes of Goldoni's 1749 *Il Cavaliere e la dama* and 1750 *Pamela nubile*, itself a reworking of Richardson's famous novel in England, as was Voltaire's own *Nanine*. More important than any specific borrowing, however, is Voltaire's acknowledgement that Goldoni was increasingly becoming for French playwrights one of the models for modern realistic drama.

For many in the French theatre world, Goldoni's name first came to prominence due to the stir caused by the charges of Diderot's plagiarism. Voltaire was, of course, aware of this controversy, but he had already been introduced to the Italian writer by a new correspondent, the Marquis Francesco Albergati-Cappacelli, with whom he began a correspondance in the fall of 1758. Albergati, a wealthy Bolognese senator and devotee of the theatre, built a private stage at his country estate in direct imitation of Les Délices, where he staged primarily his own plays and those of Voltaire in his own translations. In November of 1758, he wrote to Voltaire for advice on how to stage the ghost and to create appropriate thunder and lightning effects for his upcoming production of *Sémiramis*. Voltaire sent detailed advice, beginning a correspondance that continued over the next twenty years. On Albergati's advice, Voltaire obtained and read a number of Goldoni's plays, and was struck by their naturalness and freshness. The subject of Albergati and Goldoni came up when Casanova visited Voltaire in July of 1760. In his extended and amusing report on their conversation, Casanova quotes Voltaire as remarking that he was not personally acquainted with Albergati, "but he has sent me Goldoni's plays, some Bologna sausages, and a translation of my *Tancrède*." Casanova considered Albergati a good actor (some called him "the Garrick of Italy"), but the author of plays that would "bear neither reading nor performance." Goldoni, on the other hand, Casanova praised as "the Molière of Italy."[18] In September of this year, Voltaire wrote to Goldoni himself, in Italian (indeed, in a reasonably good Venetian dialect), praising his style and naturalness.

The stir that *L'Ecossaise* created in Paris encouraged no less than three Italian adaptations of the play in 1761, but only one, Goldoni's *La Scozzese*, was a significant success. Unable to rely on the specifically Parisian references, Goldoni deepened the characters around Frélon, especially Freeport, the bluff English merchant who had proven one of the unexpected attractions of the play in Paris. Thanks largely to Voltaire and Goldoni, the gruff English businessman with a heart of gold became a very popular figure in later eighteenth-century comedy, returning to his homeland in the 1760 *The Coffee-house* and in George Colman's *The English Merchant*. *La Scozzese* was one of Goldoni's last Venetian comedies. The Diderot affair and the praise of Voltaire had won him a considerable reputation in Paris and an invitation to come there as resident playwright for the Comédie Italienne. Discouraged by the Venetian public's current preference for the fantastic dramatic fables of his rival, Carlo Gozzi, over his own more realistic work, Goldoni happily accepted, remaining in France from 1762 until his death in 1793.

The clearing of the spectators from the Comédie stage encouraged Voltaire to complete *Tancrède*, a tragedy that he had been planning since 1755. This pathetic story of a heroic knight who believes, incorrectly, in a report of unfaithfulness in the woman he loves, anticipated romanticism in its medieval setting, which was exploited for its local color and spectacle. The first performance boasted sixty-six supernumeraries, an elaborate chevalric hall, and a public square with a palace and temple. Voltaire rejected, however, Clairon's desire for a scaffold for the heroine, which he considered beyond the bounds of propriety.

The first new play to take full advantage of the recently cleared stage, and buoyed by the talents of Clairon and Lekain in the leading roles, *Tancrède* enjoyed a great success in the fall of 1760 and eventually surpassed all other eighteenth-century tragedies at the Comédie, except *Zaïre*. Voltaire, though now sixty-six years of age and forty-two years after his first success, still, remarkably, had many plays ahead of him. This, however, was the last to have a long career in the active repertoire, being regularly revived at the Comédie until 1855.

NOTES

1. "Extrait des registres du Consistoire de Genève, 31 Juillet 1755," quoted in Lucien Perey and Gaston Maugras, *La Vie intime de Voltaire aux Délices et à Ferney* (Paris: Calmann Lévy, 1892), 93 (henceforward PVI).

2. Edward Gibbon, *Memoires of My Life*, ed. Georges A. Bonnard, (London: Nelson, 1966), 84.

3. Young Hai Park, "La Carrière scènique de *L'Orphélin de la Chine*," *Studies on Voltaire and the Eighteenth Century*, vol. 120 (1974):107.

4. *Mercure de France*, November 1755, p. 180; *Correspondence littéraire*, August 20, 1755.

5. C. S. Favart, *Mémoires et correspondance littéraires, dramatiques, et anecdotiques*, 3 vols. (Paris: Collin, 1808), 1:lxxvii. Vanloo's painting of Mme Favart in this role (illustration 6) shows all of these innovations but the bare arms, probably considered still too shocking for a portrait.

6. Pierre Larousse, *Grand dictionnaire universel du XIXe siècle*, 17 vols. (Paris: Larousse, 1866–90), 3:1055.

7. Jean François Marmontel, *Oeuvres*, 7 vols. (Paris: A. Berlin, 1819-20), 1:152.

8. Charles Collé, *Journal de Collé*, 2 vols. (Paris: Firmin Didot, 1868), 2:34.

9. James Boaden, *Private Correspondence of David Garrick*, 2 vols. (London: Henry Colburn and Richard Bentley, 1831–32), 2:405 (henceforward GC).

10. Collé, *Journal*, 1:324.

11. See Raymond Naves, *Voltaire et l'Encyclopédie* (Paris: Editions des presses modernes, 1938).

12. A tradition traced by Edith Melcher, *Stage Realism Between Diderot and Antoine* (New York: Russell and Russell, 1976).

13. Thomas Rolleston, *Life of Gotthold Ephraim Lessing* (London: W. Scott, 1889), 92–93.

14. Quoted in Adolphe Jullien, *La Comédie et la Galanterie au XIIIe siècle* (Paris: Edouard Rouveyre, 1897), 101.

15. See Pierre Peyronnet, *La mise en scène au XVIIIe siècle* (Paris: Nizet, 1974), 100–101.

16. Friedrich Melchior Grimm, *Correspondence littéraire*, 16 vols. (Paris: Garnier, 1877–82), 4:123.

17. *Année littéraire*, V, 1760, p. 215.

18. Jacques Casanova, *Mémoires*, 4 vols. (Paris: Garnier, 1880), 4:461-62.

Chapter 7

The Sage of Ferney, 1761–1769

Voltaire launched the year 1761 with a major new project. On 1 January he wrote to the Académie Française offering to undertake an edition of the complete works of Corneille, partly to honor his illustrious predecessor and partly to provide a dowry for an impoverished descendent of Corneille whom Voltaire had taken under his protection. This twelve-volume work, with minute, almost line-by-line analysis, occupied Voltaire for the next three years and thanks to his reputation and far-flung correspondence, enjoyed a huge sale. As usual, however, what would have been for most writers (even for those not yet approaching their seventieth year) a full-time occupation, was for Voltaire only one of dozens of projects, many of which, as usual, involved the theatre.

After the banning of spectators from the Comédie stage and the success of *L'Ecossaise* and *Tancrède*, there was no more talk from Voltaire of keeping his "fresh wine" to drink at home with his friends. Although he opened a new theatre at Ferney in October, which now became the center of his amateur theatre activity, he also became closely involved once again with the theatre world of Paris. In late February and early March, he followed closely the reception of Diderot's *Le Père de famille*, which had finally made its way to the Comédie stage, and the success of which Voltaire saw as an important victory for virtue after the disgrace of Palissot's *Philosophes*. Voltaire's own work, both major revivals and new plays, now dominated the Parisian stage. During the 1761–1762 season, his plays were performed more often than those of Corneille and Racine combined.[1] As usual, however, these productions were not unmarked by controversy. In August of 1761, he submitted to the Comédie a new comedy, *Le Droit de Seigneur*, under a pseudonym in hopes of disarming his enemies. The title, referring to the well-known legend of the medieval lord's right to enjoy the brides of his vassals on their wedding night, naturally aroused protest for its salaciousness, although in fact this infamous "right" is only mentioned as one abuse of the nobility, in a play primarily concerned with social egalitarianism and defending the *philosophes* in the person of an enlightened marquis.

Le Droit de Seigneur was one of the last plays submitted to Crébillon as censor, and the aging poet, possibly offended by its subject matter and possibly (it was widely reported) suspecting that it was the work of his old enemy, Voltaire, required extensive cuts and even created a new scene of his own. In the opinion of Favart, this scene was surprisingly fresh and witty "for an author ninety years of age,"[2] but naturally Voltaire was outraged at this new indignity from his old adversary, especially when the play in this adapted form received only a disappointing eight performances. Most critics agreed that the mixture of two comic opening acts and three sentimental and philosophic concluding ones (the fault of Voltaire and not Crébillon) made the play unattractive, but Voltaire, not surprisingly, blamed the censor and the actors, and he frequently staged the play at Les Délices and Ferney to demonstrate its effectiveness.

In October of 1761, while awaiting Crébillon's verdict on his new comedy, Voltaire completed a new tragedy as well. The success of *Tancrède* encouraged him to undertake a work with even greater emphasis on spectacle. This was *Olympie*, in which he returned to a classic setting, after the death of Alexander, whose daughter, Olympie, rejects the suitor selected by her mother, Statira, in favor of Cassandre, even though he was responsible for her father's death. The play, which encountered no censorship problems, was expected to premiere at the Comédie early in 1762, but was delayed due to a quarrel between Clairon and Dumesnil over who should play Olympie. As a result, the premiere in fact took place in March at Ferney, with a revival the following month, when the visiting Lekain was among the spectators. It was also given in the fall in Mannheim, Germany, before it finally received its Paris premiere in 1764.

His increasing use of "English" spectacle and violence did not prevent Voltaire from taking offense at two articles that appeared in the fall of 1760 in the *Journal Encyclopédie*, reflecting a growing passion for all things English by suggesting that Shakespeare was in certain respects superior to Corneille, and Otway to Racine. His response was the 1761 "Appel à toutes les nations de l'Europe," stressing the excesses of English works and urging that their example be used, as he had done, to refine, not replace the more elegant and refined French tradition.

Voltaire's anger at Crébillon did not cease with the latter's death in June of 1762; indeed, he published (anonymously) a satiric *Eloge de Crébillon* two weeks after his rival's death, whose cruelty and timing was deplored even by such allies as Diderot and D'Alembert. Not content with this attack, Voltaire began planning a new tragedy that would specifically challenge comparison with Crébillon's last work, *Le Triumverat*. Thinking that the highly conventional Crébillon could be best challenged by a more contemporary and innovative approach, Voltaire reworked the same material, but announced it as the work of a fledgling young dramatist who was, he claimed, much influenced by new styles. By this ruse, he hoped to take his revenge upon Crébillon while keeping his own name entirely out of the matter. In a letter of 13 July to d'Argental, he announced the new play as employing an innovative style that "will fool everybody. The play will be a bit barbarous, a bit English. There will be an assassination. It will be far removed from good manners. The spectacle will be beautiful, sometimes quite picturesque." Since the play would be announced as the product of a "promising young man who should be encouraged," its success would be an amusing joke on the French public, "so frivolous, so fickle, so changeable, so uncertain in its taste" (VC, LII, 174). All this elaborate planning went for naught. The play, one of Voltaire's weakest, was offered at the Comédie the following year, but was the clearest failure of Voltaire's long theatrical career, not even gaining a second performance. The kindest words, from Grimm, may have hurt the most—that the beginning author showed signs of promise. This experience should have convinced Voltaire of the uselessness of his continuing campaign against Crébillon, but the antagonism was too deep. He would return yet one more time to challenge his old rival.

Although he remained nominally a Catholic, Voltaire's antagonism to traditional Christianity steadily increased during his years at Ferney. The spirit of tolerance and free inquiry encouraged by the *philosophes* was rightly seen by conservative clergy as a threat to their authority, and Voltaire's most implacable and consistent enemies came not from the political or literary worlds, but from the church. Never one to shun a confrontation, Voltaire adapted as his battle cry *"Ecrasez l'Infâme"* (Crush the Beast), where *L'Infâme*, though generally referring to fanaticism and intolerance, came to be particularly associated with the established church. On the political scene, Voltaire directly engaged *L'Infâme* in perhaps his most famous cause, the defense of Jean Calas, a Toulouse Protestant merchant falsely accused and tortured on charges of murdering his son to prevent him from becoming a Catholic. Largely as a result of Voltaire's efforts, the king's council reversed the judgement, adding new laurels to Voltaire's reputation as "the conscience of Europe." Voltaire's own summation of the lesson of this case, his *Traité sur la tolérance*, one of the major documents of the Enlightenment, appeared the following year.

Voltaire's literary contributions to this struggle were often less noble, especially the most notorious of them—the play *Saül*, written and privately circulated in 1762, at the height of the Calas controversy. This freewheeling burlesque, the irreverence and outrageous tone of which recall the notorious *La Pucelle*, satirized the fanaticism, cruelty, degeneracy, and superstitions of the biblical kings, its most outrageous scenes and situations scrupulously footnoted with references to the relevant passages in the Bible. Voltaire utilized anachronisms and crude language to increase the humor, but he also delighted in more straightforward satire of biblical allusions and poetry, as when David declares to Bathsheba: "Your teeth are like a freshly-bathed sheep, your neck like a bunch of grapes, your throat like the tower on Mount Liban" (VO, V, 594). A public staging, indeed even publication of such a work was unthinkable, though private copies circulated widely in Paris. Voltaire resorted to his usual stratagem of attributing the work to an unknown English author, and in fact did use certain material in it from a 1761 tract written by an English deist, Peter Annet. He also mischievously suggested that his friends spread the rumor that Fréron was the actual author, though the style and subject matter left few doubts as to the truth in anyone's mind. Voltaire did not even stage *Saül* at his private theatres, though he did report later that a Berlin theatre had presented it in 1769 for the amusement of Frederick II, with whom Voltaire was once more on cordial terms (VC, LXXII, 228).

In 1763, Voltaire, whose relations with the authorities of Geneva remained strained, gave up his home at Les Délices and settled full time at Ferney. There, the old pattern of presenting theatre and entertaining on a grand scale continued unabated, as Edward Gibbon, who revisited the theatre in August, reports:

> The play they acted was my favourite *Orphan of China*. Voltaire himself acted *Genghis* and Madame Deny *Idamé*; but I do not know how it happened: either my taste is improved or Voltaire's talents are impaired since I last saw him: He appeared to me now a very ranting unnatural performer.... Perhaps I was too much struck with the ridiculous figure of Voltaire at seventy acting a Tartar Conqueror with a hollow broken Voice, and making love to a very ugly niece of about fifty [illustration 8]. The play began at eight in the evening and ended (entertainment and all) about half an hour after eleven. The whole Company was asked to stay and set down about twelve to a very elegant supper of a hundred Covers. The supper ended about two, the company danced till four; when we broke up, got into our Coaches and came back to Geneva just as the Gates

Illustration 8. Voltaire in his seventies performing a tragic role at Ferney.

were opened. Show me in history or fable, a famous poet of Seventy who has acted in his own plays, and has closed the scene with a supper and ball for a hundred people. I think the last is the more extraordinary of the two.[3]

The long-delayed *Olympie* at last premiered at the Comédie in March of 1764, with Clairon as Olympie, Lekain as Cassandre, and Dumesnil as Statira. Neither characters nor plot gained much praise, but the public was delighted by the spectacle, which included a procession of priests and the Temple of Diana at Ephesus, which at one point was shaken as if by an earthquake and several times opened its doors to reveal first the high altar and later the burning funeral pyre of Statira, onto which Olympie leaps after stabbing herself at the end of the play. Even more supernumeraries were used than for *Tancrède*, this time eighty-three at the first performance (subsequently reduced to twenty-eight).

In the year 1765, Voltaire enjoyed an indirect success in a genre new to (and little respected by) him, the comic opera. The great pioneer in this genre, Charles Simon Favart, turned two of Voltaire's tales, *L'Education d'une fille* and *La Fée Urgèle* into successful comic operas—the first (under the title *Isabelle et Gertrude*) premiered in Paris in August, the second in October at the court in Fontainebleau. Favart and his wife were now at the height of their popularity and influence, having resolved the quarrel between patrons of French and Italian musical theatre in the 1750s by gradually developing a distinctly new French form utilizing Italian elements. The Opéra-Comique theatre, long associated primarily with parody, gradually devoted more attention to these more ambitious works, especially after Favart succeeded his mentor, the highly successful Jean Monnet, as director in 1758. Favart's best-known work, *Les Trois Sultanes* in 1761, admirably combined his comic writing talents, the new musical approach, and the interest in historically accurate scenery and costume that he and his wife had been developing for the past decade. (The production's costumes were in fact designed and created in Constantinople.) It was regularly revived at the Opéra-Comique until the beginning of the nineteenth century, when it was transferred to the Comédie Française. There it has been occasionally revived, even in the present century.

Up until this time, the Opéra-Comique had maintained a regular, but legally ambiguous existence at the Saint-Germain fair, where the growing success of Favart and fellow artists Sedaine, Monsigny, and Philidor continued to stimulate protests from their more firmly established rivals the Comédie Française and the Comédie Italienne, but without result, thanks to the popularity of the Opéra-Comique, at court. The Comédie Italienne particularly suffered from the steadily increasing popularity of the Opéra-Comique, and at last in 1762 the two companies were officially united at the old Hôtel de Bourgogne, the Opéra-Comique thus gaining the official position of a state-supported theatre like the Opéra and the Comédie Française.

Before 1765, Favart's only association with Voltaire's work had been a one-act parody of *Mahomet* produced in 1742, one of the swarm of such ephemeral parodies that followed every major work by Voltaire or other writers in the period. The 1765 works were quite another matter. M. and Mme Favart were now among the most visible artists in Paris and at court, and their new offerings were major events. No expense was spared for the Fontainebleau performance of *La Fée Urgèle*, as the official in charge reported:

> There was a chorus and ballet, which had to be costumed in the time of King Dagomert. We had no costumes from that period, and some 200 were required. M. le Maréchal de Richelieu and M. le duc d'Aumont nevertheless gave orders for their creation, which involved great expense.This play required as many things as grand opera.[4]

Voltaire, clearly pleased by this elaboration of his work, wrote flattering letters to both artists. To M. Favart he wrote, "You are the inventor of an infinitely agreeable new genre; the Opéra will have in you its Molière, as it had its Racine in Quinault [the librettist of Lully, creator of French Opera]," while to Mme Favart he wrote, "From now on it is the Opéra-Comique that will support France's reputation. I am sorry for old Melpomene, but now the young Thalia of the Hôtel de Bourgogne has eclipsed by her delights the majesty of the former queen of the theatre."[5]

The growing international reputation of Favart also led to his version of Voltaire's story appearing as comic operas during the next several years on a number of other European stages. J.A.P. Schultz created a German *Singspiel, Die Fee Urgele*, which was premiered in Berlin in 1789. J. H. Wessel created a Danish version, using the French music, which was given in Copenhagen in 1782. There was even a marionette version in Hungary, presented in 1776 in one of Europe's most elaborate puppet theatres, at the royal residence of Esterház, where Haydn was music director. One of Haydn's most beloved students, Ignaz Pleyel, then only nineteen, made his debut as a composer with this work.

The most significant of the many European adaptations of this work was presented by David Garrick in London in 1774, the first major collaboration between Garrick and his new scenic designer, Philip Jacques de Loutherbourg, inaugurating a new era in British stage design. When he became codirector of Drury Lane in 1747, British theatres regularly relied upon a few stock pieces of scenery, used for many different plays, but by the end of the next decade, new scenery was created for certain productions, the most elaborate of which, interestingly, was Arthur Murphy's adaptation of Voltaire's *L'Orphélin de Chine* in 1759.

Jean Monnet in Paris frequently gave Garrick advice on lighting and stage spectacle, but his most significant aid was the recommendation of de Loutherbourg, who was to become Garrick's chief scenic designer, one of the first members of England's Royal Academy of Arts, and the creator of a revolution in British scenic design. The Alsatian landscape painter provided Garrick with a kind of visual spectacle until then unknown in London—fog and moonlight effects, glittering cascades of water, forests whose foliage could change in an instant from green to blood red, and so on—spectacle that in many ways anticipated romantic scenic design.

Garrick, doubtless thinking of the visual spectacles for which the Opéra-Comique was noted, created his own version of Favart's *Fée Urgèle* as the first major vehicle to display the talents of his new designer. He called it *A Christmas Tale* since it was presented for the 1773–74 Christmas season, a time when visual spectacle was the rule on most London stages. Garrick noted a variety of effects he wanted to achieve, among them: a garden whose objects could vary their colors, rocks that would split open to reveal a magic castle and a fiery lake, a burning palace, a moonlight scene, and a sea prospect and sunrise.[6] Although most critics agreed with Horace Walpole that only the scenery saved this piece "from being sent to the devil," the scenery was quite enough for most Drury Lane patrons, and *A Christmas Tale* launched a series of spectacular pantomimes, ballets, and occasional straight plays that de Loutherbourg continued to execute as Drury Lane's chief designer under Garrick, and after Garrick's retirement in 1776, under the new managers, Richard Sheridan and his partners.

Garrick's visits to Paris during this European tour coincided with a series of controversies over the continuing question of the civil and religious rights of actors in France. This long-standing problem gained fresh prominence in the 1760s, largely due to the efforts of Mlle Clairon, with the strong encouragement of Voltaire. Clairon began her campaign by protesting, as a devout Catholic, against the automatic excommunication of actors. She enlisted the aid of Huerne de la Mothe, a Parliamentary lawyer, who printed a brochure, *Liberté de la France contre le pouvoir arbitraire de l'excommunication* in 1761, summing up arguments previously advanced by Voltaire and others. This pamphlet brought the subject again to public attention, but with unhappy results. Huerne's arguments, intemperately and inelegantly written, simply stiffened resistance, and the pamphlet itself was condemned and burned.

Fresh evidence of the church's intransigence appeared the following year, when Sarrazin, a leading member of the company in the years of Voltaire's major contributions, died. Sarrazin had retired in 1759 and, following the practice of the time, renounced his profession so as to receive last rites and be buried at Saint-Sulpice, his home parish. When his comrades asked permission to have a service said in his honor, however, they were coldly refused, on the grounds that prayers could not be said at the request of those excommunicated.[7]

The Comédiens responded by arranging for an elaborate memorial service in 1763 to honor the recently deceased Crébillon. Knowing the antagonism of the archbishop of Paris, they appealed to a small church that belonged to the Order of Malta that was outside his jurisdiction, and on 6 July they organized an elaborate festival there, attended by many important members of the clergy, a deputation from the French Academy, representatives from all major theatres, and influential members of society and the court. The brilliant success of this occasion (reviewed as if it were a theatrical performance in the *Almanach des Spectacles*) aroused the fury of the archbishop, who appealed to the Order of Malta to punish the priest of the church involved. Clairon and others seized the occasion to again protest the ban of excommunication through their representatives at court, but their complaints went unheard. Voltaire, long a champion of this same cause, followed these developments with great interest, writing encouragingly to Clairon as the apparent leader of the protests.

The arrival of Garrick in October of this year provided a welcome diversion from these controversies. His numerous friends in the theatre world, led by Clairon, Préville, and Monnet, welcomed him with enthusiasm and introduced him to younger colleagues he had not previously met. He attended the theatre avidly, and was invited to the leading intellectual salons of the day, where he met most of the prominent *philosophes*—Diderot, D'Alembert, Helvétius. Often he was called upon to display his acting skill, which made an enormous impression on this company. The most famous of these occasions was reported in detail by Grimm. At a dinner party including both French and English guests, Mlle Clairon recited some passages from Racine and Voltaire, then urged Garrick to follow her example in English. He gave Hamlet's "To be or not to be," the dagger scene from *Macbeth* and, most impressively, a pantomime representation of Lear's madness, explaining that he had learned how to do the latter by observing a friend who had been driven to madness when he allowed his infant child to fall from a window.

Such observations and such an approach to acting naturally had a profound impression upon Diderot, Grimm, and their circle, who found in Garrick precisely the natural actor they felt called for in the new realistic theatre of their dreams. Grimm wrote that:

> Garrick indulges neither in grimaces nor in caricature; all the changes which take place in his features come from the manner in which his deepest feelings work. He never oversteps truth, and he knows that other inconceivable secret of making his appearance increase in beauty by no other aid than that of passion. . . . The English Roscius was the religion and church of our little flock.[8]

From Paris, Garrick travelled to Italy, and considered returning by way of Ferney, to visit Voltaire, who offered him his hospitality and an invitation to perform in his theatre. The opportunity to continue his campaign for Shakespeare at this citadel of French taste was clearly tempting, but Garrick felt this extra excursion would put too much of a strain on his feeble health, and he wrote to Voltaire an apologetic letter of regret. He could not return to London without another stop in Paris, however, arriving there in the spring of 1765.

On the eve of his departure in mid-April occurred the most serious confrontation yet between the French actors and the government over their professional rights. A certain Dubois, a minor actor at the Comédie, had been accused by a surgeon of not paying a bill. Dubois signed a formal oath that he had paid, witnessed by a fellow-actor, Blainville. The surgeon's lawyer, confronted with this document, argued that it was invalid, citing legislation in Rome which declared that the testimony of actors, members of an "infamous profession," had no legal validity.[9]

This argument, publicly circulated, naturally outraged Clairon and others, and they in turn raised an uproar about the insult to the profession. Unhappily, as the case was investigated, it became clear that Dubois and Blainville had in fact perjured themselves, and Dubois had not paid his just debt. The wrath of the actors against the colleague who had thus reinforced the prejudices of their enemies can be imagined. They demanded from the First Gentlemen that the offending parties be expelled from the company, but one of these administrators was interested in Dubois' daughter, and the request was refused.

The next announced piece in which Dubois had a significant role was De Belloy's tragedy *Le Siège de Calais*, announced for 15 April. De Belloy, an actor and playwright much influenced by Voltaire, had written a moderately successful tragedy without sexual love following the model of Voltaire's *Mérope* and *Zulime* in 1762, and *Le Siège de Calais* also followed Voltaire's example of *Adélaïde du Guesclin* in treating a French historical subject. The play appealed to patriotic interests and offered the attractive novelty of a bourgeois hero, the brave mayor of the city (one of the burghers of Calais, immortalized in Rodin's famous statue). The play was one of the great successes of its time in Paris, at Versailles and throughout France. It was even presented in San Domingo, the first tragedy printed in French in America (LFT, 484). Clairon, Lekain, Molé, Dauberval, and Brizard, all with major parts in the play, refused to perform, causing the cancellation of the most popular play of the decade. A riot broke out at the theatre which had to be contained by the police. This event became the talk of Paris, and public opinion ran overwhelmingly against Clairon and her colleagues, who were considered to have put their personal pride before their obligations to their public. As with most public matters, the controversy also reflected the now well-established cultural split between liberal and conservative factions, with writers like Fréron angrily denouncing the actors, and *philosophes* like Grimm writing in their defense (LFT, 288–93).

The Gentlemen of the Chamber, headed by the Duc de Richelieu, saw the matter as a challenge to their authority, and ordered the rebellious actors imprisoned. Dauberval and Brizard were arrested the same day. Clairon was taken to prison from her sickbed, though she was placed in the most comfortable room there, richly furnished by aristocratic admirers, who flocked to visit her in her confinement, turning it into a kind of triumph. Molé and Lekain could not immediately be found. It was rumored that Garrick sheltered them in his apartment,[10] which is not certain, but is possible, since they turned themselves in to the authorities on 17 May, and Garrick left for London the following day. In any case, Garrick was kept informed of the progress of the actors' case by a series of letters from Lekain, Molé, and Clairon (GC, II, 430–44). Clairon was released after five days, but placed under house arrest and, to reduce the celebratory atmosphere that now surrounded her, allowed no more than four visitors plus her doctor each day. The other actors, although they had submitted letters of resignation from the company, were taken from prison each day under guard to the theatre so that they could perform, but not with Dubois, who was placed on leave until the matter could be resolved.

Finally a compromise was reached. De Belloy withdrew his *Le Siège de Calais* to avoid future demonstrations; Dubois was given an early retirement and pension, and the actors withdrew their resignations and were set at liberty, after slightly more than two weeks imprisonment. Richelieu, furious with what he saw as concessions to the actors, hired Dubois for his own theatre at Bordeaux and for some time thereafter afflicted the Comédiens with a series of irritating regulations and requests. In 1764, Voltaire had written to Clairon, "If actors of talent are firm enough in declaring that they will no longer serve an ungrateful public so long as the rights that belong to them are withheld, then this cruel injustice will have to be corrected" (VC, LV, 188), and he repeatedly sent messages during the crisis of April of 1765 to Clairon urging her to stand fast (VC, LVIII, 81, 82, 99). The time had apparently come to put his advice to the test, and Clairon, Lekain, and Molé all requested permission to retire from the Comédie. As servants of the state, however, they did not have a free choice in the matter. All were refused by Richelieu, though Clairon, for reasons of health, was granted a leave until the following Easter. She travelled to Geneva, reportedly to consult with Theodore Tronchin, who enjoyed a reputation as one of the foremost doctors of the era, but the fact that Tronchin was a neighbor and close friend of her longtime champion and advisor, Voltaire, must surely have been an important element in this decision.

Voltaire, who had often urged her to visit him at Ferney, was naturally delighted. She arrived there at the end of July, and one of Garrick's correspondents reported to him the effect of her arrival on Voltaire:

> they say that when she arrived the poet was at death's door, surrounded by his
> doctor, his surgeon, and so on, but that he said that if she could recite some
> verse of his that would revive him. She willingly agreed, and declaimed with
> such power her part in L'Orphélin de la Chine that the enchanted author quite
> forgot his illness. (GC, II, 448)

Tronchin had warned Clairon that a return to the stage might well be fatal. It may be that this advice was given more for political than medical reasons or it may be that, as Voltaire suggested in a letter of 12 August to d'Argental, the stress of the "vocal outbursts and vehement action" required on the Comédie stage (VC, LIX, 12) presented a real problem. In any case, during August and September, Clairon presented a series of performances—among them Amenaide in Tancrède and Electre in Oreste—in Voltaire's theatre, rebuilt and enlarged especially for this occasion.

From Ferney, Clairon went on to Marseilles, not returning to Paris until the beginning of November. All during her absence she corresponded with her many friends in the profession and at court concerning her future plans, and the months following her return were filled with negotiations seeking to provide the actors of the Comédie with the rights they sought. While Clairon worked to rally public support to her cause, a lawyer, Jabineau de la Voute, prepared a legal case for presentation to the king. Voltaire was closely involved in this process, sending letters from Ferney to de la Voute containing not only rhetorical advice, but legal precedents, some dating all the way back to classic antiquity (VC, LX, 92–95, 133–34). One measure of the arbitrariness of the denial of civil liberties to actors was that this problem did not exist at the Opéra, for the simple reason that its official title was not "the Opéra," but the Académie Royale de Musique; thus its members were not legally actors or singers but academicians, like the members of the Académie Française! Indeed one proposal advanced in 1761 and again in 1766 to resolve the problem of the Comédie actors was to officially change the title of the organization to the Académie Royale Dramatique, a solution perhaps too simple and straightforward to be adopted.[11]

Confident of finally achieving relief for this long-standing injustice, Voltaire wrote letters to Clairon in February and March, proudly recalling his own contributions to this cause and making suggestions for her triumphant return to the stage (VC, LX, 109, 175). Alas, it was not to be. The arguments assembled by de la Voute were presented to the king in council in late March of 1766, but even when advised by his councillors that privileges granted to actors by Louis XIII had never been revoked and needed only to be reaffirmed, the king was opposed. "Actors will never be under my reign what they have been under those of my predecessors," he affirmed. "Let me hear no more of this."[12] And that was the end of the matter—until the Revolution.

Clairon remained faithful to her vow. Although only forty-two years of age, she never again performed in public, though she did make appearances at court and in private theatres. Voltaire, bitterly disappointed, took some consolation from Clairon's steadfastness. This also compensated him in some measure for his disappointment in the lack of support the actors had received from his longtime friend the Duc de Richelieu, to whom he wrote with bitter humor:

> I am most disappointed for the public and for the arts that you are willing to see the theatre deprived of Mlle Clairon in the full force of her talent. . . . She has given up excommunication, and I also, since I am in retirement. Only you remain excommunicated, since you are still First Gentleman of the Chamber and thus in charge of the works of Satan. It seems clear that the one who gives the orders is much more to be cursed than the poor devils who carry them out. (VC, LXI, 90)

Voltaire could take some consolation, however, from the happier outcome of another of his protracted theatre campaigns. In this same spring, a theatre was established in Geneva.

This surprising development was made possible by a crisis in the Genevan government. Geneva was by no means the tranquil utopia some of its champions depicted. It had a history of civil dissension, so serious that once earlier in the century (in 1737) its citizens had been forced to call upon its neighbors, France and the cantons of Berne and Zurich, to restore order. In

1766, similar unrest had developed, primarily between the traditional ruling class of the city and the rising bourgeoisie, who were demanding a greater share of the power. Voltaire put himself forward as peacemaker, with little result, and early in 1766, France, Berne, and Zurich were again appealed to as mediators.

Scarcely had the French representative arrived in Geneva, when Voltaire, as an assiduous student of history, informed him that when the foreign representatives had last come to restore order in 1737, they had relieved the tedium of their stay in this austere city by establishing a theatre. The representative, accustomed to the entertainments of Versailles, needed no convincing, and suggested to the Geneva Council (a suggestion that amounted to an order) that a theatre should be reestablished in the city. Accordingly a wooden theatre, seating approximately 800, was constructed in the spring of 1766. The nearest available company was at Carouge, today a suburb of Geneva, but then in Savoy, a territory controlled by the king of Sardinia. The king, at the request of the Genevan Council, released the company to their new theatre, which opened in July.

The repertoire of this company consisted entirely of comic opera, which after the successes of Favart in the mid-1750s was enjoying a tremendous popularity throughout France. By the end of the decade, two other major composers in this genre had appeared, Pierre-Alexandre Monsigny and François-André Philidor, and the genre's most important librettist in the eighteenth century, Michel-Jean Sedaine. Sedaine gained his first reputation as a poet, but was brought into the theatre by that unsurpassed discoverer of young talent, Jean Monnet, for whom he began writing comic burlesques and then libretti. Under the influence of his mentor, Diderot, Sedaine continually worked for the integration of music, language, and emotion, and for the realistic depiction of characters. He is thus primarily remembered for the major role he played in developing the genre of French comic opera from its status as light burlesque entertainment at mid-century to full operatic maturity at the beginning of the Revolution. Sedaine also, however, enjoyed success as a comic dramatist and opera librettist. His *Le Philosophe sans le savoir*, generally considered one of the century's best comedies, premiered at the Comédie in 1765, and in 1766 his *Aline, reine de Golconde*, with music by Monsigny, was presented at the opera, with the result that in the late 1760s Sedaine had works simultaneously playing on the three national stages of France.

One of the most fruitful collaborations in French operatic history, between Sedaine and Monsigny, began in 1761 with *On ne s'avise jamais de tout*, such a success that it was revived at court, a rare distinction for a work from the fairground theatres. It was also selected for the official opening of the merged Comédie Italienne and Opéra-Comique the following year. *Le Roi et le Fermier* in 1762 was a far more ambitious collaboration, in length (three acts), in its emotional coloring, and in its mixture of serious and comic elements, of kings and peasants (Sedaine was a great admirer of Shakespeare and of his use of such mixtures). Both of these plays were presented by the new company in Geneva, along with: Sedaine and Monsigny's 1764 *Rose et Colas*; Favart's *La Fée Urgèle*; and several works by Philidor, including his 1763 *Le Bûcheron*, written with Sedaine, and his 1765 adaptation of Henry Fielding's novel *Tom Jones*, written with his more frequent collaborator, Antoine Poinsinet.[13]

Geneva's new company played five nights a week, an unusually full schedule for a company of this time in a city of this size, suggesting a strong measure of popular interest. In mid-September they closed for a week, during which they performed twice at Ferney for Voltaire, whose ill health had prevented him from seeing them in the city. Voltaire wrote to d'Argental that he invited the entire company of "49, including the violins" to cure his "horrible melancholy," which apparently they did (VC, LXII, 205). This was Voltaire's first exposure to the genre of comic opera, of whose mixed productions he was deeply suspicious. Four works were presented for him, offering a good selection of the company's repertoire: Monsigny and Sedaine's *Le Roi et le Fermier* and *Rose et Colas*, Favart's *Annette et Lubin*, and a piece dealing with Henri IV (VC, LXII, 187). This latter may have been *Les Evénements de la Chasse* by Sticotti, created at the Comédie Italienne in 1759. Besterman identifies it as Charles Collé's *La Partie de Chasse de Henri IV*, though this seems unlikely, since it had only been privately performed in Paris in 1762 and not published until the spring of 1766. The *philosophes* often cited Henri IV as a benevolent and enlightened monarch, in contrast to the authoritarian Louis XV, and it is hardly surprising that Louis forbade a public performance of Collé's work, which was not offered in Paris until 1774. Its published version, however, was highly popular and widely circulated. Although Voltaire expressed concern about a "comic treatment" of his hero, he accurately predicted an eventual great success for Collé's play in the theatre, and wrote to friends in Paris requesting a copy this same spring (VC, LXII, 161).

The next generation's leading composer of comic operas, Grétry, was introduced to this genre in Geneva, where he settled for a time after five years of studying music in Rome. He became a regular guest at Ferney until his departure in the fall of 1767, one of the few musicians so honored (unlike the young Mozart, now ten years of age, who performed for Grétry in Geneva, but whose aspiring father requested in vain an invitation to Ferney). Grétry and Voltaire discussed at length poetry, music, and the new genre, which Voltaire feared was displacing traditional comedy and tragedy in the public's esteem. But with Voltaire's advice and encouragement, Grétry decided to try his hand at it, taking as a libretto one of Favart's works based on Voltaire, *Isabelle et Gertrude*. The music, by Blaise, was generally considered inferior to the text, and Grétry felt he could improve upon it. His first comic opera was thus premiered in Geneva in the fall of 1766 and was a great success, with an unusually long run of six performances. The composer was even summoned upon the stage to be applauded, a custom then common in Paris, but not yet seen in Geneva.[14]

Rosimond, the director of the Geneva theatre, very likely with the encouragement of Voltaire, also sought to broaden his offerings beyond comic opera by engaging several artists more trained in traditional theatre. In November, Voltaire entrusted to them his *Olympie* and exalted in its success as a triumph not only for his art but for his ideals. "*Olympie* has been performed for five consecutive days," he notes in a letter of 5 November. "You see that Jean Jacques [Rousseau] was right to say that I would corrupt the republic" (VC, LXIII, 77). Voltaire's triumph was, however, short-lived. When the peace commission departed in January of 1767, the troupe was given leave and they moved for a time to Berne, hoping soon to return, but these hopes were dashed early in February when a fire of suspicious origins completely destroyed the Geneva theatre. Another was not built until 1782, four years after Voltaire's death.

During the fall of 1766, Voltaire created *Les Scythes*, another tragedy of cultural conflict, this time with a distinctly autobiographical note, with a central character, Sozame, an elderly philosopher from the cultivated but despotic state of Persia, whose free speaking has driven him into exile among the hospitable and freedom-loving, if somewhat simple-minded people of Scythia. There is of course a love action, with a heroine who commits suicide, but much of the dialogue is made up of philosophic discussions between Sozame and his Scythian counterpart, Hermodan, revealing the author's real interest. The Comédie actors accepted the work in December, but did not present it until the following March. In the meantime, Voltaire organized a production at Ferney, to which he gave unusual attention, rehearsing it for almost three months and rewriting constantly. He finally presented it at Ferney 16 March, just ten days before the Comédie premiere. Among his guests at this time were the young dramatist La Harpe and his wife. La Harpe's first (and only) successful tragedy, *Comte de Warwick*, had been presented at the Comédie in 1763, and Voltaire reported that he was as skillful in acting as in writing, indeed calling him "the best actor in France today." As for his wife, "She performs like Mlle Clairon, although she is a good deal more sentimental." In short, he concluded, "I only hope that the play is as well performed in Paris and Bordeaux as it is in Ferney" (VC, LXV, 63). Although his praise of the La Harpes is clearly exaggerated, the Paris production was disappointing. Lekain was ineffective and Clairon's substitute worse still. Audiences considered the work cold and abstract, faults only emphasized by Voltaire's continuing interest in employing pantomime and spectacle, and *Les Scythes* achieved only four performances.

Although Voltaire still felt misgivings about the increasing popularity of comic opera, the conversations with Grétry and the performances at Ferney in 1766 encouraged him to experiment in this direction. One of the comic operas presented at Ferney dealt with Voltaire's old hero, Henry IV, whom he had glorified forty years before in his epic poem, *La Henriade*, and he now returned to this subject to create a "petit divertissement" that would offer "a little singing and dancing, some comedy, some tragedy, some joking, and a moral" (VO, VI, 343), but which due to its subject matter could clearly be offered only at private theatres. On 20 August 1768, Grétry achieved his first important success in Paris with *Le Huron*, based on Voltaire's short story, *L'Ingénu*. Soon after word of this success reached Ferney, Voltaire dispatched two new libretti, *Le Baron d'Otranto* and *Les deux tonneaux*, to Paris for Grétry's consideration. Grétry provided music for *Le Baron* and presented it to the Opéra Comique, claiming, according to Voltaire's wishes, that it was the work of an aspiring young provincial playwright.

The result of this strategy was as unfortunate as the similar presentation of *Olympie*. The actors rejected the work, but suggested that the young author showed promise and encouraged Grétry to invite him to Paris where they could work with him to improve his skills. Thus caught in his own trap, Voltaire abandoned the project and a true Voltaire/Grétry collaboration fell through, as had the Voltaire/Rameau project almost forty years before. Nevertheless, it is striking that Voltaire, whose interest in music was relatively minor, in both cases sensed and encouraged the talents of two of the century's greatest composers, before either had enjoyed even a modest success.

Les Guèbres, a new tragedy that Voltaire wrote in the late summer of 1768, fared no better, though it was significant in launching a new series of tragedies, most not presented, which were open statements of *philosophe* propaganda. Never had Voltaire so clearly pitted characters of tolerance and humanity (*Les Guèbres* was subtitled *La Tolérance*) against the forces of cruelty and religious fanaticism than in this totally imaginary series of bizarre confrontations in Syria during the Roman Empire. The author expected the play to be a great success, not only because of its message, but because, in his eyes at least, it contributed to the popular new form of "*tragédie bourgeoisie*" in which his longtime friend and correspondent, Bernard Saurin, had just achieved a great success with *Béverlei*, his adaptation of Moore's *The Gamester*. Although a preliminary *Discours* to the 1769 edition echoes Lillo and others in boasting of utilizing common characters and a simple style instead of the pomp of kings and princes (VO, VI, 491–92), the style, if a bit flat, departs little from Voltaire's earlier work. Not distinguished as literature, and dangerous in theme (in vain, Voltaire appealed to the examples of *Tartuffe* and *Mahomet*), the work was never presented, despite extensive rewriting.

To this roster of disappointments must be added Voltaire's final comedy, *Le Dépositaire*, written in 1769. Here, after his largely unsuccessful attempts to adjust to the changing dramatic tastes of the times, he attempted to return to the style of Molière and of his own first comedy, *L'Indiscret*, a success at the Comédie forty-four years before. Its subject matter also returned to his youth, an anecdote of the celebrated courtesan, Ninon de Lenclos, whom Voltaire's godfather the Abbé de Châteauneuf had taken Voltaire to meet in 1705, when he was a boy of twelve and she a formidable eighty-five. Voltaire knew well that this style of comedy was quite out of fashion, but dreamed that he might revive interest in such work. It was, however, too weak an effort to achieve so substantial an effect. The play was reluctantly accepted by the Comédie, then withdrawn, perhaps by Voltaire's own friends. Critical response to the published version was cool from friends like Grimm, and savage from enemies like Fréron, who remarked, with some justice, that comedy had never been Voltaire's strength. So this decade ended with Voltaire unable to achieve public performances in each of the major genres of the period—comedy, tragedy, and comic opera. It appeared that his long theatrical career might be over. But a final triumph in this field remained ahead, and the years of exile and frustration that preceded it would make it all the more spectacular and gratifying.

NOTES

1. See VC, XLVII, 90. Five plays by Corneille received a total of sixteen performances; six plays by Racine received eighteen; and sixteen plays by Voltaire received seventy-six.

2. Quoted in Maurice Dutrait, *Étude sur la vie et le théâtre de Crébillon* (Paris: Bordeaux, 1895), 148.

3. Edward Gibbon, *Letters of Gibbon*, ed. J. E. Norton, 3 vols. (London: Cassell, 1956), 1:154–55.

4. Quoted in Maurice Dumoulin, *Favart et Madame Favart: Un ménage d'artistes au XVIIIe siècle* (Paris: Louis-Michaud, n.d.), 91.

5. Quoted in Dumoulin, 92.

6. Cecil Price, *Theatre in the Age of Garrick* (Totowa, New Jersey: Rowman and Littlefield, 1973), 79–80.

7. Louis Bachaumont, *Mémoires secrets pour servir à l'histoire de la république des lettres in France*, 36 vols. (London: J. Adamson, 1780–89), 1:92.

8. Friedrich Grimm, *Correspondance littéraire*, 12 vols. (Paris: Garnier, 1878), 6:318–21.

9. Gaston Maugras, *Les Comédiens hors la Loi* (Paris: Calmann Lévy, 1887), 286.

10. Frank A. Hedgcock, *David Garrick and His French Friends* (London: Stanley Paul, 1912), 235.

11. Maugras, *Les Comédiens*, 319.

12. Ibid., 323.

13. A listing of all plays known to have been presented may be found in P. Long des Clavières, *La Jeunesse de Grétry* (Besançon: Jacques et Demontrond, 1920), 85.

14. André Grétry, *Mémoires ou essais sur la musique*, 3 vols. (Paris: Imprimérie de la république, 1797), 1:143.

Chapter 8

The Final Triumph, 1770–1778

The year 1770 saw major changes in the theatres of Paris. The old Opéra, located in the former palace of Cardinal Richelieu, had burned in 1763 and a new theatre was built in almost the same location, opening in 1770. In the interim, the Opéra was housed in the reopened and refurbished Salle des Machines, which Servandoni had operated in the Tuileries Palace from 1738 until 1754. Partly under the stimulus of a new Opéra, fresh attention was given to the Comédie, whose 1689 home, capacious and comfortable a century before, had long since come to seem cramped and outdated. In 1767, the architects Peyre and Wailly were commissioned to design a new theatre on the left bank, which would become today's Odéon. Construction was authorized in 1770, but the work proceeded slowly, and the new theatre was not completed until 1781. In the meantime, the Comédie left its old home in 1770 for the larger and better-equipped theatre in the Tuileries which had just sheltered the Opéra. The Tuileries theatre, indeed the wing of the Louvre in which it was housed, no longer exists, but it has left its mark on French theatre vocabulary. Stage right and left in France are still called "the garden side" and "the court side," referring to the fact that a spectator seated in the Tuileries theatre would have the Tuileries gardens to his left, the Carrousel courtyard to his right. The two great events which occurred during the decade the Comédie remained in this space were the premiere of Beaumarchais' *Barbier de Séville* in 1775 and Voltaire's triumphant return in 1778.

One of the leading salons in Paris in 1770 was that of Mme Necker, wife of the diplomatic representative of Geneva to the French court, a prosperous banker who would become Controller General of France. One spring evening this year she invited a group of prominent *philosophes* including Grimm, d'Alembert, and Diderot, and proposed the commissioning of a statue of Voltaire, an extremely rare honor for any living person and quite unheard-of for a man of letters. They enthusiastically agreed, and within a short time an astonishing range of subscibers had enrolled, including foreign monarchs and even such old enemies as Rousseau, Palissot, and Fréron (whose money was returned). In June, Pigalle, the king's own sculptor and one of the most highly regarded artists of the period, arrived at Ferney to begin the work. After some difficulty in keeping his ebullient subject still long enough to pose, Pigalle produced a work that caused considerable controversy. Influenced by a recent wave of excavations in Greece and by Wincklemann's 1764 major work on antique art, Pigalle created a nude statue in the classic style, one of the first in what would become a late eighteenth-century vogue. The good Mme Necker was quite scandalized, but the seventy-six-year-old philosopher himself only dryly remarked that "either clothed or nude, his body would not give ladies erotic notions."[1]

Early in 1768, after a series of quarrels with Voltaire, Mme Denis departed for Paris, where she remained until the fall of 1769. Her return inspired many rumors that Voltaire would follow, and indeed Mme Denis pursued this possibility through friends at court. She received little encouragement, but the dream of returning to Paris took on increasing urgency for the aging Voltaire after 1770 and, as in the past, his dreams of achieving this centered on the theatre.

Unhappily, his first such project after 1770 returned to his ongoing challenge to Crébillon, a contest that now vitally concerned almost no one but Voltaire. Still, in certain moods Voltaire seemed to consider Crébillon centrally responsible for all or most of his own theatrical failures ("Before I die," he wrote in January of 1771, "I must bury Crébillon as he has buried me" VC, LXXVIII, 23), and rarely a year passed without one or more attacks on the earlier dramatist appearing in some Voltaire work.[2] His last dramatic challenge, *Les Pélopides*, reworked Crébillon's first great success, the 1707 *Atrée et Thyeste*. In his enthusiasm, Voltaire dreamed that this new work would not only confirm him as the leading tragic writer of the age, but would be the perfect choice to be performed before the French court on the occasion of the upcoming royal marriage of Louis Stanislas Xavier, the future Louis XVIII (14 May 1771). Such a triumph, he further believed, would necessarily end his long exile (VC, LXXVIII, 78). Much to his disappointment, however, even his friends did not share his enthusiasm, and the new work was presented neither at the wedding nor at the Comédie. At this same time, Voltaire also did an adaptation of another major earlier tragedy, Mairet's *Sophonisbe*, though this more in a spirit of tribute than challenge. Published in 1770, it was eventually performed in late 1773 at Fontainebleau and on 15 January 1774 at the Comédie, where it was given only four performances. Only the superior acting of Lekain, it was generally agreed, inspired even this many.

The dream of returning to Paris in the wake of a new theatrical success continued, however. Voltaire's next attempt at this was *Les Lois de Minos*, completed in mid-January of 1772. To d'Argental he wrote that after the "warmed-over" creations of *Sophonisbe* and *Les Pélopides*, he now felt that the best way to counteract the current popularity of "comic opera and vaux-hall" and to restore a sense of grandeur to the French stage and the court was by an imposing, interesting, and "entirely new" piece with "great spectacle" (VC, LXXXI, 30). In fact, the plot and the concerns of *Les Lois de Minos* are essentially the same as those of *Les Guèbres*, with the location shifted from Roman Syria to ancient Crete. Once again, a maiden is threatened with religious sacrifice and a philosophic secular leader saves her by confronting the powers of fanaticism in the person of the high priest. The newest feature of the work, as Voltaire suggests, is the spectacle, which he proudly summarized as containing among other attractions priests and warriors, Greeks and savages, a sacrifice, and for a climax "the destruction of the high altar and a cathedral in flames" (VC, LXXXI, 60).

Such an emphasis was not without its dangers, for already Voltaire was being accused by some critics of turning the French classic stage into a "magic-lantern show,"[3] but a more serious immediate problem in the case of so outspoken a call for freedom of conscience was censorship, and all through 1772 Voltaire reworked the play in response to suggestions from the censor and the Comédie actors.

Although clearly Voltaire's interest in theatre was undiminished, his advancing age and unstable health and the absence of Mme Denis discouraged theatrical performances at Ferney. In 1769, the theatre, so long a center of entertainment at the estate, was converted into a silkworm nursery to support another of Voltaire's astonishing range of enthusiasms. On and off since 1760 a small provincial theatre had existed across the French border at Châtelaine, but it was little patronized either by the citizens of Geneva or by Voltaire. The company was not distinguished and Voltaire himself remarked that "the pleasure of seeing provincial actors is not equal to that of acting oneself" (VC, LXXXII, 72). However, in the course of 1772, with the theatre at Ferney inactive, Voltaire became more and more involved with Châtelaine. The company, well aware of the usefulness of his interest, began producing his plays and even installed a special box for him at the side of the stage. He attended a production of *Nanine* 18 June, and was so pleased that he invited the actors to Ferney to coach them for a production of *Adélaïde du Guesclin*.

Zaïre followed in July and *Olympie* in August, but the peak of Voltaire's involvement came in September, when Lekain paid another visit and presented a series of six performances at Châtelaine, which of course drew overflowing crowds from the entire region. The many anecdotes of this visit invariably involve Voltaire as much as Lekain. A correspondent wrote to Frederick II that Voltaire conducted the rehearsals of his plays and at one point in *Mahomet*, impatient with the actor playing Seïde, he cried, "I will play it for you," and "indeed he played the scene with a fire that surprised us all" (VC, LXIII, 26; illustration 9). Voltaire was equally part of the performances, as an amusing report from a Swiss observer makes clear:

> Voltaire, seated in front of the first wing, in full view of all the audience, applauded like one possessed, banging with his cane and crying out "It couldn't be better!" "Ah, Mon Dieu, how good it is!" setting an example of tender feeling by bringing his handkerchief to his eye. His enthusiasm was such that at the moment when Ninias was leaving the stage after having confronted Assur, without fear of destroying the illusion he ran after Lekain, seized his hand, and embraced him. Nothing more comically ambiguous could be imagined, for Voltaire resembled one of those comic old men of the theatre, stockings rolled over his knees and in antique costume, supporting his trembling legs only with the aid of a cane. (PVI, 463)

The comic ambiguity must have been all the greater for those who recalled Voltaire's long campaign against the illusion-breaking presence of stage spectators.

Lekain returned to Paris to lead the campaign for the staging of *Les Lois de Minos*, working on the casting and championing the play in salons and at the Comédie. After a series of delays, occasioned in part by the highly successful debuts of a major new tragic actress, Mlle Raucourt, and the publication of a mangled pirated edition in Paris, Voltaire withdrew the play from the Comédie. He still hoped that the Duc de Richelieu would arrange for a production at Fontainebleau for the wedding of the Comte d'Artois, but as a final indignity, Crébillon's *Catilina* was selected instead. So ended this phase of the campaign to reconquer Paris.

After the Fontainebleau disappointment, Voltaire removed the dedication to Richelieu from *Les Lois de Minos* and doubtless wished he had followed his original intention of dedicating it to the Russian empress, Catherine, who by this time had replaced Frederick in Voltaire's opinion as the model of an enlightened modern ruler. Voltaire had viewed Catherine's seizure of power

Illustration 9. Voltaire and Lekain rehearsing *Mahomet* at Ferney.

in 1761 with understandable misgivings, but her first attempted contact with him was shrewdly through her French secretary, François Pictet, a native of Geneva who had in fact appeared in productions of Voltaire's plays at Ferney. Pictet knew the way to appeal to Voltaire, assuring him that Catherine knew his works "almost by heart" and requesting his permission to perform his works in Russia "not with actors, whom we have not had this summer, but with Lords and Ladies of the court." In anticipation, Pictet reported, they were already rehearsing *Zaïre*, *Alzire*, and *L'Orphélin de la Chine* (VC, L, 153). Naturally, Voltaire was delighted at conquering another monarch's heart, and soon he was involved in a regular correspondence with Catherine that lasted until his death.

A permanent stage had been established at Russia's Winter Palace in 1734, which welcomed a series of foreign troupes, including Austrian ballet, Italian opera, the German company of Caroline Neuber from Germany, and a French troupe led by Raucourt, whose daughter's debut at the Comédie in 1772 was a major event. A native company of professional actors was brought from Yaroslavl in 1752 and made a state company in 1756, their repertoire consisting primarily of French dramas translated into Russian. This was the theatrical tradition inherited by Catherine, and it expanded significantly during her reign. After her initial contact with Voltaire, Catherine's correspondence has little to say about the cultural activities at her court, although she did maintain a troupe of French actors and did apparently enjoy Voltaire's plays. The major content of the correspondence for a number of years was her military campaigns, primarily against the Turks, which Voltaire supported in the cause of enlightenment and progress (like the later romantics, he dreamed especially of Greek emancipation). Theatrical matters became more important after 1772. In 1762, Catherine had opened Russia's first state educational institute for girls, nominally modeled on France's Saint-Cyr. After they had presented Voltaire's *Zaïre* and the 1751 *Semira* by Alexander Sumarokov, the leading Russian dramatist of the period and a devoted imitator of Voltaire and the French classics, Catherine asked Voltaire to perform judicious cutting of some classic works to make them more suitable for young minds. Voltaire enthusiastically promised to do so, and sent a copy of his recent *Les Lois de Minos* for possible use (VC, LXXXI, 113). He also recommended several young actors of his acquaintance to Catherine, who in fact employed them in her French company.

Encouraged by Voltaire's interest, Catherine mentioned a series of popular witty comedies that had begun to appear in St. Petersburg, the work of an anonymous young Russian. Voltaire, accustomed to this game, seems to have guessed at once that the empress herself was the author, and he pronounced the French translations that were sent to him as "worthy of Mo-lière," natural and true to life (VC, LXXXIII, 43).

During the early 1770s, a new writer came to prominence in Paris, Pierre Augustin Caron de Beaumarchais, who would become the leading dramatist of the new generation and carry on a number of Voltaire's projects and con-cerns. His theatrical debuts were not auspicious. His *Eugènie*, inspired by Diderot and the English drama, was a failure at the Comédie in 1767, al-though its prefatory essay on serious drama provided one of the major theo-retical statements on that evolving genre. In it, Beaumarchais argued that "other things being equal," the serious drama "offered a more immediate in-terest and a morality more discreet than heroic tragedy and deeper than tradi-tional comedy."[4] His second play, *Les deux amis*, in 1770, did no better. He then became involved in a complex lawsuit which left him penniless, dis-graced, and branded as a forger. Like the young Voltaire, however, the young Beaumarchais thrived on adversity, and also like Voltaire, sought revenge by his wit and his pen. He began publishing a series of pamphlets dealing with his case that became the rage of Paris, and were read with delight from Phila-delphia to St. Petersburg. Dialogue from them was staged by ladies of the court for the amusement of the king, Goethe was inspired by Beaumarchais' adventures to write his play, *Clavigo*, and Voltaire, reading each new pam-phlet with delight in Ferney, wrote in February 1774 to d'Alembert that Beaumarchais was the only current writer that he enjoyed: "He unites every-thing—buffoonery, seriousness, arguments, power, sentiment, all sorts of eloquence. He has confounded his adversaries and given lesson to his judges" (VC, LXXXVII, 83). Beaumarchais' third play, *Le Barbier de Séville* was first banned in 1774 and then, as his support grew and the legal actions against him were declared void, cleared for performance a year later. At the first performance, 22 February, the audience found the work too dark and cynical and the play did not succeed, but the resourceful author com-pletely reworked it within twenty-four hours, turning it into one of the most popular comedies of the time. The darkness and irony were put aside until a more appropriate occasion, which was indeed not long in coming. The resil-ience, the daring, and the wit of the young author must have recalled to the eighty-year-old Voltaire his own youth, and in his final years, he and Beau-marchais would develop a special literary and personal relationship.

The death of Louis XV on 10 May 1774 aroused a brief hope that royal disapproval of Voltaire would now diminish, but Louis XVI viewed the *phi-losophes* in general, and Voltaire in particular, with even deeper distrust. Voltaire again immersed himself in activities at Ferney, overseeing the arts and industries of his little community, receiving, as always, a string of visitors, and writing some forty new works during this fall, among them a new tragedy, *Don Pèdre*. Voltaire seems to have had no hope of placing this play on the stage, but saw it primarily as another contribution to his ongoing struggle against the intolerance and brutality of those in power, this time not the church, but the judges and parliaments responsible for the Calas affair and for a series of other miscarriages of justice he had involved himself with since that famous case.

Unhappily for his many English admirers, in these final years Voltaire also directed the same energy and fire he brought to political abuses to what he conceived of as a major cultural abuse, the increasing influence in France of English theatre in general, and Shakespeare in particular. Of course, it had been Voltaire more than any other single person who had stimulated this interest, but that fact doubtless helps explain his growing concern as the century progressed and young French poets increasingly looked to England not only for strategies to renew the French tradition, but, he feared, for models to replace it. Already in 1761 he had attempted to stem the tide with his "Appel à toutes les nations de l'Europe," but in vain. Even the *Encyclopédie* offered enthusiastic praise for Shakespeare in its 1765 entries on "Stratford" and "Tragedy," and Garrick's 1769 Shakespeare Jubilee at Stratford directed new attention to the dramatist throughout Europe. Mme Riccoboni even wrote to Garrick in 1770 that the Pigalle statue of Voltaire was a French attempt to honor a famous author in modest imitation of the English celebration, (GC, 572) a theory, it is to be hoped, that never reached Voltaire.

In the 1770s, the chorus of French praise increased. Jean François Ducis, with much more enthusiasm than ability, undertook a series of attempts to rework Shakespeare in French neoclassic style, a task for which his almost complete ignorance of English was probably an advantage. Voltaire dismissed Ducis' 1769 *Hamlet* as "detestable" and "a cold horror" (VC, LXIII, 135) and his 1772 *Roméo* as a "visigothic piece" (LXXXIII, 6), but both were successes at the Comédie, increasing Shakespeare's reputation. Ironically, it was Ducis who in 1778 inherited Voltaire's chair at the French Academy. In 1773, Marmontel's *Chefs-d'oeuvre dramatiques* spoke of Shakespeare's "transcendent merit,"[5] and Mercier's *Du théâtre* the same year exalted Shakespeare specifically in contrast to the "haughty poets" of France, whose highly praised tragedy "is only a phantom clothed in purple and gold, but with no life in it."[6] For Voltaire, the final straw was the publication in March of 1776 of the first two volumes of a complete and much more faithful translation by Pierre Le Tourneur, with a preface lauding Shakespeare as the world's greatest dramatic genius. The 160-page preface gave distinctly lesser praise to Corneille and Racine, while Voltaire was not even mentioned.

Voltaire's wrath was first expressed in a public letter of 19 July to his old friend, d'Argental, who was also a subscriber to the translation (as were the king and queen of France, the king of England, Catherine of Russia, Diderot, and many of the most famous names in Europe). "I was the first to show to the French some pearls that I had found in his enormous dung heap," Voltaire raged. "I did not expect that I would serve one day to trample under foot the crowns of Racine and Corneille in order to adorn the brow of a barbarian mountebank" (VC, XCIV, 204).

This letter was immediately followed by a more substantial salvo. D'Alembert read before the French Academy on 25 August 1776 a *Discours* prepared by Voltaire recalling to the Academy that it had been founded to deal with the literary dispute surrounding Corneille's *Le Cid* and suggesting that now, 140 years later, they should again protect French literature by pronouncing judgement upon Shakespeare, the product of a barbarian age whose sins against the proprieties and decorum were far greater than those condemned by the Academy in *Le Cid*. By way of illustration, Voltaire cited numerous examples of the low, indecent, and outrageously improbable in Shakespeare.

The displeasure of the English representatives at the occasion can be imagined, especially that of Shakespeare's champion, Elizabeth Montague, who had already published in 1760 an "Essay on the writings and genius of Shakespeare . . . with some remarks upon the misrepresentations of M. de Voltaire." The great majority of the French listeners, however, were reportedly much amused, and the occasion was on the whole a triumph for Voltaire.

This same summer also saw Voltaire much more involved with theatrical matters at home. Saint-Gérand, the impresario of the Châtelaine theatre, persuaded Voltaire to allow him to construct a new theatre at Ferney. An abandoned barn was accordingly converted into a comfortable and well-equipped modern stage. Voltaire wanted Lekain to inaugurate this new theatre, but since Lekain was a member of the royal company, an official leave from the court was necessary. Voltaire appealed through intermediaries to the new queen, Marie Antoinette, who graciously granted the request, a gesture that signaled the beginning of at least a partial reconciliation between Voltaire and the court. Lekain arrived at the end of July and gave eight extremely popular performances at Châtelaine and Ferney. In a letter of 5 August, Lekain marveled how Voltaire, at the age of eighty-three, "worked regularly ten hours a day," but whose literary tasks "do not prevent him from working on his community, increasing its commerce, and increasing in every way its happiness and fortune." Lekain found his host witty and charming as ever, except when raging against the current vogue for English drama, Shakespeare, and tragedies in prose (VC, XCV, 9).

Neither the Lekain visit nor the triumph at the Academy gave Voltaire the satisfaction he anticipated. In a letter to d'Argental, Voltaire complained that at Ferney Lekain had appeared in De Belloy's 1771 *Gaston et Bayard*, "in which he achieved no other success than in remaining in bed for a quarter of an hour," and Du Ryer's "ancient declamatory piece," the 1646 *Scévole*. Lekain, Voltaire complained, no longer gave him any consideration, particularly in the matter of reviving *Olympie*, which had not been seen at the Comédie since its premiere in 1764 and which Voltaire urged Lekain, in vain, to perform at court for the new queen.

The Shakespeare campaign was also encountering disappointments. Subscriptions for Le Tourneur were not falling off, as Voltaire predicted they would, but steadily increasing, probably in part due to the controversy. Voltaire's address to the Academy was denied publication rights, ironically on the grounds that his many quotations of the improprieties in Shakespeare offended public decency. More predictably, a campaign of refutations of his attack was soon underway in both England and France, the most important contributors to which were: Lady Montague, whose earlier work was translated into French as a response to Voltaire in 1777; and Joseph Baretti, an Italian living in London, whose "Discours sur Shakespeare et sur Monsieur de Voltaire" appeared this same year. The battle raged up until and even into the Revolution, then died away, only to reemerge and be refought, with a clear defeat for Voltaire's position, in the battles of romanticism in the early nineteenth century.

Discouraged by Lekain's lack of support and the resistence to his campaign against Shakespeare, Voltaire wrote to D'Alembert in the fall of 1776 that he felt like the pamphleteer Beaumarchais, an isolated individual with no power left but his pen. Even in far-off America, whose Revolution seemed to be foundering, he saw the forces of darkness on the rise: "You know that the troops of Doctor Franklin have been beaten by those of the King of England," he wrote. "Alas, the *philosophes* are being beaten everywhere. Reason and liberty are badly received in this world" (VC, XCV, 131).

And yet Voltaire never entirely gave up his dream of some measure of reconciliation with the court. The new king seemed implacable, but the queen offered some hope. In May of 1776, she actually requested that Lekain perform *Tancrède* for the court, and in September Voltaire responded with alacrity to a request from the Comte de Province for a *divertissement* to entertain the queen at a party the Comte was giving. Although he had only a bit over two weeks for this project, he eagerly agreed, updating an entertainment of some sixty years before from the queen's home court of Vienna, *L'Hote et L'Hotesse*. Not surprisingly, the work had little artistic merit, but Voltaire was delighted to receive such a commission, his first since *La Princesse de Navarre*, over thirty years before.

These marks of royal interest seem to have encouraged in Voltaire an urge to make one last attempt at a triumphant new tragedy. At any rate, he announces beginning work on it in the same letter (18 October) to d'Argental in which he requests news of the success of his divertissement at the festival (VC, XCV, 121). The work went slowly, with Voltaire complaining of the folly of undertaking such a project in his eighty-third year (VC, XCV, 151). Early in the new year, 1777, he became so discouraged that he put aside this work, *Alexis*, and began another, *Agathocle*. During the summer he continued work on both, with the result that a rough draft of *Agathocle* was staged at Ferney in September and a basically complete version of *Alexis* in November. The octogenarian playwright, who a year before had expressed doubts that he could complete another play, now had two ready for submission. Voltaire felt *Alexis*, now renamed *Irène*, was nearer its final form and asked the Comédie to consider it first. The play was read to the actors 2 January 1778 by Monvel, Lekain being absent due to illness. It was enthusiastically accepted, but a few days later a major scandal erupted when Lekain refused to accept the leading role, created especially for him by Voltaire. The Comédie administrators demanded that Lekain write to Voltaire to explain, which he did on 13 January, pleading that his uncertain health prevented him from undertaking youthful and vigorous new roles, and offering to accept a minor part instead (VC, XCVIII, 22). Voltaire's response was cooly ironic, noting that despite his own bad health he had worked night and day to complete the work. He also noted that the papers reported that Lekain was remarrying, though he doubted this was true since Lekain would surely have informed him, and concluded that if in fact it were true, he hoped that the "fatigues of getting married" would not prevent Lekain from assuming the smaller role he proposed (VC, XCVIII, 33). Lekain wrote back in apology, denying the marriage as a foolish rumor, but the damage was done. There was no further contact between Voltaire and his protege. Unfortunately, Lekain's illness, unlike his marriage, was all too real, and he died before Voltaire's play could be presented.

The defection of Lekain and the remembrance of all the tensions of mounting a play and weathering the inevitable criticisms of it swept over Voltaire, and only the continued insistence of d'Argental and other friends in

Paris prevented him from abandoning the project altogether. With Lekain gone, the focus of the play shifted from the romantic hero, now played by the less distinguished Molé, to the heroine, played by Mme Vestris, torn, in traditional neoclassic fashion, between love and duty, and the play was renamed *Irène*. Rehearsals continued, anticipation grew, and Voltaire, whose exile had never been official, but who had been clearly warned for years that arrest and imprisonment probably awaited him in Paris, decided to risk a return. On 5 February 1778, he departed for the capital.

His return was a triumph, one of the great events of the century, and although Voltaire's enemies were still numerous and powerful, it was clear that any action against him at this moment was impossible. He settled at the elegant town house of the Marquis de Villette, who had married an impoverished girl Voltaire had taken under his wing, and upon these grounds claimed a kind of son-in-law relationship to the philosopher. Visitors by the hundreds descended on the house, three hundred the first day alone. The first was Voltaire's old friend d'Argental, who with his joy also brought the sad tidings that Lekain had died on 8 February, two days before Voltaire's arrival. This sad note was quickly absorbed in the flood of acclamations. The Academy sent a delegation to call, as did the Comédie. Dr. Franklin came. As the representative of the American cause in France, he had become a center of Parisian attention since the French decision on 8 February to openly support this cause. Beaumarchais came, now hailed as a leading supporter of the American cause (and deeply involved in the illegal but generally ackowledged supplying of arms to the revolutionaries), as well as a major new playwright. "All my hopes," Voltaire is reported to have said, "are centered on Beaumarchais."[7] Goldoni came, no longer a significant creator of new work (his single successful play in France had been *Le Bourru bienfaisant* in 1771), and now living in Paris on a royal pension. Richelieu came to help with the casting and other preparations for *Irène*. Under all this stimulation, Voltaire's already frail physical condition sharply worsened. The faithful Tronchin managed at least to keep him from the stress of attending rehearsals of *Irène*, which were being held in the house, but not from coaching sessions with individual actors, whom Voltaire was well aware were much inferior to the great names available to him in the past.

The play opened on 16 March, with Voltaire too ill to attend. Marie Antoinette was present, however, and much of the court from Versailles. Messengers were dispatched at the end of each act to bring news to the invalid. Although certainly one of Voltaire's weaker efforts, under the circumstances it could hardly have been anything but a triumph. The greatest occasion was still to come, however. By 21 March, Voltaire had recovered enough to leave the house and by 30 March to attend *Irène*'s sixth performance. A blue star-spangled coach picked him up at four in the afternoon (a bent little figure in the wig and fancy dress of forty years before, covered with a sable pelisse from Catherine of Russia), and took him to the Louvre, where a crowd of two thousand met his coach. The French Academy (only the churchmen absent) met him in their outer hall—an honor never before accorded to anyone, and unanimously elected him to their presidency.

Then it was on to the Comédie where he was placed in a front box and crowned with laurel by the actor Brizard. For twenty minutes he was applauded by actors and audience before the play could begin, and the applause continued almost line by line. At its conclusion, Voltaire's bust was carried onto the stage and crowned with flowers and laurels, after which Mme Vestris recited an ode in Voltaire's honor (illustration 10). *Nanine* was given as afterpiece, to further enthusiasm, and afterward Voltaire made his way through cheering crowds to his carriage which was escorted back to the Hôtel Villette by dancing, shouting, and weeping multitudes. Voltaire himself was reduced to tears. He summarized the occasion in his last letter to Frederick the Great, exulting, in addition to the personal triumph, in the thunderous applause which had greeted every line attacking his old enemies, tyranny, and superstition. He concluded: "It is then true, Sire, that in the end men will be enlightened, and those who believe that it pays to blind them will not always be able to keep their eyes closed" (VC, XCVIII, 171–72).

There were more visits, more correction of manuscripts, more letters, more campaigns (including launching the Academy on the writing of the famous Dictionary which has been its best-known achievement), since Voltaire, typically, remained staggeringly active until the very end, but the end was now almost at hand. During the month of May he failed rapidly, and died 30 May 1778.

Although Voltaire never left the church and made a confession of faith a few weeks before his death, he allowed no priests in his chamber during his final days. This, with the known animosity of church and king, led his friends to conceal his death and remove his body secretly from Paris, dressed as a sleeping traveler in a coach. He was taken to the Abbey of Scellières, a hundred miles out of Paris, whose prior had approved an honorable Christian burial with full rights. This took place on 2 June, only a day before a mandate forbidding it arrived from the bishop. The news now reached Paris, where all newspapers were forbidden to print obituaries, and the Academy was forbidden to hold its customary service upon the death of a member. Such petty restrictions, of course, only added to the Voltaire legend and

Illustration 10. Crowning of the bust of Voltaire on the stage of the Comédie.

helped prepare him for his final role in the century, as one of the secular saints of the Revolution.

NOTES

1. E. H. Gaullier, "Anecdotes inédites sur Voltaire racontées par François Tronchin," *Etrenne nationales, troisième année* (Geneva: Institute et Musée Voltaire, 1855), 215.

2. See Paul O. LeClerc, "Voltaire and Crébillon *pére*: History of an enmity," *SVEC*, 115 (1973):esp. 137–48.

3. Gustave Desnoiresterres, *Voltaire et la Société au XVIIIe Siècle*, 8 vols. (Paris: Didier, 1876), 8:14.

4. Beaumarchais, *Oeuvres complètes*, 6 vols. (Paris: Furne, 1828), 1:8.

5. Marmontel, *Oeuvres*, 7 vols. (Paris: A. Belin, 1820), 7:380.

6. Louis-Sébastien Mercier, *Du théâtre* (Amsterdam: E. van Harrenvelt, 1773), 97.

7. Georges Lemaitre, *Beaumarchais* (New York: Knopf, 1949), 260.

Chapter 9

The Path to the Pantheon, 1778–1791

Apparently fearing public disturbances, the authorities banned all productions of Voltaire plays in Paris for twenty-one days following the announcement of his death. Beginning in late June, however, the Comédie regularly presented an average of four or five Voltaire works each month, primarily such tragedies as *Tancrède*, *L'Orphélin de la Chine*, and *Zaïre*, even though the current leading players, Mlle Sainval and Larive, were clearly far inferior to their models, Clairon and Lekain.

The fame of Voltaire arose to new heights after his death along with an enormous demand for copies of his works, most of which had been banned by various governments of Europe and were extremely difficult to obtain. A Parisian publisher, Charles Panckoucke, seeing a business opportunity, began accumulating Voltaire publications and manuscripts, purchasing a large number from Mme Denis, including the complete correspondence with Frederick the Great. He soon realized that the project would be far more difficult than he had anticipated. Voltaire had been so prolific that the publication would be the largest ever undertaken in France, more than twice the size of the thirty-three-volume *Encyclopédie*. Moreover, many of the writings were still officially banned in France, and although smaller works published elsewhere, in Amsterdam for example, normally circulated there with little difficulty, a project as visible and expensive as this would have to have a firmer guarantee of protection. Catherine the Great, hearing of Panckoucke's dilemma, offered to carry out the project in Russia, but then Beaumarchais stepped forward and convinced the sympathetic prime minister, Maurepas, that he, as a Frenchman, should oversee this important national project. Somehow Maurepas gained the permission of Louis XVI, but only on condition that the printing be done outside France and with no government support. Beaumarchais founded a publishing firm, the "Société Philosophique, Littéraire et Typographique," of which he was the sole member, bought three paper factories in Lorraine, and rented an abandoned fortress in Germany where he set up a press. Public interest was enormous, since the Paris celebrations so shortly followed by the philosopher's death had made a profound effect. For the first six months of 1779, the first anniversary of these events, almost half the performances at the Comédie were of Voltaire plays, supplemented by several special festivals. After a production of *Tancrède* 1 February, an occasional piece showed the muses arguing over which Voltaire favored. Finally, Apollo (played by Molé) decided in favor of Melpomene (played by Vestris). A procession of characters from Voltaire's plays then marched across the stage to the sound of fanfares, while Melpomene crowned a bust of the poet.[1]

The season ended 20 March with *L'Orphélin de la Chine*, following which the actor Bernard Fleury, the company's newest member, praised Voltaire as "the French Sophocles, who had rivals but it may be, no equals," and who achieved "the first rank in Parnassus and the immortal crown which belongs only to genius."[2]

The first anniversary of Voltaire's death fell just a month after the spring reopening of the theatre, and Mme Denis proposed an offering on this occasion of his last play, *Agathocle*, a draft of which had been performed in 1777 at Ferney. The story revisited familiar grounds of warrior brother rivals in love, and a royal father agonizing between them, containing nothing remarkable, but that of course was of minor import. The event provided another occasion to celebrate this remarkable career, extending literally up to the final days of life. Before the production began, the actor Brizard begged the audience's indulgence, to "pardon our zeal for his memory, or rather approve it, rendering to his ashes the honors that you have so often rendered to his person" (VO, VII, 393).

Early in 1780, Beaumarchais distributed a prospectus for two editions of Voltaire's works, one in seventy volumes octavo, the other in ninety-two volumes duodecimo, fifteen thousand copies of each to be sold by private subscription. He pursued this task with a zeal worthy of Voltaire himself, personally reading, correcting, and revising thousands of pages of text, negotiating with representatives of Frederick and Catherine, who insisted that their correspondence be heavily edited, and handling the infinite material and legal demands of this vast project. Like Voltaire, he also managed to successfully pursue a bewildering variety of other business and literary matters on the side. It was well that he did so, since only a few wealthy subscribers could afford the necessarily high subscription rates, and eventually there were only two thousand, while Beaumarchais had hoped for fifteen times that number. The work was completed in 1788 and widely hailed as one of the great publishing achievements of the century, but Beaumarchais himself lost over a million livres on it, surviving only because of his simultaneous success in shipping and a variety of other businesses.

In the public mind, Beaumarchais the financier and Beaumarchais the editor were, however, quite eclipsed during these years by Beaumarchais the playwright. In April of 1782, the Comédie finally moved from the Tuileries into the lavish new home built for them back on the left bank near the Luxembourg Palace. Voltaire remained the most frequently offered playwright, with fifty-six productions this year, but the repertoire was badly overbalanced in favor of tragedy, where the loss of Lekain and Clairon was keenly felt. Molière and Lesage were revived with some frequency, but the public of the time found them rather too boisterous and farcical, and more recent comic works either overly sentimental or cold and sterile. Except for Beaumarchais' *Le Barbier de Séville* in 1775, a number of years had passed without the premiere of any comedy of lasting interest.

At this point Beaumarchais came forward with a new work, *Le Mariage de Figaro*, a sequel to his earlier popular success. The Comédiens happily accepted it, and it passed the censor with no problem. Marie Antoinette read it with delight and suggested a production at Versailles, a proposal which brought the work at last to the attention of Louis XVI who, to everyone's surprise, was enraged by it. Mme de Campan, who read it to him, recorded his famous and ironically prescient reaction: "Detestable! This play must never be given! The man mocks everything that should be respected in government. Before this play could be performed, the Bastille would have to be torn down."[3]

Beaumarchais, like Voltaire, knew how to thrive on opposition, and well aware that his play now had the additional attraction of forbidden fruit, he willingly acceded to the barrage of requests he now received for readings of it at all the capital's most fashionable salons. The grand duke of Russia offered an official premiere at St. Petersburg. Beaumarchais declined, "for the honor of France," but made certain that Marie Antoinette heard of the offer. This spurred the queen to arrange for a private performance at court in June of 1783 with actors from the Comédie, but the king again expressed his displeasure and the project was cancelled.

All of this simply increased pressure for a production, especially among the aristocracy, and at last in September the Comte de Vaudreuil offered the play privately at his chateau, with most of the court in attendance. Rather than relieving the pressure, the production gained Beaumarchais new supporters, and Louis, after calling in a series of five censors, none of whom could be convinced to condemn the play, finally capitulated. *Le Mariage de Figaro* opened at the Comédie 27 April 1784. It was a huge success, especially for the young Louise Contat, who established herself as a major actress with her interpretation as Suzanne. The play ran for a triumphant seventy-five nights, with people coming from distant parts of the country to applaud its revolutionary sentiments. Probably even more important than Figaro's challenges to the count, at a time when public defiance of authority was steadily increasing, was the spectacle of the bourgeois Beaumarchais successfully confronting and triumphing over the arbitary rulings of the king. Inevitably, Beaumarchais was also attacked by conservative critics, and he was imprudent enough to respond to one by boasting of his conquering of "lions and tigers to get a comedy performed."[4] The result was that he was briefly imprisoned for disrespect to the royal family in Saint-Lazare, a facility for juvenile offenders. This insult deeply wounded Beaumarchais, but it satisfied Louis, who even relented to the point of permitting a court performance of *Le Mariage de Figaro*, with the queen appearing as Rosine.

Louis did not even raise any protest about Beaumarchais' next work, a strange mixture of philosophic drama, fairy-tale play, opera, and spectacle named *Tarare*, which dealt with a struggle between an omnipotent and arbitrary oriental despot and a modest and honest commoner who eventually replaces him on the throne. The production, with music by Antonio Salieri, opened at the Opéra 8 June 1787, and was warmly received by a public that looked forward to a new age of freedom and tolerance that, they sensed, was already on the horizon.

Since the death of Lekain, a number of young actors had made their debut at the Comédie, often in works by Voltaire, but it was not until November of 1787 that the major serious actor of the next generation made his appearance, François-Joseph Talma, in the role of Seïde in *Mahomet*. After a series of successful debuts, Talma was accepted as a member of the society on 26 December, after appearing as Egisthe in *Mérope*. Since Larive and others controlled the major tragic parts, however, the young actor, despite his talent, faced a long period of minor roles.

He nevertheless found ways of attracting attention. He became intrigued by the costume reforms of Lekain and Clairon, which had been largely ignored by their conservative successors, and in January 1789, cast in a tiny, seventeen-line part of a tribune in Voltaire's *Brutus*, he appeared in an authentic Roman costume, researched and designed by his friend, the painter Jacques-Louis David. The solitary figure in toga, sandals, bare arms, and

natural hair surrounded by eighteenth-century breeches and wigs scandalized his fellow actors and delighted the public. Since each actor was responsible for his own costume, however, the others had no recourse but to
gradually follow his example or ignore his reform, and some did each.

The split in the Comédie over the question of authentic costume echoed a
split between progressive and conservative members generally, a split that
steadily widened in the turbulent political situation following the fall of the
Bastille, 14 July 1789, and the king's enforced return to Paris from Versailles
in October. A key element in the division was a new tragedy by Marie-
Joseph Chénier, *Charles IX*, which sought to capitalize on the revolutionary
spirit of the time by focusing on the historic massacre of Protestants on St.
Bartholomew's Day and the weakness and intolerance of King Charles.
Such a subject would have been unthinkable in Voltaire's lifetime, although
he was well aware of how congruent it was to his own interests. Indeed, he
correctly predicted in a 1764 letter that when "the horror of fanaticism is
aroused in all enlightened souls," the Saint Bartholomew massacre "will be
the subject of a tragedy" (VC, LIV, 138).

Charles IX was, in fact, at first banned by the censor and resisted by conservative members of the Comédie, but patriotic supporters inside and outside the theatre campaigned for it, and it was at last presented on 4 November
1789. The usual leading actors refused to play the unsympathetic king, and
the part was taken by Talma, his first major creation and his first great triumph. The play remained for some time a focus of division within and without the theatre, and it established Chénier as the first dramatic poet of the
Revolution. In the closing days of December, the National Assembly finally
granted to actors their long-denied rights of citizenship, a reform championed by such leading political figures as Mirabeau and Robespierre. Representatives of the church led the opposition, and such religious rights as
baptism, marriage, and burial were still denied. Clearly the actors owed
much to the new order, but the older actors, accustomed to the often generous support of the court, tended to remain loyal to the old authorities. The
split between the two factions at the Comédie became official in the spring of
1790, when Talma and others departed to establish a rival theatre, more sympathetic to the progress of the Revolution.

The popularity of Voltaire as a dramatist immediately following his death
grew even greater during the Revolution, many of whose leaders regarded
him as a spiritual father. In the decade between his death and the beginning
of the Revolution, his works were performed at the Comédie 553 times,
while during the decade of the Revolution itself he received 896 performances in Paris. In fact, this represents a smaller percentage of the total offer-

ings, since the abolishment of the old theatre monopolies in January of 1791 stimulated a flood of new competing enterprises, but the number is still impressive. The Voltaire that appealed to Revolutionary audiences was distinctly different from the dramatist of the previous decade. His five most frequently performed plays between 1778 and 1789 were *Tancrède, Zaïre, Alzire, Mahomet*, and *L'Orphélin de la Chine*, essentially the plays that modern critics still consider his best. Only one of these five also appears among the most performed of the next decade, *Mahomet*. The others are *Nanine, Brutus, L'Enfant prodigue, Mérope*, and *La Mort de César*. The appearance of the two comedies, especially of *Nanine*, with an astonishing 192 performances, roughly twice as many as the next most popular, suggests the often neglected importance of lighter entertainment during the Revolution, though *Nanine*'s egalitarian political statement surely contributed to its popularity. The shift in the serious plays clearly suggests a search for political relevance, especially in the case of *Brutus*, presented only three times between 1778 and 1789, and 107 times between 1789 and 1799. Its revival in November of 1790 served, like Chénier's *Charles IX*, as a focus for political demonstrations, and the Comédie even created niches on either side of the stage to hold busts of Voltaire and Brutus. During 1793, *Brutus* was one of a small group of plays (in fact the only pre-Revolutionary one) selected by the Committee of Public Safety to be presented once a week at public expense to inspire revolutionary fervor.[5]

Voltaire was thus from the beginning of the Revolution considered one of its champions, both within and outside the theatre. At the first great revolutionary festival, held in the Champ de Mars to celebrate the first anniversary of the fall of the Bastille, verses from Voltaire were carved on the central altar erected to the nation. Not surprisingly, voices began at this time to be raised in Paris in favor of a festival or public memorial to honor the memory of the great philosopher. One of the first was Chénier, who in a 1789 pamphlet complained that "Voltaire's ashes have been dishonored, whereas a public monument ought to be displayed for the respect of his fellow citizens and foreigners."[6] Chénier's suggestion was warmly supported by Beaumarchais and other leading figures from the literary, theatrical, and political world of Paris, but it was Charles Villette who soon emerged as leader of the campaign. Villette, in whose house Voltaire had died, assumed something of the role of heir, purchasing Ferney, erecting a mausoleum there, and dedicating himself to celebrating Voltaire's memory.

Plans were proposed in the fall of 1789 for the city of Paris to honor Voltaire with a memorial in the church of St. Sulpice, where a number of former actors (who had renounced their profession) were buried, but Villette attacked this plan in a 21 December article in the *Chronique de Paris*, arguing that the nation rather than the city should pay tribute, and that Voltaire's body should be placed in St. Geneviève, Paris' newest church, and considered by many its most beautiful. Villette also pointed out that since church property was nationalized in 1789, the monastery where Voltaire rested now belonged to the state, but it could fall into private hands if some action were not taken.

Clerical influence was still strong enough in the National Assembly to reject Villette's proposal. He then conceived another plan, first proposed in the *Chronique* on 27 May 1790, to convert St. Geneviève into a Pantheon, following the Greek and Roman example, where the great men of the new nation, beginning with Voltaire, would be interred. He also read this proposal publicly at the Comédie at a revival of *Brutus*, to an understandably enthusiastic audience, after which most of the papers of Paris took up the campaign.[7] The death on 2 April 1791 of the famous orator Mirabeau, one of the most revered figures of the Revolution, provided the impetus Villette's proposal required. The National Assembly quickly decided to give Mirabeau the honor of being the first to be placed in St. Geneviève, rechristened the Panthéon and made a perpetual shrine to the great men of the nation. Voltaire, Descartes, and Rousseau were mentioned as future possibilities, their religious status now irrelevant since, much to the irritation of the clerics, the church was desacralized. The decision about whether to so honor Voltaire was forced upon the National Assembly soon after, when word came that the Jacobin society of Troyes, the town nearest the former monastery where Voltaire was buried, was planning to buy the property and carry the remains off to their own shrine. After a brief debate, the assembly voted to take over the body. It was exhumed, given a service in the local parish church, and placed on brief display under guard to assure that it would not be appropriated by zealous Troyeans.

The funeral convoy made a triumphant four-day procession to the capital, arriving in Paris on 9 July 1791, where the coffin was placed amid flowers and wreaths amid the ruins of the Bastille, the prison which had once held Voltaire, as it had so many other enemies of the old order. That evening, many of the capital's theatres presented special occasional pieces honoring Voltaire or revivals of his works. The Comédie offered the premiere of a new Chénier play, *Calas*, based, of course, on Voltaire's most famous campaign for social justice.

The transfer of Voltaire's remains to the Panthéon the following day was one of the major celebrations of the Revolution, a "festival of philosophy" inspired in part by the memory of the first national festival the previous summer, but focusing more on the contributions of artists, authors, and musicians. Chénier led the planning committee. The music was composed by François

Gossec, whose contributions to the Mirabeau funeral had been much admired. The decorations were designed by Jacques-Louis David, now emerging as the leading artist of the period and a champion of neoclassic style. This
triumvirate, first assembled for this "*pompe vraiment antique*," remained the
standard committee organizing future revolutionary festivals.[8]

A driving rain prevented the ceremonies from beginning for several hours,
but at last the skies cleared and the procession left the Bastille. Its composition provided a catalogue of the cultural and political icons of the day. First
came a cavalry troop, then delegations from schools, clubs, and fraternal so-
cieties, then large relief portraits of Voltaire, Rousseau, and Mirabeau. Next
came the workers involved in the demolition of the Bastille, carrying balls and
chains found in the prison and followed by a model of it (a standard feature of
revolutionary processions). After a delegation of national electors came a
deputation from the theatres, with a golden statue of Voltaire carried by four
men in classic costume and surrounded by Beaux Arts students, similarly
dressed and bearing banners with the names of Voltaire's principal works.
Next came the academicians, accompanying a golden casket containing the
complete edition of Voltaire's works, donated by Beaumarchais, who himself
led a delegation of authors. The sarcophagus itself was preceded by a full orchestra, supported by wheels of bronze and drawn by twelve white horses.
Above it rose a statue of Immortality placing a crown of stars on the author's
head. Amid the carved classic decorations and theatrical masks on its sides
appeared the legend "Poet, philosopher, historian, he made a great step forward in the human spirit. He prepared us to become free."[9] Behind the sarcophagus came the deputation from the National Assembly, the judiciary, and
the municipality of Paris, headed by the mayor.

The first stop of the procession was before the Opéra, its facade decorated
with draperies and foliage, a bust of Voltaire, and medallions inscribed to his
operas *Pandore*, *Le Temple de la Gloire*, and *Samson*. Gossec had created
choral arrangements for some particularly revolutionary verses from the latter work, which were performed by singers from this theatre. After the bust
was crowned, the procession moved on to its next station, the home of the
Marquis de Villette on what was now called the Quai de Voltaire (illustration
11). There an amphitheatre covered with foliage had been erected in front of
the house, which bore the banner "His spirit is everywhere; his heart is here"
(indeed this was literally true, as the Marquis had retained Voltaire's heart).
Mme de Villette and the daughters of Calas, dressed in mourning and surrounded by youngsters in classic robes singing a chorus by Gossec, saluted
the statue.

Illustration 11. The Voltaire funeral procession crossing the Seine.

Turning down the rue Dauphine, the cortege made a brief stop before the old home of the Comédie, its facade decorated with the usual bust of the poet, garlands, and a banner recalling "At the age of seventeen he created *Oedipe*." Night was falling as the procession reached the nearby new Comédie, also festooned with garlands, but with twenty-two medallions devoted to different theatrical works and a banner balancing that of the old Comédie: "At the age of eighty-four he created *Irène*." When the procession arrived, a curtain parted to reveal the lobby, with an illuminated statue of Voltaire and actors dressed as characters from his plays appearing to do him homage. At last, near midnight the procession moved on to the Panthéon, where Voltaire's remains were finally put to rest, just a few streets away from the spot where, ninety-seven years before, his remarkable life had begun.

These years, from his birth to his final apotheosis, are almost precisely those of the eighteenth century, and there is surely no figure who occupies so commanding a position in the cultural life of that century as Voltaire. He was unquestionably the leading figure of the theatre of this century, not only in France, but, thanks in part to France's cultural dominance, throughout Europe. This was partly due to his incredible literary productivity and influence, but also to his astonishing lifelong correspondence, thousands of letters to kings and commoners, actors and playwrights, indeed to most of the cultural leaders of the era. No understanding of the theatre, indeed of the cultural life of Europe in this century is possible without some familiarity with the astonishing career of Voltaire. This is true even though his many plays themselves, so dominant internationally in their own time, today are known only to scholars. He lies firmly on the other side of that great divide created in western literature by romanticism, and has suffered the fate of association with the old order. It is the revolutionary side of Voltaire, his political and social thought, that lives on today, while his conservative side, from which his theatre never escaped, has faded in the public memory. Could Voltaire return today, this situation would probably surprise him, for he always assumed that fame, even immortality, was to be sought in literary achievement, but on the whole he would probably not be displeased to be remembered less as a great poet than as a champion of freedom and liberty.

NOTES

1. *Journal de Paris* 34 (3 February 1779): 136.

2. Ibid., 80 (21 March 1779): 321–22.

3. Madame de Campan, *Mémoires sur la vie de Marie-Antoinette* (Paris: Firmin Didot, 1849), 3.

4. Louis de Loménie, *Beaumarchais et son temps*, 4 vols. (Paris: Michel Lévy, 1856), 2:365.

5. Alfred Copin, *Talma et la Révolution* (Paris: Perrin, 1888), 168–69.

6. Marie-Joseph Chénier, "Denonciation des inquisiteurs de la pensée" (Paris: La Grange, 1789), 43.

7. Gustave Desnoireterres, *Voltaire et la Société au XVIIIe Siècle*, 8 vols. (Paris: Didier, 1876), 8:479.

8. Alfred Bingham, *Marie-Joseph Chénier* (New York: privately printed, 1939), 23–25.

9. Most of the details of this festival come from Desnoireterres, *Voltaire*, 8:493–501.

Chronology of Voltaire's Life

Date	Events in Voltaire's Life	Theatre and Opera	Public Life
1694	November 21, born in Paris		
1695		Congreve, *Love for Love*	
1696		Cibber, *Love's Last Shift* Regnard, *Le Joueur*	
1697		Italian actors banned from Paris	
1699		Death of Racine	
1700		Congreve, *The Way of the World*	
1702			War of the Spanish Succession Anne queen of England
1703			Bach, first *Organ Works*
1704	Enrolled in Louis-le-Grand	Cibber, *The Careless Husband*	Battle of Blenheim Newton, *Optics*
1705		Motteux, *Arsinoe*	
1707		Farquhar, *The Beaux' Stratagem* Crébillon, *Atrée et Thyeste*	
1708		Crébillon, *Electre*	
1709		Lesage, *Turcaret* First *opera buffa*, in Naples	
1710		Death of Betterton	
1711	Graduates, Louis-le-Grand	Crébillon, *Rhadamiste et Zénobie*	
1712		Philips, *The Distrest Mother*	
1713	Returns to Paris	Addison, *Cato*	Peace of Utrecht
1714	*Anti-Giton*, dedicated to Duclos		George I king of England

Date	Events in Voltaire's Life	Theatre and Opera	Public Life
1715			Defoe, *Robinson Crusoe*
1716		Reopening of Comédie Italienne	Death of Louis XIV
1717		Rich, *Harlequin sorcerer*	
1718	May–October, confined in the Bastille November 18, premiere of *Oedipe*	Italian actors return to Paris	
1719			Mississippi Bubble
1720	February 15, premiere of *Artémire*	Marivaux, *Arlequin poli par l'amour*	
1721		Steele, *The Conscious Lovers* Deslile, *Arlequin sauvage*	
1722		Marivaux, *Surprise d'amour*	
1723			Louis XV crowned Bach, *Magnificat*
1724	March 6, premiere of *Mariamne*		
1725	August 18, premiere of *L'Indiscret*		
1726	May, goes to London		Swift, *Gulliver's Travels* Vivaldi, *The Four Seasons*
1727		Destouches, *Le Philosophe marié*	George II king of England
1728	*The Henriade* Fall, returns to France	Gay, *Beggar's Opera*	
1729		Death of Oldfield	
1730	December 11, premiere of *Brutus*	Death of Lecouvreur Thompson, *Sophonisba* Marivaux, *Jeu de l'amour et du hasard*	
1731		Gottsched, *Sterbende Cato* Fielding, *Tragedy of Tragedies*	
1732	March 7, premiere of *Eriphyle* August 13, premiere of *Zaire*	Covent Garden opens Destouches, *Le Glorieux*	
1733		Rameau, *Hippolyte et Aricie* Lachaussée, *La fausse Antipathie* Pergolesi, *La Serva padrona*	Pope, *Essay on Man*
1734	January 18, premiere of *Adélaide du Guesclin* *Lettres philosophiques*		
1735		Hill, *Zara* Rameau, *Les Indes galants* Lachaussée, *Préjugé à la mode*	Hogarth, *The Rake's Progress*

Date	Events in Voltaire's Life	Theatre and Opera	Public Life
1736	January 27, premiere of *Alzire* October 10, premiere of *L'Enfant prodique*		
1740	June 8, *Zulime*		Frederick II king of Prussia Frederick Invades Silesia Richardson, *Pamela*
1741		Schlegel, *Hermann*	Handel, *Messiah*
1742	August 9, premiere of *Mahomet*	Schönemann in Berlin	Peace of Breslau Piranesi, *Prisons*
1743	February 10, premiere of *Mérope* August 20, premiere of *La Mort de César*	Debut of Clairon	
1745	January, invited to Versailles February 12, *La Princesse de Navarre* April, elected to French Academy November 27, *Le Temple de la Gloire*		
1746		Rousseau, *Les Fêtes de Ramire*	Frederick V king of Denmark
1747		Petits cabinets inaugurated	
1748	August 28, premiere of *Sémiramis*	Crébillon, *Catilina*	Peace of Aix-la-Chapelle Buffon, *Histoire Universelle*
1749	June 16, premiere of *Nanine*		Diderot, *Lettre sur les aveugles* Fielding, *Tom Jones*
1750	January 12, premiere of *Oreste* April, leaves for Berlin	Debut of Lekain	
1751	*Siècle de Louis XIV*	Sumarokov, *Semira*	First volume of the *Encyclopédie*
1752	February 14, premiere of *Rome sauvée* August 17, premiere of *Le Duc de Foix*	Goldoni, *La Locandiera*	
1753	March, leaves Berlin	The *Querelle des Bouffons* Rousseau, *Le Devin du village* Favart, *Bastien et Bastienne*	
1755	Settles at Les Délices	Lessing, *Miss Sarah Sampson*	Lisbon earthquake
1756		Russian state theatre founded	Beginning of Seven Years' War
1757	Gibbon visits	Diderot, *Le fils naturel*	"Genève" article
1758		Diderot, *Le Père de famille*	Rousseau, *Lettre à d'Alembert*
1759	*Candide* Purchases Ferney		Stern, *Tristram Shandy*
1760	July 26, premiere of *L'Ecossaise* September 3, premiere of *Tancrède*	Palissot, *Les Philosophes*	George III king of England

Date	Events in Voltaire's Life	Theatre and Opera	Public Life
1761	Begins Corneille Edition *Appel à tous les nations*	Favart, *Lestrois Sultanes*	Catherine empress of Russia
1762	January 18, premiere of *Le droit de Seigneur* *Saül* written Beginning of Calas Affair		Rousseau, *Contract Social*
1763	*Traité sur la Tolérance* Second Gibbon visit	Garrick in Paris	Treaty of Paris
1764	March 17, premiere of *Olympie*		
1765		Sedaine, *Le Philosophe sans le savoir* Favart, *La Fée Urgèle*	
1767	March 16, premiere of *Les Scythes* Visit from Grétry	Beaumarchais, *Eugènie* Lessing, *Minna von Barnhelm* *Hamburgisch Dramaturgie*	
1768	*Les Guèbres, Le Baron* *Les deux tonneaux*	Grétry, *Le Huron*	
1769	*Le Depositaire*	Saurin, *Béverlei* Ducis, *Hamlet* Shakespeare Jubilee	
1770		New Opéra opens Comédie moves to the Tuileries	Rousseau finishes his *Confessions*
1772	Lekain performs for Voltaire *Les Lois de Minos*	Goldsmith, *She Stoops to Conquer* Goldoni, *Le bourru bienfaisant*	
1773		Mercier, *Du théâtre* Goethe, *Goetz von Berlichingen*	
1774	January 15, premiere of *Les Pélopides* *Don Pèdre*	Garrick, *A Christmas Tale*	Death of Louis XV Goethe, *Werther*
1775		Beaumarchais, *Barbier de Séville*	
1776	*Lettre à l'Académie Française* *Le Hôte et la Hôtesse*	Garrick retires Le Tourneur translations of Shakespeare	Declaration of Independence Gibbon, *Decline and Fall of the Roman Empire* Smith, *The Wealth of Nations*
1777		Sheridan, *The School for Scandal*	
1778	March 16, premiere of *Irène* March 30, feted at the Comédie May 30, death in Paris		
1779	March 31, premiere of *Agathocle*		
1782		Opening of new Comédie	
1783	Kehl edition of works		End of American Revolution

Date	Events in Voltaire's Life	Theatre and Opera	Public Life
1784		Beaumarchais, *Mariage de Figaro*	
1785		Schiller, *Don Carlos*	
1786			Death of Frederick the Great
1787		Beaumarchais, *Tarare* Debut of Talma	
1789		Chénier, *Charles IX*	Beginning of French Revolution
1791	July 10, body moved to the Pantheon		

Further Reading

PRIMARY SOURCES

French

Voltaire. *Correspondence*. Edited by Theodore Besterman. 107 vols. Geneva: Institute et Musée Voltaire, 1953–1965.
————. *Oeuvres*. 52 vols. Paris: Garnier, 1877.

English

Voltaire. *The Works of Voltaire*. Translated by William F. Fleming. 22 vols. New York: E. R. Dumont, 1901.

BIOGRAPHY

Beaune, Henri. *Voltaire au collége*. Paris: Amyot, 1868.
Besterman, Theodore. *Voltaire*. Chicago: University of Chicago Press, 1966.
Chase, Cleveland B. *The Young Voltaire*. New York: Longmans, Green, 1926.
Perey, Lucien, and Gaston Maugras. *La Vie intime de Voltaire aux Délices et à Ferney*. Paris: Calmann Lévy, 1892.
Tallentyre, S. G. *The Life of Voltaire*. 2 vols. London: Smith, Elder, 1903.

STAGE HISTORY

Alasseur, Claude. *La Comédie Française au 18e siècle: Étude économique*. Paris: Mouton, 1967.
Albert, Maurice. *Les Théâtres de la Foire*. Paris: Hachette, 1900.
Baldensperger, Fernand. "La chronologie du séjour de Voltaire en Angleterre et les *Lettres philosophiques*." *Archiv für das Studium der neueren Sprachen*, 129 (1912):137–53.

Bengesco, Georges. *Comédiennes de Voltaire*. Paris: Perrin, 1912.

Bonnassies, Jules. *La Comédie-Française: Histoire administrative*. Paris: Didier, 1874.

Clairon. *Mémoires*. Paris: Firmin Didot, 1846.

De Manne, E.-D. *Galerie historique de la troupe de Voltaire*. Lyon: N. Scheuring, 1877.

Hawkins, Frederick. *The French Stage in the Eighteenth Century*. 2 vols. London: Chapman and Hall, 1888.

Jullien, Adolphe. *La Comédie à la cour*. Paris: Firmin Didot, 1883.

Lekain. *Mémoires*. Paris: Ponthieu, 1825.

Olivier, Jean-Jacques. *Voltaire et les comédiens*. Paris: Société Française d'Imprimerie, 1899.

Park, Young Hai. "La Carrière scènique de *L'Orphélin de la Chine*." *Studies on Voltaire and the Eighteenth Century*, 120 (1974): 93–138.

Robinove, Phyllis S. "Voltaire's Theatre on the Parisian Stage 1789–1799." *French Review* 32 (1958–1959): 534-38.

CRITICISM

Besterman, Theodore, ed. *Voltaire on Shakespeare, Studies on Voltaire*, vol. 54. (Geneva: Institute et Musée Voltaire, 1967).

Carr, Thomas M., Jr. "Dramatic Structure and Philosophy in *Brutus, Alzire* and *Mahomet*." *Studies on Voltaire and the Eighteenth Century*, vol. 143 (1975): 7–48.

Deschanel, Emile. *Le Théâtre de Voltaire*, Paris: Calmann Lévy, 1888.

Lancaster, Henry Carrington. *French Tragedy in the Time of Louis XV and Voltaire*. 2 vols. Baltimore: Johns Hopkins, 1950.

———. *Sunset: A History of Parisian Drama in the Last Years of Louis XIV*. Baltimore: Johns Hopkins, 1945.

LeClerc, Paul O. *Voltaire and Crébillon père: History of an Enmity. Studies on Voltaire and the Eighteenth Century*, vol. 115 (1973).

Lion, Henri. *Les Tragédies et les théories dramatiques de Voltaire*. Paris: Hachette, 1895.

Pappas, John. "Voltaire et le drame bourgeois." *Diderot Studies* 20 (1981), 225-44.

Ridgway, Ronald S. *La Propagande philosophique dans les tragédies de Voltaire. Studies on Voltaire and the Eighteenth Century*, vol. 15 (1961).

———. "Voltaire's Operas." *Studies on Voltaire and the Eighteenth Century*, vol. 189 (1980):119-52.

Vance, Sylvia. *History as Dramatic Reinforcement: Voltaire's Use of History in Four Tragedies Set in the Middle Ages. Studies on Voltaire and the Eighteenth Century*, vol. 150 (1976).

Vrooman, Jack Rochford. *Voltaire's Theatre: The Cycle from Oedipe to Mérope. Studies on Voltaire and the Eighteenth Century*, vol. 75 (1970).

Wellington, Marie. *The Art of Voltaire's Theater*. New York: Peter Lang, 1987.

Willens, Lilian. *Voltaire's Comic Theatre: Composition, Conflict, and Critics. Studies on Voltaire and the Eighteenth Century*, vol. 136 (1975).

Index

About the Author

MARVIN CARLSON is Sidney E. Cohn Professor of Theatre and Comparative Literature at the Graduate Center of the City University of New York. He is the author of numerous books and articles on theatrical theory, theatre history, and current performance and is the founding editor of the journal *Western European Stages*.

Recent Titles in
Contributions in Drama and Theatre Studies